Love
IS A
Verb
DEVOTIONAL

Love

IS A

Verb

DEVOTIONAL

365 DAILY INSPIRATIONS
to Bring LOVE ALIVE

GARY CHAPMAN

with JAMES STUART BELL

BETHANY HOUSE PUBLISHERS

a division of Baker Publishing Group
Minneapolis, Minnesota

© 2011 by Gary Chapman

Published by Bethany House Publishers
11400 Hampshire Avenue South
Bloomington, Minnesota 55438
www.bethanyhouse.com

Bethany House Publishers is a division of
Baker Publishing Group, Grand Rapids, Michigan.

Printed in the United States of America

ISBN 978-0-7642-0970-3 (hardcover)
ISBN 978-0-7642-1068-6 (pbk.)

Library of Congress Cataloging-in-Publication Data
Chapman, Gary D.
    Love is a verb devotional : 365 daily inspirations to bring love alive / Gary Chapman with James Stuart Bell.
       p. cm.
    Summary: "A 365-day devotional exploring how to put love into action. Each day's reading includes a Scripture verse, brief true story, and concluding devotional thought"—Provided by publisher.
    ISBN 978-0-7642-0970-3 (hardcover : alk. paper) 1. Love—Religious aspects—Christianity—Prayers and devotions. 2. Devotional calendars. I. Bell, James S. II. Title.
BV4639.C4245 2011
241'.677—dc23   2011025397

Unless otherwise indicated, Scripture quotations are from the *Holy Bible*, New Living Translation, copyright © 1996, 2004, 2007 by Tyndale House Foundation. Used by permission of Tyndale House Publishers, Inc., Carol Stream, Illinois 60188. All rights reserved.

Scripture quotations identified NIV are from the Holy Bible, New International Version®. NIV®. Copyright © 1973, 1978, 1984, 2011 by Biblica, Inc.™ Used by permission of Zondervan. All rights reserved worldwide. www.zondervan.com

Scripture quotations identified KJV are from the King James Version of the Bible.

The following are true stories, but some details and names have been changed in order to protect privacy.

Cover design by Lookout Design, Inc.

12   13   14   15   16   17   18   7   6   5   4   3   2   1

To all of the contributors to this volume:
Your stories of your love and God's love in action are
heartwarming and encouraging.

— Gary Chapman —

To Caitlin Bell, may you have an ever deeper experience of the
love of Jesus and those around you.

— James Stuart Bell —

Acknowledgments

To Kyle Duncan, for his continuing vision of love in action. To Julie Smith and Ellen Chalifoux, for their excellent editorial supervision. Special thanks for assistance from my longtime partner in inspirational story development, Jeanette Littleton.

— James Stuart Bell —

Introduction

You can give without loving, but you cannot love without giving.
This is one of the truths Irish missionary Amy Carmichael learned during her fifty-five years of service in India. Love is not just good feelings for someone—it is an act of the will. Love, by its very essence, results in action.

Action may take different forms, as our contributors demonstrated in our previous volumes, *Love is a Verb* and *Love is a Flame*. It may be found in serving others, or love may be expressed in words of encouragement. It might be displayed through supplying gifts of love, or manifested in gentle touches. Love might even mean praying for another or just being there for someone. Our expressions of love may come naturally. Or they may be steps of faith and obedience that we learn from the Holy Spirit.

In the pages of this devotional book, you'll see how God has led others to express their love . . . and you'll find how others have experienced God revealing His love to them. You'll see how the ultimate expression of love, God's Word, has inspired and challenged people just like you to reach out to others—friends and family, total strangers, and even perceived enemies.

So we welcome you to explore the actions of love in these nuggets of spiritual gold, and to learn more about the God who so loved us that He gave—over and over and over again—with His presence, His provision, His words of encouragement and hope, and even His life.

May the Lord's gifts of love be so real in your life that you too are inspired to put His, and your, love into action.

— Gary Chapman and James Stuart Bell —

Faith for the Future

I entrust my spirit into your hand.

—Psalm 31:5

I'm nostalgic. Cleaning out my parents' estate has been tough this year because I like to keep ties to the past. I like its security. I tend to resist change and would just like to stay put—especially when life is comfortable.

Peter also wanted to stay put in Luke 9. Jesus went to the mountain to pray, and while the disciples slept, Moses and Elijah arrived to chat with Jesus—perhaps to cheer Him on.

When Peter woke up and saw the hero party going on, he was ready to set up permanent tents and stay. That was much better than the imminent death Jesus was talking about!

But the glory moments ended and the men had to move on.

As we enter a new year, I'm reminded that we can't cling to the security of the past, or even today. We have to keep moving on into an insecure future, where we don't know what will happen. But we don't move into the future alone. The One who loves us best will be there with us every step of the way.

❉ *We can enter the future confidently, remembering that God goes with us.*

— Julie Durham —

New Every Day

Great is his faithfulness;
his mercies begin afresh each morning.

—LAMENTATIONS 3:23

"Hi, babe. Think it'll snow today?"

I couldn't believe my father was as cheery as ever. The night before, we'd had one of those parent/child skirmishes that happen in families. I came out of my bedroom that morning hesitant to face Dad. I thought he and I were at odds—but apparently he didn't. He acted as if nothing had happened.

Dad followed that same motif all through my growing-up years. He was quick to forgive, to forget, and to move on. And I could always feel free to approach him knowing that even if we'd had a tiff, he still loved me.

What a wonderful picture that has become in my life of God's care. God has reminded me that it doesn't matter what went on the day before. Whether I failed or succeeded, He is so faithful that He offers me new mercy, love, acceptance, and forgiveness when necessary, every day of my life.

✳ *Every day is a new day with God and His love.*

— Jeanette Gardner Littleton —

Have to or Want to?

Do all that you can to live in peace with everyone.

—ROMANS 12:18

*H*appy [expletive] New Year! I hope I never see you again!" my stepdaughter announced.

I sighed. It wasn't the first time my stepdaughter had been angry with me. She was a person who took offense easily and dramatically. As I'd raised her, I'd noticed her tendency was to assume everyone was against her—like popular kids at school—when I suspected they didn't think of her at all. I wondered if she had some strains of her mother's paranoia issues.

In the past, estrangements from my stepdaughter had honestly been a bit of a relief—after all, if she wasn't talking to us, she couldn't wreak emotional havoc and our lives were simpler.

But this time, something was different. When Ann wouldn't respond to apologies I left on her voicemail, I couldn't just say "I've done my part" and release it as I had in the past. I became distressed. I began to fervently pray that God would soften Ann's heart. I actually missed her and deeply longed to have the relationship healed.

I realized I'd finally learned to really love her.

❊ *When we really love someone, we don't seek healing in relationships just because it's right—but because we long for it.*

— Jane Doelan —

Keeping Them in Prayer

God knows how often I pray for you. Day and night
I bring you and your needs in prayer to God.

—ROMANS 1:9

I tumbled out hard words about my situation. Needing a job. Behind in the bills. Struggling every day just to keep afloat. The group listened quietly. A few asked questions. "Have you tried this place?" "Would you consider relocating?" "What about taking out a home equity loan to tide you over?"

I gave the answers, feeling even more despondent. I'd tried everything. Then someone said, "Come on, let's pray about this together."

What followed was about fifteen minutes of solid, God-exalting prayer for my family and me. I listened raptly, amazed at how eloquent each person was. They were impassioned, pleading, crying out to God to get me out of the miry clay, as Psalm 40:2 put it.

I went home that night greatly encouraged. The battle remained tough, but we kept praying together. I realized the prayers all came from hearts of love. That kind of love can keep a person going, even when it seems no hope is left.

❖ *True love responds to real needs and gets involved through prayer.*

— Mac Thurston —

Trust His Love

We know how much God loves us, and we
have put our trust in his love.

—1 JOHN 4:16

*S*tuck! Stuck, Mommy!"

"I know. It's okay. Everything is going to be okay. Just a few more minutes," I said, trying to calm my son.

Two-year-old Evan was stuck lying snugly wrapped as the doctor glued the wound on his cheek back together.

"Stuck, Mommy!" he tried again.

"I know. I know. It's okay." I smoothed his hair back from his forehead to comfort him.

Still, he pleaded, "Go, *go*, Mommy!"

My voice, touch, and love continued to calm him until the doctor finished.

How often I have cried out to my heavenly Father, "I'm trapped in this situation that I can't change. Take me out of this misery!"

I'm comforted that my heavenly Daddy is saying, "I know. I know. This will take some time, but it is going to be okay."

I may not feel like it is okay—or maybe like it will ever be okay—but I can trust His love just as surely as Evan felt my love and assurance as I stroked his head.

✳ *What we believe in frightening moments is not as important as Who we believe.*

— Sheila Sattler Kale —

A Lesson in Patience

Love is patient and kind.

—1 CORINTHIANS 13:4

*M*y patience was wearing thin after five minutes of watching my father struggle to sign the Mother's Day card I bought for him to give Mom.

His Alzheimer's had affected his motor skills as well as his memory. It was hard for him to hold a pen, let alone write with it. When I asked him for the third time if he needed help, he said, "I can't decide what to write."

"What do you mean, Daddy?"

"I can't decide whether I want to sign the card 'Love, Bud' or 'I love you. Bud.'"

After hearing those simple words, I gladly waited another twenty minutes as Daddy patiently struggled to sign the card for the woman he'd loved since high school. When he finished at last, there was no doubt about it. Although scribbly and shaky, he had managed to write "I love you. Bud."

Daddy died a few months later. Mom cherished that Mother's Day card. And I cherish the lesson Daddy taught me that day—that patience is love in action.

❖ *The patience of love never gives up.*

— Linda Cox —

Personal Presence

If I had such faith that I could move mountains,
but didn't love others, I would be nothing.

—1 CORINTHIANS 13:2

*E*njoy your time with Ben!" my husband called as I started the car. I gripped the steering wheel and went to pick up my brother for coffee. Several years earlier, my relationship with Ben had been strictly biological. But now a simple friendship sprouted from our semi-soiled past. Even so, I still felt more like a stranger than a sibling to my brother. I also felt pressured to shine my "Christian light" brighter than usual since we viewed life through very different lenses.

Tonight, however, I didn't have the energy to preach. "Lord," I prayed, "please help me love my brother and not make him into a witnessing project. If you want me to speak of you, please open a natural door in our conversation and help me know what to say."

God answered my prayer and helped me point to Him as my brother and I discussed life goals. I had a relaxing, relationship-deepening visit.

✣ *God calls us into personal relationships with Him. We share Him best when we personally relate to others.*

— Katherine Mitchell —

A Meeting of Hearts

You have stayed with me in my time of trial.

—LUKE 22:28

I met Linda at a writers' conference last year. She was an author seeking to tap in to her inner poet; I felt like a frazzled mental case, bent on escape.

"I ran away from home," I said with a strained chuckle. "It's been a rough couple of weeks."

With pent-up emotion, I proceeded to tell my month's story to her. I whined about my husband's absence and our leaky roof. I complained about our son's job loss and his move back into our home with his pregnant wife, toddler, and hairy dog.

"I actually registered for this conference because I was interested in the workshops," I said, "but it's my solitary hotel room I appreciate most right now."

At the end of the day, I bumped into Linda again. "I don't usually spill my guts to total strangers," I said, "but I appreciate your taking the time to listen to me. I'm glad I came to the conference, and I'm glad I met you."

Linda hugged me. Then she prayed, "Heavenly Father, be with my new friend . . ."

✳ *God knows just when we need a friend.*

— Dawn Lilly —

God Sticks With You

Don't you see how wonderfully kind, tolerant,
and patient God is with you?

—ROMANS 2:4

Days after my conversion and the joy and exhilaration I felt as a new Christian, someone asked how old I was. "Twenty-one," I answered.

"So that means God stuck with you for twenty-one years trying to get you to listen to Him, huh?"

I hadn't thought of it that way. But yes, that was a truth I needed to realize. God hadn't given up on me the many times I refused to listen to Him. He never pushed me aside after I heard the gospel and didn't accept it.

Nowadays, when I talk to new Christians, I often raise this issue. "How does it feel to realize God hung in there with you for all those years?"

One time, someone said, "You mean to say He was working on me even as a little kid?"

I told him, "I think that's what the Bible teaches."

How long did you put God off before recognizing His love in Christ? God sticks with us even when we're stuck in our sin. He loves us that much.

✽ *God doesn't give up. His love is greater than our refusal to listen.*

— Richard Holland —

A Risk Worth Taking

Dear friend, you are being faithful to God when you
care for the traveling teachers who pass through,
even though they are strangers to you.

—3 JOHN 1:5

I was desperately lonely.

My husband's job had landed us in our fifteenth home in nine years, and I was a stay-at-home mom with a toddler. As we walked into a couples' Sunday school class, I prayed someone would want to invest in friendship. The class had the usual introductions and then someone asked how we'd arrived in their community.

As we explained about contract engineering and our nomadic lifestyle, one couple was listening to God. "Wow, how can we pray for you?"

I decided to take a chance. I confessed my loneliness and how I craved a friend.

In the short silence, I felt the room weighing the cost of friendship. But Susan didn't even hesitate. "Come over and have lunch with us today after church."

Her husband echoed the invitation with a grin. "It'll give us a chance to visit."

I've never forgotten their gift that day and have found many dear friends when I invest in others.

✴ *Investing in friendship and love always brings great returns.*

— Edie Melson —

Finding Love in an African Slum

Do not be afraid or discouraged. For the Lord
your God is with you wherever you go.

—JOSHUA 1:9

I could barely see the woman in the dark corner of the hovel
she called home. She had no water, power, or comforts besides a cot, a tiny coal firepot, and a couple of boxes to sit on.

Only days before, my four healthy children surrounded me in our
spacious, well-loved home. Now, across the ocean and in a world
that might have been on another planet, I sat in a squalid African
hut watching a woman dying of AIDS struggle for each breath.

On the plane ride to Ethiopia, doubts had plagued my thoughts.
*What are you doing leaving your children for two weeks? Why go
all the way to Africa to help the poor? Why you?*

For this exact moment, answered a voice in my spirit. I crossed
the room, held her hand, and, bending near, whispered life-giving
Scripture. In that moment love was as elemental to life as breath.
Love is extending my hand, sharing a prayer, and, sometimes, leaving all I've ever known to find what I truly have to give.

✻ *When you go to unfamiliar places, you will discover opportunities
to share love you never knew you had to give.*

— Alyssa Santos —

Chosen by Him

And having chosen them, he called them to come to him.

—ROMANS 8:30

I remember the moment like yesterday. I had applied to a seminary—only one—to study for the ministry. I heard one of the seminary teachers preach on several tapes. He made me laugh, cry, and feel emboldened to live more strongly for Christ. When I applied, the seminary dean informed me I was very late. They'd already selected most of the incoming class, and he recommended I apply for the next semester.

After praying, I decided to go for it. The wait was awful. But one day I received a letter from the school. I opened it with trepidation. It said, "You have been chosen to enter our school for this school year."

Chosen. Have you ever thought about that in reference to God choosing you? He chose you and me to be His children, His friends, His servants.

He chose us because He loves us. Only love could choose people like us, don't you think? And that love is greater than any in this world.

❊ *God's love reached out to us and chose us even before we ever thought of Him.*

— Lloyd O'Donnell —

Always Watching

The Lord keeps you from all harm
and watches over your life.

—PSALM 121:7

I sat in the ER cubicle, my chair pulled as close as possible to my six-year-old's inert form on the bed. I stroked the blond hair away from her face and watched as her tiny body—aided by IV fluids—fought the high fever. It was the third ER visit of her young life.

Over the past thirteen years, I have spent hours upon hours in ERs and hospital rooms. A son born with a heart problem, then facing injuries and accidental poisoning when he was a toddler. A stepdaughter with a staph infection and allergic reaction. A husband with heart issues and chronic kidney stones. An elderly father with a disintegrating body. A stepmother with gall stones and infections. By now I know the routines almost as well as the nurses.

Scripture tells us that God watches over us. I picture Him watching over us as I watch over my loved ones in the ER—anticipating their needs and making sure they're okay. He watches, and waits, and steps in when He needs to. Because we're precious to Him.

�֍ *God's watch care is active—ready to spring to meet our needs at any time.*

— Jeanette Gardner Littleton —

The Too-Big House

Cheerfully share your home with those
who need a meal or a place to stay.

—1 PETER 4:9

I didn't realize it would be this big!" I exclaimed, walking
through our newly built retirement home.

"Neither did I," said my husband. "What were we thinking?"

We had chosen a plan far bigger than our needs dictated, even
with a second kitchen downstairs. After moving in, we felt guilty
over having so much when so many in the world have so little. We
got on our knees and dedicated our home to hospitality.

Over the years, study groups met in our home, and many meals
were served.

One day a call came. "A young single mom and her four-year-old
need a place to stay for a few months while she trains for a job in
your area. Would you let them live with you, free of charge, and
care for her little one?"

Without giving it a second thought, we replied, "Of course!"

Friends and relatives warned, "You're too old to put up with a
youngster."

Too old? Never! And suddenly, the too-big house we'd built was
just the right size.

✳ *We enjoy God's blessings much more when we share them with
others.*

— Margaret M. Marty —

Softened by His Love

God blesses those who work for peace, for
they will be called the children of God.

—MATTHEW 5:9

*J*udy and I seemed destined to antagonize each other. I couldn't
figure out why. We were both Christians who were serious
about our faith.

One day, after we had another round of stinging jabs at each
other, I took the matter to the Lord. He seemed to say, *Invite her
over to your home. Get to know her better.*

Reluctantly, I obeyed, and she accepted the invitation.

While we were together, I talked with Judy about the problem
we seemed to have. She didn't know why we rubbed each other
the wrong way either. So we prayed together and asked the Lord
to help us understand and love each other.

During our talk, we discovered that we had a number of common
interests. We began to like each other. Eventually, our conversation shifted to the Lord. We both truly wanted to please Him. We
apologized for our attitudes. We smiled at each other, and God
did an amazing thing. He softened our hearts and love blossomed.
Today we are good friends.

✢ *Love blossoms when we water it with prayer.*

— Donna J. Howard —

Receiving to Give

In his grace, God has given us different
gifts for doing certain things well.

—ROMANS 12:6

*H*arley was one of those guys who never appeared to have a lot going for him. Factory job. Minimum wage. Widower. Messed-up adult kids. I met him one day in a Toastmasters group at our church. He gave a speech and then sat down.

At the break, I walked over to him. "You could give that speech in a lot of places," I told Harley.

"I'm trying," he said. "But it's slow going. There are other things I do better."

"Like what?"

"Well, after my wife died, I talked to the pastor and said I wanted to start a grief recovery group here. I did it, and now we have fifty people coming. It really charges me up."

Afterward I thought about this. Harley had a gift from God. His gift was the ability to give of himself and to love others. And God used him.

✻ *Love compels us to use the gifts God has given us to serve Him and others.*

— Joseph Compaine —

ABCs of Love

I weep with sorrow; encourage me by your word.

—PSALM 119:28

*G*ardner, come to dinner. Now!"

My thirteen-year-old son sniffled in the other room. He was having a bad night. He'd been furious with his little sister, he'd spoken inappropriately with me, and he'd gotten a rebuke from his father.

"Was I really that mean, Elizabeth?" he quietly asked his sister as he shuffled to the table, his head down. I could tell he felt terrible for the way he'd acted. After the occasional anger episode like this, Gardner tended to beat himself up emotionally.

"Alphabet for Gardner!" I called as we filled our tortillas with taco ingredients. I'd started doing the game a few days earlier for my daughter and husband. I'd systematically go through the alphabet, for each letter naming a word that described the person.

"*A* is for adorable," I said. "Gardner is such a cutie!"

"*B*—brave," his sister announced. "Gardner is a brave person."

"*C* is for creative," my husband added.

And on we went. Once in a while Gardner would throw in a negative word, but we clearly overrode him—no negative traits allowed; only good ones.

�֣ *Just as God encourages us with His Word, we can encourage others with our words.*

— Jeanette Gardner Littleton —

A Sister's Unfailing Love

But I trust in your unfailing love.

—PSALM 13:5

Go to the car right now!" my sister demanded.

"No," I snapped, "you can't tell me what to do!"

"Yes, I can. I'm your big sister," she shouted.

There wasn't a lot of sisterly love between us while we were growing up. My sister, Sheryl, was a drill sergeant.

After high school, I attended college two states away—in part to get away from her.

We seldom spoke, but one February day I received a phone call.

"So what's up, Sheryl?" I asked in a surprised tone.

There was a long pause, followed by the words, "God took Aaron home!"

My sister's oldest son died of no apparent cause; he was just seventeen years old.

I flew out for the funeral, holding my sister's hand and wiping away her tears.

When I returned to my family in Pennsylvania, I promised to keep in touch, and I kept my word!

It's been twenty years since Aaron's death, and last Christmas my sister gave me a heart-shaped frame with a picture of us in matching Easter dresses with the words, "A sister's love *never* fails." For the first time, I *felt* my sister's love, and she felt mine.

✤ *Sometimes it takes years to develop, but there's nothing like the love of family.*

— Connie Pombo —

Great Performance

A person with a changed heart seeks praise
from God, not from people.

—ROMANS 2:29

My friend waxed eloquent about the concert he'd been to where a famous opera tenor had performed. "He was amazing. I was in tears at many points, the music was so touching. The applause was overwhelming."

We talked more and I said, "I wonder how such people keep their humility in such situations."

He laughed. "You know, it's kind of a weird thing. But whenever people started to applaud, he didn't bow. He didn't eat it up and grin. No, he stepped back and bowed his head, as if praying. I think he realized everything he had was from God, and that God should get the real applause."

I thought about it a long time. Yes, in love God gave us gifts. In love He keeps us going. In love He trains us and makes us even better at what we do. And in love He applauds us, letting us know He is pleased.

⁂ *Using our gifts is a way of praising God.*

— Harry Erb —

Finding Land Again—Together

He lifted me out of the pit of despair,
out of the mud and the mire.
He set my feet on solid ground.

—PSALM 40:2

I barely knew Sharon. Even though we served with the same mission organization and attended the same church, our paths never crossed personally—until my whole world fell apart.

My husband and I discovered our beautiful eighteen-year-old daughter was struggling with an eating disorder. Life quickly became about treatment centers, counselors, dieticians, and plaguing guilt and questions. How could this happen?

I was drowning. I did the daily routine—and gulped for air. I attended church—and swallowed more water. I did ministry—and went further under. I even choked on prayer and Bible reading.

Then a lifeguard appeared at the door.

"So how are you holding up?" Sharon asked sincerely as many others had.

"I'm not," I replied tearfully. "And I have no idea what to do about it."

But Sharon did. She found a support group and drove me there every Tuesday evening. She even listened as I poured my heart out there and back.

Sharon held me afloat when I couldn't swim for myself. And I found land again.

Now I'm becoming a lifeguard as well.

❊ *Kind, encouraging words from shore won't rescue the drowning. Love dives in.*

— Debbie Burgett —

Kevin's Lifelong Lesson

Let your conversation be gracious and attractive so
that you will have the right response for everyone.

—COLOSSIANS 4:6

*S*ometimes I think you don't like me at all!" my friend Kevin
exclaimed.

I looked at him in surprise. He couldn't have been more mistaken!
Kevin was truly one of my favorite people. I saw him every week
when we had rehearsal for a music group we both sang in. And
honestly, I always looked forward to seeing Kevin. We seemed to
have a special friendship and camaraderie.

I finally found my voice. "Why in the world would you say that?"

"Well, you tease me so much," he explained. "Sometimes it
sounds mean. And sometimes I think you're serious. It hurts my
feelings."

I started thinking about my words to Kevin. He was right; I did
tease him a lot. And yes, sometimes it was negative teasing. But
anything negative wasn't really how I felt. Surely he knew that. . . .

Apparently not.

I was distraught when I realized I'd hurt this man of whom I was
so fond. Kevin taught me a lesson that changed my life. From that
time, I dropped my sarcasm and less-than-complimentary teasing.
I learned that the last people I want to hurt with my words are the
ones I'm most fond of.

✻ *Our words should always reflect the love we feel for others.*

— Jenni Davenport —

Heavenly Perfection

Our bodies are buried in brokenness, but they will
be raised in glory. They are buried in weakness,
but they will be raised in strength.

—1 CORINTHIANS 15:43

I love hearing speaker, author, and disability advocate Joni Eareckson Tada talk about heaven. She has such hope and light in her eyes and a lilt in her voice. Her confidence cries out that one day she will shed her broken, paralyzed body and have a new one that's resplendent, powerful, and glorious. When she talks about heaven she adds, "I just hope that day comes soon."

So it is for all of us. I sometimes tell my wife, "I can't wait till I'm a trim 140 pounds, in perfect shape, and able to run a mile in four minutes."

We talk about things like being able to eat anything we want and not gain weight, having the power to go anywhere at a mere thought, and seeing God's face. But one thing I can't wait for is being able to love everyone perfectly.

I mean it. I long for the day when I never say a mean word again, never make a mistake, and always show perfect love. That's something to look forward to.

✴ *Don't be discouraged. One day God will make you perfect—in goodness, compassion, and love.*

— Mark Littleton —

Meatloaf Blessing

Don't give reluctantly or in response to pressure.
"For God loves a person who gives cheerfully."

—2 CORINTHIANS 9:7

*T*he aroma of meatloaf from the backseat permeated my car, giving me heartburn in more ways than one. Stopping at the white frame house, I sighed. After contributing four meals of mercy in two weeks, my spirit grumbled—*enough is enough.*

With a plastered smile, I carried the meatloaf and marched to the door of this woman recently home from surgery. She tried to smile back at me. The right side of her face was horribly distorted, one scar still raw with healing. Then I recalled that this was the latest of several surgeries for cancerous tumors.

Seeing the meatloaf, the left side of her face lit with radiance. She praised God for all His goodness. Humbled, I was suddenly filled with a renewed spirit—the privilege of being God's ambassador of blessing. *I had almost missed it!* I will never again think about meatloaf without remembering God's special lesson.

❉ *A grace-filled attitude is a blessing to everyone—even yourself.*

— Patricia L. Stebelton —

Pay It Forward

He comforts us in all our troubles so that we can comfort others.

—2 CORINTHIANS 1:4

*N*ancy, I don't know how I'm going to live without Burton," Renee said between sniffles.

"I understand," I said.

"I know you do," Renee answered, "you've been through this."

Renee had called to tell my new husband and me that her spouse had suddenly died. As she spoke to me of her grief, my mind traveled back four years earlier to when I lost my first husband, Jim, the same way Renee lost her husband.

"Renee," I said, "God loves you and has your healing in His plan. He carried me through the grief and gave me a new life. I never thought I could go on living, much less love and marry again. But here I am."

"I'm so glad God brought you into my life," Renee said. "It helps so much to talk to another woman who survived something like this."

When the Lord took Jim home, I couldn't imagine that He would bring Renee or others into my life to love and encourage, just as He has loved and encouraged me.

✳ *When we show love and compassion to others, we are blessed as much as they are.*

— Nancy Reinke —

For Us All the Way

If God is for us, who can ever be against us?
—ROMANS 8:31

*M*y boss definitely didn't like me. I'd let him know I was a Christian. And now he took advantage of me at work in any way he could. Like the day he told me, "You'll do this dirty job because you're a Christian, right? God says so."

He soon had some other distasteful jobs just for me. I kept on doing the jobs and praying, "God, I know you're with me. So just help me to do these things with a smile."

After weeks of this, my boss called me into his office one day. Then he asked, "Why are you putting up with this stuff from me?"

I sat there amazed. An answer came to me. "I know you probably will think this weird, but it's because I love God, and loving Him makes me love you, even if you don't like me much."

He just shook his head. "Get out of here. Oh, and I'm giving you a raise."

Our relationship improved and I felt for the first time love had won the day.

✻ *Love even the unlovely. God sees and will reward you.*

— Mark Littleton —

Fresh Clothes, Fresh Perspective

Most important of all, continue to show deep love for
each other, for love covers a multitude of sins.

—1 PETER 4:8

It was day three of my hospital stay with our sick daughter. My clothes were feeling saggy and uncomfortable. What a relief it was when my husband walked into the hospital room with a Walmart bag stuffed with an outfit that didn't match and clean underwear. Fresh flowers and chocolates could not have communicated his commitment to me any better than that pair of clean underwear.

This was our third trip to the hospital in two months. Friends didn't stop by anymore to offer comfort. They had families of their own to care for. In the past, they had always been there for me when I felt like my husband wasn't.

But this time my friends didn't make sure I had dinner every night, a toothbrush, and fresh clothes. My husband did. It doesn't sound like much, but his provision in those basics was the beginning of a renewed trust and passion for him.

✻ *Sometimes love is best communicated in quiet service to one another.*

— Jennifer C. Hoggatt —

Mommy Meltdowns

I tell you, her sins—and they are many—have been forgiven, so she has shown me much love. But a person who is forgiven little shows only a little love.

—LUKE 7:47

*A*drenaline-rushed, mommy meltdown mornings weren't my proudest moments. My yelling hurt my sons' feelings, leaving me burdened with guilt. I prayed, *God, I don't want to emotionally damage my sons. Please forgive me.*

After I pitched a toddleresque tantrum one morning, I realized I faced two options: rationalize my behavior or ask my sons for forgiveness. So before the boys left for school, I said, "I'm sorry for blowing up. It's not your fault. Mommy was wrong. Will you please forgive me?"

Like the Lord, they eagerly forgave me. Reconciled, we parted with hugs and kisses.

After a stressful, exhausting day, I picked up my sons from school. Too tired to referee my sons' war of words, it took all my emotional strength to keep from yelling, "Be quiet!"

Then, during a lull in the hostilities, four-year-old Kyle innocently asked his brother, "Kristoffer, do you love me?"

Kristoffer sweetly replied, "Yes, I do, Kyle. I know I don't act like it sometimes. Will you forgive me?"

"Yes, Kris, I forgive you."

I knew the verbal warfare wasn't over, but they had learned to enjoy truces of forgiveness.

❊ *The Lord is ready to forgive—may that also be said about us.*

— Scoti Springfield Domeij —

Not Another Refugee!

Blessed are those who help the poor.
—PROVERBS 14:21

The night my husband brought Mike home with him to eat dinner, I knew Mike was just another con artist, and I refused to accept him. I said, "Never again! No more refugees!"

Mike had used heavy drugs and had lived under a bridge for months before straightening up enough to find work. My husband had a penchant for taking on those who were down on their luck, and soon he persuaded me to take Mike to a Bible conference with us.

After one of the teaching sessions, I looked over at Mike. He just sat there with tears in his eyes.

"Why hasn't anyone ever told me about this before?" he asked.

Putting aside my judgmental spirit, I allowed God's unconditional love for Mike to fill me and flood over me and through me. Before long, we had a new son in the Lord. What a blessing I would have missed if I hadn't allowed God to pour out His love through me.

✳ *God's unconditional love often sneaks up on us when we least expect it!*

— Ann Varnum —

The Blessings of Expressing Love

This is my command: Love each other.

—JOHN 15:17

I rang the doorbell of my elderly friend and I heard her say from behind the door, "Come on in."

So I entered and saw her smiling face as she wheeled across the floor in her motorized chair.

"How are you doing?" I asked.

"I'm taking one day at a time. God is so good to me," she replied.

As we talked, I noticed she was as concerned about my struggles as I was about hers. Each of us shared how hard life was at times in our own particular situations, and our bond in Christ deepened.

After more than two hours of conversation, we prayed for each other and bid our farewell. We each committed to pray for each other's concerns and to pray that we would remain steadfast in trusting God to provide strength to cope with life.

As I walked to my car, I thought of how, in my effort to show love toward my friend, she had expressed love toward me. In my attempt to bless another, I was blessed as well.

✳ *As we show others our love, sometimes we also receive love in return.*

— Michael K. Farrar —

The Boy With the Stony Heart

And I will give them singleness of heart and put a new
spirit within them. I will take away their stony, stubborn
heart and give them a tender, responsive heart.

—EZEKIEL 11:19

*L*ord, I just don't think anything is going to ever have any effect," I told God one day when talking with Him about my son.

My husband and I had raised him to know God and Scripture. We'd tried to live our faith consistently. We'd prayed.

But he said he didn't want anyone running his life, not even God. And though we'd kept an open relationship with him over the years, if anything, the more I prayed, the harder his heart seemed to get.

"I'm just wasting my time," I reiterated to the Lord. "He's as hard as a rock."

A little later the Holy Spirit responded. He reminded me that even though a rock may look hard, it has little cracks, holes, and crevices in it that water, dirt, and even bugs can get into. He reminded me that a rock isn't really solid at all. *Keep praying and loving,* the Holy Spirit seemed to whisper. *I can get in places that you can't even see.*

✳ *Don't give up on the "rocks" you know. Keep praying and loving and trusting God to reach the places you can't.*

— Jossy Grey —

In God We Trust

I know the Lord is always with me.
I will not be shaken, for he is right beside me.

—PSALM 16:8

"In God we trust."

I repeated those words as I touched a special dime in my pocket. I had found it on the car seat on the way to the funeral home. At the time, all I wanted to do was crawl into bed, but even as I picked up the dime, God said, "Trust me!"

I put the dime in my pocket. My attitude changed, and I enjoyed hearing others' remembrances about Dad and sharing my memories. With a dime, my heavenly Father comforted me when I lost my earthly father.

Since then I have found other coins—usually dimes—when I needed God's comfort and guidance most: when receiving radiation treatments, when scared about test results, during Mother's final illness.

People often hear me exclaim, "Yes!" when I find a coin and ask why I'm so excited. I tell my dime story and explain how touching the special dime in my pocket reminds me to trust God's presence, promises, and love. At other times, it reminds me to love others.

✽ *Carrying a tangible object can remind us to trust and share God's love.*

— Deb Vellines —

My Family Next Door

When God's people are in need, be ready to help
them. Always be eager to practice hospitality.

—ROMANS 12:13

Brrrrrring!
I was becoming annoyed. The shrill sound of the basic
doorbell that someone had decided to install in my little house
in a remote part of Kenya grated on me. Why would the person
ringing the doorbell not give up? I had been through some difficult
circumstances and I just wanted to be left alone. I did not want to
entertain any visitors.

But the visitor did not give up.

Brrrrrring!

There it was again. I wondered if the neighborhood kids were
just having a little fun. But, no, there was a pause and it rang firmly
again. Alarmed that some sort of emergency might have arisen, I
went to the door.

My neighbor, a local pastor who spoke no English but who
possessed a gentle and compassionate spirit, looked at me with
love in his eyes and told me, "Sister, you must join us for dinner."

He knew I was hurting and would not give up ringing that doorbell. He wanted me to know that I was part of their family too.

✳ *Often it takes persistent love to reach out to others and include them.*

— Laura Chevalier —

Tackling the Love Challenge

Beware that you don't look down on any of these
little ones. For I tell you that in heaven their angels are
always in the presence of my heavenly Father.

—MATTHEW 18:10

*A*nd then, I had to tackle her in the hall. Unfortunately, I'd worn a skirt to work," my friend Rhonda said with a grin as she told me about having to chase a run-away middle school student.

I love hearing Rhonda talk about her job as a teacher of special needs kids—even when she's not doing something dramatic like using restraining holds to keep a child from hurting himself, her, or other students.

Whether they're loving and sweet, defiant and angry, high-functioning, or nearly comatose, Rhonda loves them all. She finds ways to help the students reach their best abilities. And often she also finds ways to minister to their families, who usually have more challenges to face than a special-needs child.

Best of all, Rhonda cares for their souls by faithfully praying. "Even if I can't do anything else of lifelong value for my students, I can pray," Rhonda says.

Hearing about Rhonda's days wears me out. But it also inspires me to love like she does—like Jesus does.

✣ *Never underestimate the power love has on any kind of person.*

— Jeanette Gardner Littleton —

Don't Tire, Even When Tired

So let's not get tired of doing what is good.

—GALATIANS 6:9

My daughter Lizzie's party was scheduled early on a Saturday, a day I usually slept in. But since my wife worked late the night before, I told her I'd take Lizzie to the party so she could sleep.

When morning came, Lizzie stepped up close to my face and said, "Daddy, what time is it?"

I looked at the clock and it was time to go. I lay back, caught two more winks, and then rolled out of bed, feeling like a ton of dirt. I was tired, grumpy, and didn't want to do this. But I'd promised.

Looking at the comfortable figure on the other side of my bed, I prayed, "Please, God, help me do this, or nudge my wife to jump up and say she wants to do it."

No movement from my wife. I pulled on my clothes and got Lizzie to her party. She was very happy and told me I was "the best daddy in the world."

Do good—even in little things. God sees them all.

— Jerry Hamilton —

Courageous Friends

The heartfelt counsel of a friend
is sweet as perfume and incense.

—PROVERBS 27:9

I felt powerless to resist the sin pulling me toward disaster.
Desperate for help, I called five friends.

Two said, "Follow your heart."

The third walked me through the question, "What will happen
if you do this?"

The fourth rebuked me. I felt well-deserved shame—godly
shame—but not a shame that motivated me to change. It's like
being told you're gaining weight and need to cut calories. You feel
so bad about yourself that you reach for some comfort. Chocolate
ice cream works.

The fifth friend looked at me with tears in her eyes and said,
"You are going to be so hurt."

She's the one who kept me from making a huge mistake with
repercussions that would have been disastrous for me and for others I love.

A true friend finds the courage to speak truth. The truth was:
#1—She loved me. #2—I was absolutely wrong. And, #3—She
loved me.

As I looked at my friend, I saw God. I saw His sorrow, His
justice, and His merciful love.

✣ *A true friend cares more about what is right than about pleasing you.*

— Sheila Sattler Kale —

Victim to Victor

You must have the same attitude that Christ Jesus had.

—PHILIPPIANS 2:5

*A*nger encroached on my thoughts. *I hate my life.* I hunkered down in the pew, ready to ignore the message. *The pastor can't help me.*

I normally avoid showing my feelings by staying on a superficial level. Today was my breaking point. My roommates and I no longer spoke because of a disagreement. But my hostility had grown, unchecked. I felt I had been wronged.

Resentment churned within me until the preacher's voice intruded.

"What's wrong with being a victim?" he asked. "Jesus was."

My heart stilled. Darkness retreated and scales fell from my eyes. I could see. So what if I had been wronged, or that I was even *right*? Jesus did not defend himself. He did not say, "You can't do this to me—I'm God!" He had nothing to prove, only people to love.

And so did I. The realization stunned me. I loved my roommates more truly and with more purity at that moment than ever before. Love threw open prison doors of my own making and I walked into freedom—victim to victor.

❊ *Christ's attitude of love frees us from ourselves, letting us rise above circumstances.*

— Katherine A. Fuller —

Through God's Eyes

When he saw the crowds, he had compassion on them because
they were confused and helpless, like sheep without a shepherd.

—MATTHEW 9:36

*S*he wasn't much to look at. Her hair was tangled. Her clothes
were a mismatch of colors, too large for her frail body. Her
shoes were scuffed and worn. The Lord knew I was avoiding her.
I would walk past her quickly, but our paths still crossed often.

One day when I saw her and began my usual walk-by, she
dropped the paper bag she was holding. Very clearly I heard the
Lord say, "Pick it up."

Begrudgingly, I obeyed and we made eye contact. Her lovely
green eyes said, "Thank you." When she smiled, I didn't notice
the missing teeth. I saw a lovely woman who needed to be shown
the love of Jesus.

Because of God's amazing love for me, I determined that I would
show that same love to her. Shirley and I became good friends. I was
able to lead her to salvation and help her find self-worth through
Jesus Christ. Because of obedience, my life will never be the same.

✳ *Only when we see others through God's eyes can we love them as*
He does.

— Bobbie Roper —

A Father's Care

The Lord your God . . . will take delight in you with gladness.
With his love, he will calm all your fears.

—ZEPHANIAH 3:17

*H*oney, don't go near the swing set until I can anchor it down, okay?"

My innocent green eyes said *Okay*. My six-year-old mind decided otherwise. When Daddy disappeared into the garage, I hopped on, and within seconds was soaring high . . . before crashing to the ground.

I remember lying there, scared, the wind knocked out of me. I remember Daddy hovering over me, tenderly caring for me. I remember thinking how I deserved punishment for disobeying. I remember receiving a loving word from him instead, saying he'd wanted me to wait so I wouldn't get hurt. I remember him holding me tight, telling me he loved me.

And that's about all I remember about Daddy. Soon he would be gone from my life forever. That's when God—Father to the fatherless—lovingly stepped in.

I cherish that memory of my earthly father demonstrating my heavenly Father's love, not leaving me alone to suffer the consequences of my disobedience, but hovering over me, granting His tender mercy, teaching me life's harsh lessons with love's gentle touch.

✢ *Undeserving as we are, our heavenly Father hovers over us, rejoicing, caring for us, loving us with an everlasting love.*

— Sandi Banks —

Never Give Up

We are pressed on every side by troubles, but we are not
crushed. We are perplexed, but not driven to despair.

—2 CORINTHIANS 4:8

J read Winston Churchill's speech to Parliament at the beginning of World War II with my heart hammering. "We shall
fight on the beaches, we shall fight in the hills. . . . We shall never
surrender."

I had been suffering a clinical depression so awful I constantly
thought of suicide. It's so easy to get crushed in the battle of life.
I read Scriptures—the words of Paul, Jesus, and others. I looked
for encouragement everywhere, and there in 2 Corinthians 4:8 and
even in Churchill's words I found some hope.

Everywhere it seemed God told me, "Hang in there. Believe.
Keep on. Don't give up."

A turning point came one day when a friend visited and gave
me a little Matchbox truck.

"Put this on a shelf," he said, "and remember I'm there with you
in that truck, driving down the road and praising God."

I've lost the truck, but I still read Churchill now and then, and
I still read my Bible and have the truth that God and others are
with me through the battle of discouragement.

✵ *Battles come, but God is there. Accept His love, even if you can't
feel it at the moment.*

— Joseph Compaine —

The Silence of Love

It is foolish to belittle one's neighbor;
a sensible person keeps quiet.

—PROVERBS 11:12

I always loved church activities, and on this crisp fall afternoon, I enjoyed walking back from the campfire with my sixth-grade Sunday school teacher, Mrs. Showalter.

"Janet, you know, the boys will never like you until you lose weight," she suddenly said.

She continued in that strain, and I was stunned. I'd never realized the boys didn't like me. At times kids had teased me about my size, but that hadn't bothered me much—kids always teased other kids about something.

Now Mrs. Showalter was letting me know that adults—even those at church who were supposed to represent Jesus—also felt I was unacceptable because of the way I looked.

My little girl heart shriveled up in humiliation.

The next summer the baby fat naturally melted off my body. But the shame that I wasn't a person who could be loved as I was overwhelmed me for years.

As an adult, I realize Mrs. Showalter probably justified her criticisms under the guise of "speaking the truth in love." But I still wish she had just kept quiet.

✳ *Sometimes "speaking the truth in love" is not really a loving thing to do.*

— Janet Graham —

When Love Isn't Easy

If someone has enough money to live well and sees a
brother or sister in need but shows no compassion—
how can God's love be in that person?

—1 JOHN 3:17

*D*addy has no food at his house," our seven-year-old grand-daughter confided.

We were heartbroken over our daughter's divorce, so we wondered if God really expected us to reach into our pockets to help our former son-in-law. Our stretched finances already helped to support our daughter and three grandchildren.

My husband and I wrestled between anger and following God's Word. We took our emotional bundles before the Lord. As we prayed, God's love seeped through the barrier of resentment and enabled us to reach beyond our pain to show compassion. We purchased a grocery store gift card and drove straight to his house.

There was an awkward moment of silence when he opened the door. My husband handed him the gift card. A bewildered look crossed his face. "One of the kids said you needed food."

Tears dripped down his cheeks. I wrapped my arms around him. "We still care about you."

It's far from the ideal family picture I had in mind on our daughter's wedding day, but God's love and three precious children bind us together.

✻ *God's love compels us beyond bitter heartaches that we might show
genuine compassion.*

— Kathleen Kohler —

The Blessing of Blessing

How I praise the Lord that you are concerned about
me again. I know you have always been concerned for
me, but you didn't have the chance to help me.

—PHILIPPIANS 4:10

The missionary family spoke at our church, telling us the marvelous things God was doing in Kenya: "We have built a school, we now have an orphanage with more than a hundred kids in it, and we're starting a seminary for some of the new believers."

Of course, they showed us videos. They spoke in glowing terms about how their financial needs had been met.

"God is so good," the husband said. "I never thought I'd love living in another country, without air-conditioning, the food not so great, bugs everywhere. But we are immensely happy."

Afterward, I talked to him. When he looked at my name tag, he apparently recognized my name as one who had sent their family financial gifts.

"Thank you, thank you, thank you for your support. We couldn't do it without you. One day God will reward you for all your help."

I thought about everything the family had told us that night about their work in Kenya. "He already has," I said, tears in my eyes.

✻ *One way to show our love for God is by giving to those on the mission field.*

— Mark Littleton —

Thank You, God, for Mr. Wrong

And we know that God causes everything to work
together for the good of those who love God and
are called according to his purpose for them.

—ROMANS 8:28

*M*r. *Very* Wrong was manipulative and mean, but I was so dazzled by his charm and grand romantic gestures, I stayed in the relationship for two years.

Afterward, I struggled with many questions. Why had I allowed him into my life? Why hadn't God opened my eyes sooner? Would I be foolish enough to make this mistake again?

I didn't know it, but God was already blessing me.

When I met my Mr. Right, he was different. He didn't make grand gestures; he made quiet ones. Keeping my car running well replaced extravagant gifts. Helping me build the garden of my dreams replaced buying a dozen roses. Cooking and doing the dishes together so we could stay within our budgets replaced fancy dinners out. Mr. Right took care of me in ways I would have taken for granted had I not known Mr. Very Wrong. Grand gestures no longer impress me—real love does.

✶ *God can use any situation for our good.*

— Cynthia Owens —

The Most Unlikely Place

For everyone has sinned; we all fall short of God's
glorious standard. Yet God, with undeserved
kindness, declares that we are righteous.

—ROMANS 3:23–24

I stood and took a deep breath. Terrified to speak in public
and the only woman in a room full of men, I obviously didn't
belong. My stomach clenched as I scanned the expectant faces. I
gripped the podium for support. *How in the world did I get here?*

But this place was special and the worship time was powerful. I
wanted to be brave. The Spirit emboldened me to lead the prayer.

Was I in church? A Bible study? No. I was in a maximum-security
men's prison.

How this suburban-dwelling, college-educated mom got there
is one story. Why I choose to return frequently is another.

In the prison, I see God's love in action. I meet men who love
Jesus, whose lives are being transformed by the Holy Spirit. And
their vibrant faith inspires my own. As I worship shoulder to shoulder with thieves, abusers, and murderers, God's gift of grace becomes startlingly clear—Jesus died for *all* of us, and His blood
covers our sins the same.

✢ *In unlikely places, God frees our hearts to love our neighbors, His
children. Inmates, addicts, outcasts. All of them.*

— Kelli Regan —

Late for an Important Date

Give honor to marriage, and remain faithful
to one another in marriage.

—HEBREWS 13:4

I was late for my Valentine's Day date with my wife, losing track of time as I was immersed in a writing deadline. I hurried to the car and went a notch over the speed limit as she waited by herself at the restaurant. Would she be a bit peeved with me for not being prompt on this most romantic of occasions?

I spotted her at a table, my Irish wife's green eyes already glued to mine, two bright emeralds over a wide smile. She proudly told the waitress, "This is my Valentine!" I added that she made the choice to first be my Valentine thirty-five years ago, but I better keep my act together.

Anniversaries mark the duration of years spent together, but Valentine's Day for married couples poses a challenge—do we still love each other deeply and do we show it? I quietly promised myself I would do better next year, feeling undeserving of this priceless treasure with the emerald eyes.

❊ *Valentine's Day is a day to be expressive and grateful to the one you love.*

— James Stuart Bell —

Growing Love

Dear brothers and sisters, we can't help but thank
God for you, because your faith is flourishing
and your love for one another is growing.

—2 THESSALONIANS 1:3

*I*t always startles me to see my kids grow up and develop in
different areas of their lives, especially in the way they love.
For instance, my twenty-one-year-old daughter at one time loved
me for the things I did and bought for her. The latest Barbie doll.
The trip to the Disney Store at the mall. The array of Christmas
presents.

This moved into a time when she seemed to love me for the
things I was to her. "Daddy!" A friend. A counselor.

In time, though, she moved even beyond that. One day she said
to me, "You're my best friend, Dad."

I felt humbled by that, but I asked, "What do you mean?"

"You're always there. No matter how bad my world gets, I can
always come to you and I'll get your ear. I love you today for who
you are. You're godly. And I love that."

It struck me that she had grown in love quite a bit these last
few years.

✳ *When it comes to loving, we'll never completely arrive—we can
always love more.*

— Sam Donato —

One Horse, Three Friends

He does great things too marvelous to understand.
He performs countless miracles.

—JOB 5:9

*I*t was time to say good-bye. The vet frowned, "I'll be back at ten to put him down."

Colic is the number one killer of horses, and Cash's condition was much worse. His twisted gut left no room for hope.

Without hope, I went down on my knees crying out to God. My year had been much like Job's. "He's my best friend—the only one who loves me, and now you're taking him too. Please God, no!"

I called my friends with the news. Within an hour, Debbie and Patti came to pray and, I thought, say their good-byes. Instead, Debbie pulled out her anointing oil and prayed like I'd never heard.

"Where's your faith?" was her only comment as we applied heating pads, oil, and rubbed his stomach for hours.

Finally Debbie stood. "He's going to live."

Within minutes, Cash lifted his head and pounded the barn door. I let him out and he ran full speed. The vet returned to scratch her head. "This is not possible."

With the love of friends and a horse, God chose to perform a miracle that night in the same place He did two thousand years ago: a stable.

✣ *When God shows His love through a miracle, our lives are never the same.*

— Renee Shuping Cassidy —

Warm Feet

If you are wise . . . prove it by living an honorable life, doing good works with the humility that comes from wisdom.

—JAMES 3:13

One rainy April day I had to do a follow-up visit on a child living in a migrant camp who had tested positive for TB.

The children don't even have shoes, I noted sadly. After dinner that evening, I described my visit to my dad, who had been a J.C. Penney Company shoe salesman.

"No shoes?" Dad said. "When do you go out next? I'll get some shoes for you to take to those kids."

At my next visit to that camp, I carried six shoe boxes along with my nursing bag. The children's moms helped me to match shoe sizes with feet. It was raining as I left. Would the kids walk in the mud puddles wearing their new shoes?

"Jose!" one mom called. With my limited Spanish I only caught the word for *shoe* as a little fellow hurried to his mom and disappeared into his cabin. His feet stayed warm and dry in those new shoes.

✳ *When we hear of needs and try to meet them with the resources we have, we love wisely.*

— Julia D. Emblen —

Redeeming the Years

The Lord says, "I will give you back what you lost
to the swarming locusts."

—JOEL 2:25

I know this is part of God's plan," Lisa said about her husband's death. "And I don't like God's plan."

I hear her. I was molested as a child. Divorced—twice! Subject to panic attacks and depression. Terribly overweight. Lonely, often afraid, awkward around other people.

"What a loser!" I'd say to myself.

And yet . . . I've helped countless emotionally disturbed children because I know what they're going through. I can't judge other women in difficult marriages, and they know I understand their pain. Don't try to tell me that depression is due to lack of faith; I know better. I've lost over eighty pounds; I co-lead a Bible study; I've found an unexpected store of empathy and compassion.

Did God cause my problems so I could help others? Not a chance. But He doesn't waste anything, even my pain.

✳ *God loves us enough to redeem everything in our lives.*

— Elsi Dodge —

Reflect, Unite, and Conquer

> You know the saying, "Four months between
> planting and harvest." But I say, wake up and look
> around. The fields are already ripe for harvest.
>
> —JOHN 4:35

I wanted to grow a tomato—lots of them. Year after year I failed. I could not get a vine to produce even one tomato. "Think like a tomato," I told myself.

I did. I determined that if I were a tomato plant, I actually would not be happiest in my own yard. Instead, I'd prefer a narrow strip of my neighbor's south-facing front yard that was right next to my sidewalk and garage wall. Here, vines would get the great southern exposure of my neighbor Patty's yard and the additional heat radiating from my concrete and bricks.

So I went to see Patty. "Patty, let's team up and plant tomatoes!" I suggested, telling her my plan. She agreed.

We amazed ourselves and others as we harvested bushel after bushel of the delicious red globes. Patty had been my neighbor for twenty years, but until this year neither of us had seen the field ripe for harvesting that lay between our houses.

✷ *With a different perspective and collaboration, what field in your life could become ripe for harvest?*

— Sunny Marie Hackman —

Honor Your Leaders

Dear brothers and sisters, honor those who are
your leaders in the Lord's work. They work hard
among you and give you spiritual guidance.

—1 Thessalonians 5:12

*O*ur pastor stood humbly before the congregation. "I never thought this day would come," he said with tears in his eyes. "But it is here. We have plans to spend time traveling and with family, but I will never forget the time you've given me here. I will take with me memories of great times, good times, and even some tough times. But you all have seen me through."

One of the elders came forward with a package. "Something we want to present to you, Pastor, for your many years of service. I hope you will find these things a refreshment."

The pastor opened the gifts right there. One was a plaque honoring his years of service. A second was a card with a large check. We'd collected the money in gratitude for the many sacrifices he'd made for us, as well as his love and constant concern for our needs.

I went home that day realizing that honoring our leaders isn't just something we should do when they retire, but frequently.

✻ *God calls our leaders to serve Him in this way. As we honor them we show love to them and to God.*

— Sam Donato —

A Reason to Pray

Stay alert and be persistent in your prayers
for all believers everywhere.

—EPHESIANS 6:18

*W*hile visiting my neighbor Linda, I realized that every time she hears sirens, she stops what she's doing and prays for the injured person, family members, emergency workers, and hospital staff.

One day when my husband and I were out shopping, I heard an ambulance in the distance. I thought of Linda's example and began to pray. "Father, be with the person injured and their family members. Meet their needs. Protect. Heal. Keep them from being afraid."

Soon after we got home, the phone rang. It was Pauline, the mother of our daughter, Libby's, boyfriend.

"Jean, I don't want you to worry. Libby is okay, but . . ."

Pauline went on to say that our sixteen-year-old daughter was injured in a car wreck earlier that afternoon near the mall where I heard the ambulance. The person I had prayed for had turned out to be my own daughter, and our family.

✻ *Loving others means praying, even if we never know how needed and valuable our prayers are.*

— Jean Davis —

From Friends to Family

There are "friends" who destroy each other,
but a real friend sticks closer than a brother.
—PROVERBS 18:24

*M*ike! Wayne! Bernice!"
The room was filled with people—some I hadn't seen for more than twenty years. But the warmth and love permeated the atmosphere as we all caught up on each others' lives. We instantly picked up right where we'd left off so many years before.

It wasn't a high school reunion—I hadn't had a thing to talk about to people at those. Instead, it was a gathering of people who'd worked together as staff in a youth ministry organization decades earlier.

When one of the men, George, and I talked about the odd family feeling we all had, he offered this insight: "I think it's because we all worked together on so many projects. Even though over a hundred people worked in different areas, when something needed to be done, all the departments worked together. The weekly youth rallies, the fund-raisers, the prayer meetings . . . we all spent all those hours together working on common goals. And that's what builds relationships that last."

✳ *When we get involved in projects with others, we're bound to find friends that turn into family.*

— Jenni Davenport —

The Sanctity of Forgiveness

Lord, if you kept a record of our sins,
who, O Lord, could ever survive?
But you offer forgiveness,
that we might learn to fear you.

—PSALM 130:3–4

*M*y Christian workplace buzzed. Mary, a twenty-something former co-worker, was pregnant. Her unmarried status sent tongues into wagging mode. Mary visited our ministry often. Staunch Christians I admired expressed strong opinions: "She's not ready to be a mom." "Mary should give that baby up for adoption." "If she keeps that child, it has no future."

I thought of another unwed mom I knew who had chosen life for her child. As a result, her pro-life church ostracized her. She said, "I almost wish I'd aborted. If no one knew, I'd still be welcome."

One day I saw Mary and said, "I'm so proud of you."

"You *are*?" Her eyes registered surprise.

"When abortion is an easy option, I admire your courage to choose life for your baby."

Real love keeps no record of wrongs (1 Corinthians 13:5). Just as in Christ God forgave me, I relinquished my holier-than-thou attitudes to demonstrate kindness and compassion to Mary.

✣ *Since God forgives all my regrettable choices, how can I offer less to others?*

— Scoti Springfield Domeij —

Noah's Best Gift

Be happy with those who are happy, and
weep with those who weep.

—ROMANS 12:15

*W*hy are you crying, Daddy?"
    I hadn't noticed three-year-old Noah enter the living
room. I hurriedly swiped my bare arm across my tear-slickened
face. The obituary sheet I'd been trying to complete lay unfinished
beside me.

How could I condense my brother's life to one fill-in-the-blank
page?

As children, Daniel and I looked out for each other while Mom
worked. Now my best buddy and only sibling was gone, snatched
from our family at age twenty-nine.

I choked out words. "I'm sad because Uncle D died."

Noah said nothing, just gazed at me for a moment, then toddled
away.

When he returned, he held out his favorite toy, a Pooh Bear attached to a silky blanket.

"Feel how soft, Daddy," he said, caressing my wet hand, then
my cheek, with the blue satin border. "Doesn't that make you feel
better?"

A smile took my face by surprise. With something as simple
as a stuffed toy, God reached out to start to heal my broken heart
through the love of my new best buddy.

✻ *Sometimes love is best shown by sharing what is precious to us.*

— Benjamin Venable, as told to Jeanette Levellie —

She Didn't Thank Me

Sensible people control their temper;
they earn respect by overlooking wrongs.

—PROVERBS 19:11

*Y*ears ago I worked as a volunteer receptionist at a local charity. The recipients were mostly elderly individuals who were grateful for everything the charity provided. Well, usually.

One afternoon I received a call from a recipient. Even though what she complained about was only a minor inconvenience, she was outraged and described her disgust in explicit terms.

I was stunned. Who did this woman think she was?

Then, my thinking changed. *Why was she so angry? Had she lost her independence? Did she feel she had no control over her life? Was she sick, tired, lonely, overwhelmed?*

As I considered the potential answers, peace came over me. I answered her politely. She hung up on me. A few minutes later she called again, much calmer, and I transferred her to someone who could help.

Since that day, I see people differently. Actions that once angered me now compel me to consider how that person is hurting and how I can help.

✻ *Consider the person, not the action. God calls us to love.*

— Cynthia Owens —

Renewed Spirits

The human spirit can endure a sick body,
but who can bear a crushed spirit?

—PROVERBS 18:14

*W*e hadn't visited our son-in-law since he'd been diagnosed with brain tumors. When we did finally see him, I listened as he explained his sadness of not being able to see his "little man" or his beautiful daughter grow up. His spirit was crushed.

After dinner, I took him aside. "Steve, I've prayed about telling you something for a while. I need you to listen for a moment. You're a good man, you turned your life around from what it used to be, and, most important, you're a wonderful father."

His eyes widened.

My husband added, "We couldn't be prouder of you."

A rim of moisture crept over Steve's eyes. He wrapped his arms around my neck.

"You don't know how much that means to me," he said. "I didn't think anyone noticed that I was a good father except Pam. Pam and the kids are my life."

"Well, I'm sorry we didn't say anything sooner," my husband said. He and Steve shook hands. As they walked to the kitchen, Steve stepped with his body held a little taller. His spirit was renewed.

✳ *Love accepts opportunities to help those whose spirits are crushed.*

— Marge Gower —

A Better Way

*You have the authority to correct them when necessary,
so don't let anyone disregard what you say.*

—TITUS 2:15

It was one of those times when the church was up in arms. Some supported the new pastor's plan of action for building on to the church. Others thought it was foolhardy. The business meeting where it was being discussed was falling apart, though, until the youth pastor stood up and said, "Look, these options are all good ideas. Why don't we come up with a list of pluses and minuses about each one, and then vote on them. One at a time."

Someone said, "Here, here," but others resisted.

We talked more, but the youth pastor stood his ground.

"I've done this with the youth many times," he said. "It's simple. Just divide the paper in half. Write the proposition at the top, and then put the pluses on one side, and the negatives on the other."

Some people grumbled but finally everyone started cooperating. And together they solved the problem.

✳ *When you have some authority, use it to promote love, respect, and cooperation.*

— Gene Farmer —

An Uncomfortable Choice

I was sick, and you cared for me.

—MATTHEW 25:36

*T*he doctors say I don't have much time left," the young woman told me when she entered the bookstore where I worked. Crystal, desperate to reconnect with a faith she'd discarded years earlier, asked my advice on Christian books that would help her.

During her bookstore visits over the coming months, we talked, laughed, and prayed. When she was confined to her house as her disease progressed, she asked if I could bring by inspirational items for her to purchase.

My own fears of sickness and death caused me to hesitate.

"I'll get back to you," I said. I agonized between obeying God's Word and looking the other way.

As I prayed, God's love helped me step beyond my fears and into Crystal's world. While her health continued to decline, I relied on the Lord's strength as I wiped her face with a damp cloth, helped her with the bedpan, prayed, and read to her. Though I never grew comfortable and dreaded each encounter, Christ's example empowered me to love not with mere words but actions.

✻ *God's love enables us to minister to others beyond what we feel capable of doing.*

— Kathleen Kohler —

"Fix It, Daddy"

Jesus looked at them intently and said, "Humanly speaking,
it is impossible. But with God everything is possible."
—MATTHEW 19:26

O ur boys learned early in life that Daddy could fix almost
anything. It took years of maturity for them to insert the
important *almost.*

The hard fact of life is that not everything can be glued, duct
taped, or stapled together. While a scraped knee can be washed
and bandaged, hurt feelings are a little more difficult to treat. A
broken heart can seem impossible to fix, but our heavenly Daddy
can do what our earthly one cannot. Our loving God does not
insert an *almost.* He promises in Matthew 19:26 that with God,
all things are possible.

Just as my sons stood at the doorway to Daddy's workshop with
the broken pieces of a favorite toy and cried out, "Fix it, Daddy,"
all Christians have to do is stand before God's mercy seat with their
broken hearts and dreams, and cry out to Him, "Fix it, Daddy."

✻ *The loving God of the universe might not always fix it the way we
expect, but He will fix it.*

— Joyce McDonald Hoskins —

Rabbit Rabbit Day

Surely your goodness and unfailing love will pursue me
all the days of my life.

—PSALM 23:6

*R*abbit Rabbit," I said, peeking out from the covers.
My husband smiled at me.

Saying *Rabbit Rabbit* is a practice believed to have originated long ago in England. But for me, the tradition started with my second-grade teacher.

"If the first words you say on the first day of the month are *Rabbit Rabbit*," Miss Rosa told us, eyes twinkling, "you'll have a good month."

Faithfully I obeyed. Then one morning, I forgot.

I was doomed. While the other kids went to recess, I sulked at my desk.

"What's wrong?" Miss Rosa touched my shoulder.

"I forgot *Rabbit Rabbit*," I sniffed.

Miss Rosa spoke gently. "You know, *Rabbit Rabbit* is just for fun. You can still have a good month . . . if you try."

Now I remember those words. When I start my day thinking it's going to be good, chances are I find the positive.

"Thank you, God, for this day," I pray as I get out of bed, "and for rabbits too."

✴ *Start each day with a smile and confidence in a beautiful day, knowing the Lord who loves you has created it.*

— Peggy Frezon —

A Special Rest

So there is a special rest still waiting for the people of God.

—HEBREWS 4:9

I was visiting my alma mater the year after I graduated. I had become a Christian after graduating and I longed to tell all my friends still in school about this wonderful new life I was experiencing. However, I found it hard going.

One friend told me I was "condescending and acted like I knew all the answers."

Others said, "Christianity is just a big lie people use to keep others under control."

One told me this new change in my life all went back to my "need for a father figure," even though I already had a strong relationship with my great dad.

I walked over to the Arts building one afternoon, thinking I could look at some art projects and also pray about the frustration in my heart. There I ran into another old friend. She looked at me and said, "You look different. Something's changed. What happened?"

I told her about my conversion and the way my life was changing. She said, "You're at peace. You've made your peace with God and that's why you're no longer fighting everything."

Yes, God gives us peace, and we are different forever.

�❖ *God in His love gives us rest for our souls when we invite Him into our lives.*

— Mark Littleton —

Drawing on the Past

Everyone enjoys a fitting reply;
it is wonderful to say the right thing at the right time!
—Proverbs 15:23

"Oh, good grief! You've *ruined* our picture! Your man is too small!" The horror in the voice of my fellow first grader spread like fiery lava over my scarlet face and blackened my spirit.

I was timid and new to this Sunday school. I'd arrived late, just in time to ruin their mural with my addition. Our perceptive teacher came to my defense. "Haven't you children learned about perspective? This man is down the road, quite a distance from the others, and that's why he *must* look smaller."

I sat a little straighter and my red face cooled to a comfortable pink. This kind woman had saved me from a life of shame.

When I became an elementary school teacher, I was ever-vigilant with my shy students.

"Mrs. Ramsden, I so appreciate how sensitive you are to our child's needs," was a comment I often heard at parent-teacher conferences. I couldn't really bask in the compliment, because I remembered how I'd learned to love through kindly, Christian people like my Sunday school teacher.

⁂ *God teaches us gentleness and kindness through the sensitivity and loving actions of His obedient servants.*

— Susan E. Ramsden —

Blessing Circle

I helped those without hope, and they blessed me.

—JOB 29:13

I approached Sue at church. "I think God's calling me to support caregivers right now. Could I offer massages to you to support you through your husband's terminal cancer?"

I'd eaten dinner in this lady's perfect Martha Stewart-like home. Would she trust me enough to be so vulnerable? She did! Three times so far she's come and three times she's left looking more relaxed.

When she arrived at my door the other day, she thrust an armful of tiny yellow roses at me. "Here . . . and I also thought you could use a case of water since you're always handing it out to people." She got the case and pushed it into my kitchen.

I laughed and hugged her. My intention was to bless her during a difficult time, yet she insisted on blessing me. We both know harder times lie ahead, but she also knows she will not be facing them alone. She belongs to a community who wants to walk alongside, and she has the courage to allow them.

✳ *Sometimes the best way to forget our own difficulties is to reach out and bless someone else.*

— Linda Jett —

Praying in a Holy Way

In every place of worship, I want men to pray with holy
hands lifted up to God, free from anger and controversy.

—1 TIMOTHY 2:8

I went to church that night with anger in my heart. My wife
and I had a bad argument about certain things in our home,
and I didn't agree with her. I didn't think we needed any adjust-
ments. We called each other names, and then I left in a huff. Finally,
I ended up at the church and went to my men's support group,
where we usually talked about our lives, participated in a Bible
study, and prayed together.

When Jerry, the leader, raised the usual issue about how things
were going in our lives, I resisted the impulse to tell the guys what
had happened at home. Finally, I broke down and told them.

They were full of counsel and help. I realized I had been wrong
and needed to apologize to my wife right away. Before I felt comfortable entering the prayer time with my group, I left the room and
called her. She was so relieved and apologized too. By the time I got
home, we were right with each other and ready to talk honestly.

✳ *No one can pray honestly without real love and forgiveness in his
heart.*

— Kenneth Santoro —

Changed My Attitude

Teach me your ways, O Lord,
that I may live according to your truth!
Grant me purity of heart,
that I may honor you.

—PSALM 86:11

I enjoyed visiting with a young lady at church. We talked about housework, our husbands, children's antics, crafts, and various topics. I valued her friendship. I didn't think about her age.

One day, I found out she was the same age as my daughter. I suddenly realized I still thought of my daughter, Ginger, as my little girl. I wanted Ginger to exemplify perfection so I would look good as a mother. Therefore, I gave continual advice.

God showed me I needed to change my thoughts and actions toward Ginger. Yes, she would always be my daughter, but she was grown, married, and had her own child. I should treat her as a friend, not with the attitude of the all-knowing, all-wise mother.

My attitude didn't change overnight. But as I sought to please God and follow Him, I learned to love Ginger with God's unconditional love instead of my own self-serving attitude. I now enjoy visiting with her without questioning her decisions.

✻ *Loving unconditionally always leads to improved relationships.*

— Helen L. Hoover —

Power Lunch

> But I say, love your enemies! Pray for those who
> persecute you! In that way, you will be acting as
> true children of your Father in heaven.
>
> —MATTHEW 5:44–45

*M*anagement consolidated our Boston and New York offices, and I became Connie's supervisor. She was twenty years my senior, had previously been a journalist, and was uncooperative and incorrigible. My youth and insecurity were no match for this bold newspaperwoman. I finally spoke to the boss.

"Funny, you say things aren't working out," he said. "Connie's already complained."

"Complained? About me?" I felt outraged. My problematic subordinate had become my *enemy*!

"Invite her to lunch," he said. "Do something nice for her."

I hated the idea. For weeks I'd struggled with her obstreperous behavior. How could a sandwich help? But I had lunch with her anyway.

Over lunch I learned she'd moved to New York expecting to work for the department head, not a mid-level supervisor. I listened. I sympathized, realizing she'd relocated hundreds of miles under a false impression.

Lunch nourished a new relationship. Friendship soon blossomed and I credit my boss's advice: "Do something nice for her," which echoed Jesus's admonition, "Do good to those who persecute you" (see Matthew 5:44).

✳ *Love those you find unlovable. The Lord has promised to reward you.*

— Helene C. Kuoni —

I'm Included

And you are included among those Gentiles who
have been called to belong to Jesus Christ.

—ROMANS 1:6

*W*hen I learned some of my friends planned to drive from our school in New York to Florida for spring break, I really wanted to go. But would they include me?

I hurried down to Hoag's room to ask. He was the driver and his small car had only four seats. The middle of the backseat was a hump. When I asked if I might go, he said pretty much what I expected: "There's no room."

"I could sit on a pillow on the hump," I countered.

He answered, "I'll ask the other guys."

I really wanted to go on this trip. But I knew that although the other guys were my friends, they wouldn't want to be crowded for such a long trip. Then Hoag called home. He came to my room and said, "My father will let me take his car. It's big enough. So you're in."

I rejoiced and we ended up having a great trip.

Inclusion in something like that can be great. For the Gentiles in Jesus's day, the fact that they were included in God's plan of salvation was a wonder. God had made a way for all of us to live together in peace and love. That includes you.

✣ *When love drives us, we find ways to include others in our plans.*

— Mark Littleton —

Put on the Armor of God

Put on all of God's armor so that you will be able
to stand firm against all strategies of the devil.

—EPHESIANS 6:11

*E*very morning I pray the armor of God over my church leaders—my pastors and elders.

I ask God to bind them together and swaddle them with His belt of truth. I request that He walk them into His peace, which is beyond understanding, and help them leave peace behind them wherever they go.

I ask the Lord to filter their input and output—everything they see and hear, feel and think, say and do—through His helmet of salvation and the breastplate of righteousness.

Then I ask that He arm them with the sword of His Spirit, which is the Word of God, and the shield of faith, so that their hands hold only those essentials.

And I find, as I pray for them by name each day, that my love and respect for them grows.

✣ *Love your leaders by praying for them!*

— Elsi Dodge —

God's Plan

"For I know the plans I have for you," says the
Lord. "They are plans for good and not for
disaster, to give you a future and a hope."

—JEREMIAH 29:11

*W*hen I was eight years old, I was admitted to the hospital
with a kidney infection. My memories are sketchy, but they
directed my life. While I was in the children's ward, the nurse I had
wasn't very nice. She was angry that I wet the bed. She put the rails
up on my bed and left me: wet, lonely, and scared.

My family gave me several coloring books and paper dolls to
keep me entertained. The nurse gave some of them away to others,
saying I had too many. She didn't even ask, but just did it. That's
when I decided in my heart to become a nurse so that I could be
nice to my patients.

I did go on to become a nurse. When I had trouble and wanted to
quit, I remembered why I was there. It was in training that I found
Christ through one of my instructors whose life portrayed Him. I
wanted the peace and love I saw reflected in her face and actions.

✳ *When trouble comes, and it will, remember God has a plan.*

— Kay E. Combs —

What Can I Do for You?

If you sinful people know how to give good gifts to
your children, how much more will your heavenly
Father give good gifts to those who ask him.

—MATTHEW 7:11

*W*ith Jesus inside me, I try to help others. But sometimes I
find it hard to ask for the help I myself need.

One day, I sat in church needing advice, but I could not bring
myself to directly ask anyone for it. Suddenly, the priest I spoke to
asked, "What can I do for you?"

I felt the door open for me to describe my struggle.

He then spent time and energy to offer practical guidance and
names of several people to contact who could help me further.
That was a true moment of grace for me. I knew the Lord had
heard my heart's groanings.

The Lord then called me to do this for others.

I have prayed to be bold enough to say, "What can I do for you?"
Sometimes I can be that open, even while knowing that what the
person really needs may be very difficult for me to give. I never
forget how much this caring question helped me.

✳ *A true gift is providing what someone really needs. Don't hesitate
to ask others how you can help.*

— Jane M. Abeln —

A Bucket of Paint

Grace, mercy, and peace, which come from God the
Father and from Jesus Christ—the Son of the Father—
will continue to be with us who live in truth and love.

—2 JOHN 1:3

*W*ayne! Don't move your stepladder with the paint bucket
still sitting on it," ordered my dad, a paint contractor who
was also my boss.

"Oh, it'll be okay," I insisted, and pushed the stepladder a few
inches across the client's front porch. Instantly, a white paint tsu-
nami splashed my overalls and shoes, soaked the drop cloth, and
surged across the floor.

From his ladder perch, my dad, weary from working in the Au-
gust heat, eyed the damage and his not-too-bright teenager. Calmly,
he stepped down and said, "Well, let's clean it up."

I deserved an angry reprimand, but instead he helped me mop
up the mess. Dad's forgiving mercy taught me godly love.

The heavenly Father warns me against wrong attitudes and actions. Yet, at times, I foolishly ignore Him and disobey. The result is
always harmful—sometimes disastrous. Yet my loving Lord is gracious and merciful. He forgives me and helps me mop up the mess.

✶ *Thankfully, God loves us even when we foolishly disregard His*
Word.

— Wayne A. Pearson —

The Power of Anonymous Giving

Give your gifts in private, and your Father,
who sees everything, will reward you.

—MATTHEW 6:4

Standing at my door, the deliveryman handed me a dozen perfectly arranged red roses.

"Who are they from?" I asked.

Just a week before, a two-year relationship I'd been in had ended, leaving me broken and facing my thirtieth birthday alone.

The next afternoon, after I taught all day at school, I hurried into the florist and begged one of my high school students who worked there to tell me who sent the flowers. Reluctantly, he revealed the source.

Twenty-five years later, I park down a street in a subdivision. The husband lost his job. The wife just had a baby. Gift bag in hand, I ring the doorbell. Then I run back and jump behind the steering wheel of my getaway van. Smiling, I drive home.

I'm following a habit I began years earlier, following the example set for me that damp March morning when a much older teacher down the hall introduced anonymous giving to me with that extravagant bouquet of flowers. She spoke not words, but love to my disappointed and discouraged heart.

✳ *Giving is sometimes sweeter and purer when no card or signature is included.*

— Diane Buller —

Two Wounded Hearts, One Healing Touch

How precious is your unfailing love, O God!
—PSALM 36:7

I dreaded meeting her. I didn't want to like her, much less love her—after all, she was the wayward woman who had been waiting in the wings when my thirty-two-year marriage died.

Now a family event had brought us together; friends back home prayed for me concerning this encounter.

What does a "replacement wife" look like? I wondered. *What's she have that I don't? We were married for three decades. Over half my life. Been traded in.*

Thoughts, painful and relentless, taunted me.

The awkward moment finally came. *Help me, Lord!*

"Nice meeting you," she drawled. I responded politely.

As we chatted, I learned this was her fourth marriage. I sensed the baggage, the scars, the fears. Then, amazingly, I sensed something else: God working, helping me see her with *His* eyes of compassion and love.

She extended her hand to say good-night. Impulsively, I hugged her. She hugged back tightly and sobbed.

"You're so beautiful," she said, seeing *Jesus's* love shining through.

Two wounded hearts, miraculously bound together by His loving, healing touch.

✳ *Just when we think it's impossible, God's "precious, unfailing love" steps in, transcending our greatest fears, healing our deepest hurts.*

— Carrie Shepherd —

Impulse Spending

If your gift is to encourage others, be encouraging.

—Romans 12:8

Late Saturday afternoon, as I filled my car with gas, I noticed a garbage truck filling up on the other side of the station. Three men standing behind it shrugged out of green jumpsuits and washed off their hands and faces.

I finished before they did, so I decided to add a little excitement to their day. Driving over to the truck, I spoke to the man closest to me.

"Do you gentlemen work on this truck?"

Cautiously, the man nodded his head. The other two men watched our conversation, both faces wary. They had no reason to expect anything other than a complaint.

I pulled some money out of my wallet. As I handed each of the men a five-dollar bill, I said, "Thanks for doing such a good job keeping our city clean. Have a hamburger on me."

I looked in my rearview mirror as I drove off. They were staring at each other in confusion, wondering what had just happened.

⁂ *Delight in doing simple deeds of loving-kindness.*

— Lynnda Ell —

Promise Made, Promise Kept

Has he ever spoken and failed to act?
Has he ever promised and not carried it through?

—NUMBERS 23:19

Steve's cancer has returned. This time, we will have to remove his eye and half his skull. If he survives the surgery, he will need extensive reconstruction."

I sat rigid, stunned by the doctor's words. My five-year-old son had already endured a four-hour procedure to remove the neurofibrosarcoma from his sinuses. But now, new growth had appeared.

Where could I turn? Although I had accepted Christ in my teens, I had drifted away from Him and gone my own way. Would God even hear me now? Desperate, I searched for answers elsewhere, but found none.

Finally, the night before the surgery, I admitted I was helpless. I begged the Lord for mercy and promised if He would bring Steve through this, I would live for Him the rest of my life. Immediately, He comforted me with an overwhelming peace and assurance the cancer was gone.

The next day, the surgeon found no cancer—just a bone rounding itself off. God kept His promise, I strive daily to keep mine, and Steve, now forty-five, is cancer free!

* *God meets us in the tough places and grants us hope and peace.*

— Loretta Boyett —

Share Your Life

> We loved you so much that we shared with you not
> only God's Good News but our own lives, too.
>
> —1 THESSALONIANS 2:8

*J*he teen had come to my wife and me out of terror.

"I'm pregnant and everyone says I should have an abortion. But I don't want one," she said through her tears.

We talked about options for this baby—adoption, raising it herself, finding a home where she knew it would be raised with Christian values.

"But where would I live if I don't have an abortion? My dad won't let me come home. He says I disgraced our family."

Near our church was a home for unwed mothers. I told the girl, "We'll take you there tonight. You'll have a bed and a place to live until the baby comes."

We drove her over, got her settled in, then visited regularly and took her to church activities for the rest of her pregnancy. In the end, she made an adoption plan and the baby was placed into a good home.

Later she said, "You gave me not only the Bible but yourselves. I'll never forget it."

✵ *The truth of the Bible goes far—especially when we put it into practice to touch others with our lives and love.*

— James Hopkins —

My To-Do List

This is my commandment: Love each other
in the same way I have loved you.

—JOHN 15:12

With my neatly penned to-do list, I was ready for my day! Until my phone rang. My mother-in-law wanted to know how the kids were. I cut the call short, because my to-do list was long. She sounded a little down, but talking on the phone wasn't on my agenda. I promised to bring everyone over to see her soon.

I quickly moved to the next item on my list. The doorbell rang. Oh no! It was my friend Shelly with tears streaming down her face as she poured out her marriage problems. I tried very hard not to look at the clock—or my organizer—too often. Finally she left.

I rushed to complete my list. Two more delays. My neighbor asked me to feed her cats while she left town to help her sister who had cancer. Then I turned to see my daughter in tears. Her best friend told her they weren't friends anymore.

I felt the pressure to finish my list. The last item was prayer. Bowing my head, I thanked God for letting me complete my list. All the hurting people I encountered came to mind. "Lord, please send someone to help comfort these people."

I did came a quiet thought. *I sent you.*

✻ *People are always more important than any item on our to-do list!*

— Eva Juliuson —

The Little Red Sports Car

God will generously provide all you need. Then
you will always have everything you need and
plenty left over to share with others.

—2 CORINTHIANS 9:8

*A*t our house when a teenager started to drive, he or she had to drive a beat-up old car so we didn't have to pay so much insurance.

Our youngest daughter didn't want to drive the old beater. She wanted to drive the little red sports car. So she got a job and paid the insurance. She loved driving that car.

Then the church she loved outgrew their building. The leaders asked the members to give sacrificially so the church could enlarge.

One day, my daughter came to me in tears and placed the keys to the sports car in my hand. "I think we need a bigger church more than I need to drive the sports car."

She pledged a thousand dollars besides her regular tithe. Between the insurance amount and working as a waitress after school, she paid the pledge before she went to college.

Someday if she wants a red sports car, I think God will make sure she gets one.

✳ *God sees and cares when we love until it hurts.*

— Brenda J. Young —

A Confident Love

I am very happy now because I have complete confidence in you.
—2 CORINTHIANS 7:16

*T*he apostle Paul encouraged those he touched by believing in them. He understood that sometimes when a word of prayer doesn't seem to help, a word of encouragement from the Lord does.

When Brian entered my office, I sensed immediately that he was a man who had been down on his luck. Released from prison that day with only twenty dollars in his pocket, he slumped in the chair adjacent to my desk, discouraged and down-trodden.

He spoke eloquently, apologetically, but seldom lifted his eyes. Brian had stolen some cars to get by, and the law caught up with him. Even though he asked me for money, I knew he needed something money could not buy—confidence.

I told Brian that I saw something in him: a spark he had yet to ignite. He only needed to believe in himself as God loved and believed in him. He wept, and then left.

Several months later, Brian returned wearing a new suit and walking tall. All because someone shared God's love and confidence in him.

❖ *Because of God's confidence in us, we can love others confidently.*

— Jim Zabloski —

All in the Family

Your love for one another will prove to the
world that you are my disciples.

—JOHN 13:35

I picked up the mystery package from my doorstep and read
the sender's name. *I don't know her.* Moments later, I pulled
out its hidden treasures, each with a note from a woman named
Dee. A cancer survivor, she simply wanted to express her love and
support to me as I battled lymphoma.

I chuckled at a black velvet hat trimmed in feathery pink fur
to cover my bald head. Golden retrievers on a new T-shirt offered
me their puppy love. A box of chocolates, perfumed soaps, and a
yellow rubber ducky put a smile on my weary face. This Idaho girl
even sent two spud candies to honor her home state.

I was still amazed at the box of unexpected gifts when an auto-
graphed copy of *Praying Through Cancer* showed up in my mailbox
the next day—again from a stranger. Soon a CD of songs, written
by another cancer survivor, left me shaking my head.

Bonded by suffering, united in Christ as family, these angels of
God touched my heart with wings of love.

✣ *May we serve as God's messengers through love in action.*

— Nora Peacock —

Great-Grandma, God, and Me

For if ye love them which love you, what reward have ye?
—MATTHEW 5:46 KJV

*B*efore Great-grandma and I locked horns, I had never met anyone I disliked.

The eldest of six children, I cooked, cleaned, and bossed my siblings. When Grandma, as we called her, came to live with us, she took charge of our new baby brother, referring to him as "my baby boy." *She* ordered *me* around.

The situation became unbearable, and I went to Mom with my complaints. She listened, smiling and nodding, but I gasped at her solution. "Grandma has always been this way, so you'll have to change."

Night after night, I prayed for God to straighten out Grandma's hard-boiled heart. In the meanwhile, I attempted to keep some distance between us.

One day, Grandma told me about the time she saw the stagecoach robber, Jesse James, ride into town. When she finished, I said, "Tell me another story, Grandma."

After several Wild West tales, Grandma allowed me to hold my baby brother. We exchanged smiles. God had His hands in things when I grew to love Great-grandma and all her flaws.

✢ *When we turn our situations over to God, He sometimes answers in subtle ways.*

— Jean Ann Williams —

A Child's Love

Jesus said, "Let the children come to me. Don't
stop them! For the Kingdom of Heaven belongs
to those who are like these children."

—MATTHEW 19:14

The week after I retired from an engineering career, I began
volunteering in my church's weekday preschool.

Many times my role with the children is just being there to listen.
Like one day when Jordan drew at an art center in the weekday
preschool four-year-old class. As I stood nearby, she looked up and
said, "Grandpa John, my little dog Jenny died."

"I am sorry. What happened?" I asked.

Jordan said, "Jenny and a big dog were let out together at the
kennel. The big dog bit Jenny, and Jenny died. I miss Jenny, and
so does my mommy. When Mommy talks on the telephone about
Jenny, sometimes she cries."

At other times, I'm the one who is blessed, like when I helped
Annie in the three-year-old class put some paper on the easel so
she could paint blue and green. She leaned her head back, looked
into my eyes, and softly said, "I love you, Grandpa John."

It was then that I knew how God must feel when I say, "I love
you, God."

✣ *Have you expressed your love for God today?*

— John C. Westervelt —

Burdens Shared in the Parking Lot

Share each other's burdens, and in this
way obey the law of Christ.

—GALATIANS 6:2

*T*ime was tight. I needed to return to the office when I met her in the mall parking lot. The bumper sticker on her car said: "Someone I Love Was Murdered."

"Someone you love was murdered?" I asked.

"Yes, my twenty-seven-year-old son, seventeen years ago—beaten by thugs with two-by-fours." She spoke softly.

"I'm so sorry," I said. "Would you like a hug?"

"Yes, I'd love a hug." She asked if I'd lost a child too.

"No," I said. "I've never experienced the awful grief you have. But I have lost loved ones—a brother and a father just a month apart, many years ago."

We talked a bit more, then she told me she'd lost a sister to suicide.

"That grief, I know," I said. "That's how my father died."

There we were, two strangers in a parking lot—hugging and sharing our long-ago but still present grief. We clasped hands and wished each other God's blessings.

Suddenly office obligations shifted to a much lower priority.

✳ *Grief is a common denominator through which God's love can flow.*

— Mary Fran Heitzman —

Heart Rocks

From the ends of the earth,
I cry to you for help
when my heart is overwhelmed.
Lead me to the towering rock of safety.

—PSALM 61:2

*W*hile taking my daily walk on a nearby rock road, I noticed a rock in the shape of a heart. I picked it up. I knew my daughter would be fascinated with it too, and looked for one for my son. I searched for days but could find no "heart rock."

A few weeks later, while walking the same road, I saw a "heart rock" the size of my hand. *Where was it a few weeks earlier when I was looking so fervently?* I wondered.

God's responding message to me seemed to be, "Trust my heart. Take this rock to remind you that I am with you."

For three months I have been finding "heart rocks"—more than a hundred so far. Some of them look freshly chiseled; some are well worn. But each serves as a reminder that the Rock of all ages is fighting for me, and He will bring me through my battles victoriously.

✳ *We can lean on God who is our rock, our salvation, and our fortress.*

— Debra R. Stacey —

Total Love

I would be willing to be forever cursed—cut off
from Christ!—if that would save them.

—ROMANS 9:3

I went to our high school reunion with one purpose: to tell
my old friends about Jesus. I'd grown up with this tight-knit
group of guys long before I gave my life to Christ.

Chris was one of my closest pals. Though I hadn't seen him in
thirty years, he was as affable as I remembered.

When I mentioned that I'd become a Christian, he said, "I'm
an atheist."

I said, "It's okay. God can convert atheists too."

He laughed, but he had some questions: "How does God feel
about drinking beer?" he asked me. "How does God feel about
smoking cigars? What about gambling?"

I answered the questions as clearly as I could, ultimately saying,
"These things are really peripheral. God's more interested in your
soul. The important thing is believing in Christ, not a list of rules."

We exchanged email addresses and parted, him saying, "You
know, I like your brand of Christianity."

I keep praying that one day he'll look beyond his religious per-
ceptions to see the loving Jesus.

✳ *Loving others is the key to bringing them to the loving Jesus.*

— Clay Taylor —

Love That Knows No Borders

Never stop praying.

—1 Thessalonians 5:17

*A*fter preparing a care package for an unknown little girl in an unknown country, my eight-year-old daughter began to pray fervently for its recipient. "Please help my box get there safely. Please help the one who will get my box and bless her family."

Jessica prayed. And prayed. And prayed. For more than a year-and-a-half, every night.

In exasperation and unkindness, Jessica's older brother finally told her, "I think your box has made it there. You can stop praying now." But Jeb Daniel didn't understand the love that God had given Jessica for a little girl she had never met.

Less than a week later, Jessica received in the mail a torn letter on blue stationery. The only word we recognized amongst the foreign symbols was *India*. But we could see the beautiful face of a precious little girl in a photograph.

As only God could arrange, a church friend who had grown up in India read the letter to Jessica, word for word.

It was worth the wait. And the prayers.

✻ *I want to love the unknowns like Jessica, for they are not unknown to God.*

— Julie Lavender —

It Takes Togetherness

Two people are better off than one, for
they can help each other succeed.

—ECCLESIASTES 4:9

A rainbow of balloons floated out of the bag I was holding. "Can you choose a balloon," I asked my preschool class, "and find something in the room with the same color?"

As the children scurried off, Sherrie, the afternoon teacher, popped in. "Morning, Doris—just checking to see if everything's going okay."

I appreciated Sherrie's morning welcomes and decided to return the favor. As I peeked into her room that afternoon, children were running around with a balloon in one hand and brightly colored objects in the other. I couldn't believe Sherrie was using my hard-worked plans and had been for some time.

"I'm sorry," she apologized. "I've been so busy and always considered us a team that helps each other."

For her part, Sherrie did start putting more effort into her lessons. And me? I realized Who gave me everything to begin with and am learning to be more generous in sharing my time and talents with others. After all, we're all a part of God's team!

✣ *Sometimes God wants me to work as we.*

— Doris Schuchard —

Real Comfort

Now, however, it is time to forgive and comfort him.
Otherwise he may be overcome by discouragement.

—2 CORINTHIANS 2:7

*O*ur meeting at the boardwalk chapel was crowded, but I saw the tall man in mirrored sunglasses step in and sit down. Suddenly, he was on his feet.

"I killed six men in Vietnam. Where does that put God and me?"

I sat there frozen in place. What did this guy intend to do? We'd been taught not to engage with hecklers. But . . . he stood again, adding, "Hey, I'm talkin' to you, preacher."

No one moved. Finally, I prayed, *God, send someone to talk to him.*

God said, "How about you?"

I cringed, but got up, walked back to the man, and started talking. He was a Vietnam vet with many problems. I went out with him, spoke of God's forgiveness and comfort, and walked on the boardwalk with him.

An hour later, he left me saying, "You've really helped me. I'll never forget it."

Forgiveness and comfort: so many people need it. Is that what you tell them about?

✻ *When you comfort the hurting, God is pleased.*

— Don Richards —

Love in the Buttercups

The flowers are springing up,
the season of singing birds has come,
and the cooing of turtledoves fills the air.

—SONG OF SONGS 2:12

*P*oet Eugene Field wrote, "Buttercup shareth the joy of day, Glinting with gold the hours of play." The calendar may say spring, but the indicator that causes my heart to skip a beat is my first sighting of a buttercup. It is sunny confirmation that winter's snowy wraps will soon be packed away in exchange for yellow-green leaves and the scent of freshly turned earth.

When God presented the rainbowed promise to Noah to never destroy the earth by flood, He was compelled by a divine love for His creation. His reign over the world is fair and He will fully restore it at just the right time. Whenever the seasons begin to change, I remember that the everlasting God who spoke to Noah, visited Abraham, dwelled with Moses, and lived a lifetime in the person of Jesus Christ is loving His creation in winter, spring, summer, and fall.

I find comfort and confidence in God's abiding love that is constant even in the phases of the moon and in the buttercups of spring.

✣ *Whenever you enter a season of change, remember to look to the God of Creation who loves you in and out of season.*

— Alyssa Santos —

Cracked Pots Patched by Love

We now have this light shining in our hearts, but we ourselves are like fragile clay jars containing this great treasure. This makes it clear that our great power is from God, not from ourselves.

—2 CORINTHIANS 4:7

At my friend's house, a miniature flowerpot sits proudly displayed in the center of the patio table. It is painted with bright colors in a watermelon motif—the work of an enthusiastic child.

My friend appreciates the clay pot as a masterpiece. On close examination, though, you can easily spot cracks. The pot has been broken many times and its shards glued back together, not particularly artfully. Yet there it stands, welcoming visitors to my friend's home and representing the love that can be found there.

Like that cracked and broken pot, we humans are flawed. We have been damaged by pain, persecution, and disappointment. Yet God sees the value in each of us and continues to use us as His messengers, witnesses, and examples. The glue of His love patches our wounds so we can keep serving as His vessels, His treasures in fragile clay jars. Despite our flaws, we are worthy to share His love.

✻ *God's love patches our wounds so we can do the same for others.*

— Kim Sheard —

Foolish or Wise?

Instead, God chose things the world considers foolish
in order to shame those who think they are wise.

—1 Corinthians 1:27

I have heard forever that I should make more of an effort
to share my faith. But I don't seem to naturally get many
opportunities. So I decided, after prayer and seeking God, to become more proactive about it. I began carrying tracts with me
everywhere I went. I gave them to people like cashiers at Walmart
and others I met.

In time, I got another idea: *What if I said directly to some of
these people, "Have you ever heard of the gospel? Do you know
what it is?"*

And if they said yes, I'd ask, "Do you believe it?" As I've started
asking these questions, I've received many interesting responses.

Of course a few people get nasty and don't like it. And some
regard me as some "stupid Christian" or a real fool. I tell people,
"I guess I'm just a fool for God. If that's what it takes to show love
to others, I'm all for it."

Anyway, it's not a problem. I'll live with that criticism since out
of my foolishness, God may be able to bring His love, light, and
wisdom into someone else's life.

❖ *We're never foolish to try to reach others with God's love.*

— Mark Littleton —

The Lovable Girl

The Lord doesn't see things the way you see them. People judge
by outward appearance, but the Lord looks at the heart.

—1 SAMUEL 16:7

*W*hen I found out the big secret in the neighborhood, I nearly
blew a fuse. My son was dating Nicole, and no one dared
to tell me. Everybody knew how judgmental I was—everyone
except me.

I didn't want to be alienated from my son, so I said to God,
"Please help me love Nicole."

You see, when I heard "tattoos" and "tongue ring," I thought
"biker chick." Well, in walked this sweet girl with a Tinkerbell
purse and beautiful blue eyes that lit up every time she looked at
our son. We all fell in love with her instantly.

From that point on, God opened my eyes to the blossoming of
Nicole's new faith, the winsomeness of her personality, and the
tenderness of her warm heart.

She's in the family now. She's the one who makes everybody's
birthday special. She's the one who helps family members in need.
She loves others deeply and sweetly. I'm so glad she's our Nicole.

✳ *When we ask God to help us love, He can answer in ways that*
amaze and delight us.

— Cindy Sipula —

A Baggie of Love

Don't just pretend to love others. Really love them.

—ROMANS 12:9

I was sitting next to my husband's hospital bed when I got a call.

"Robbie, this is Jan. I'd love to see you. Can you come to the waiting room?"

Two days earlier, my husband had been in a serious motorcycle accident. It would be a very difficult time for my family, and John would spend a month in hospitals. I was exhausted, but I knew Jan would lift me up.

"I'll be right there."

Jan greeted me with a hug. We sat and talked and, before she left, she prayed for me and gave me a bag.

"Just a few things you might need."

Back in John's room, I opened my gift. Some snacks, a book, a candle. And then I saw a Baggie filled with coins. A note attached said, "For the hospital vending machines."

Tears came. Jan had taken the time to love me with genuine affection. That simple gift ushered my heart into the presence of God. I prayed, thanking Him for Jan, for the strength He gave me through friends, and for a simple Baggie that blessed me so much.

I used every one of those coins.

✳ *Using creativity in giving is a way of loving others with genuine affection.*

— Robbie Iobst —

Show and Tell

Direct your children onto the right path,
and when they are older, they will not leave it.

—PROVERBS 22:6

*A*s I left a local discount store, I reached inside my pocket for my cell phone and unknowingly pulled out loose bills. A lady behind me shouted, "Mister, your money is blowing away."

I turned and saw her son chasing the dollar bills. I gave chase too. It was dark and the wind blew the money in all directions. We sprinted after it beneath the floodlights. I laughed as I raced him toward the final bill with the wind kicking it away one more time.

I grabbed it. The boy looked to be about seven or eight years old. When he handed me the money he had collected, I thanked him and gave him the dollar I had chased down. With a laugh and a handshake, we went our separate ways.

I marveled at what I had witnessed. What a wonderful example of doing the right thing: treating others as they would want to be treated. This mom had taught her son by putting action to her words. She had *shown* him honesty.

✻ *The best way we can make sure kids will grow up to be considerate adults is to demonstrate love for others while they're still small.*

— Jim D. Ferguson —

Is It Friday Yet?

I have not come to call those who think they are righteous,
but those who know they are sinners and need to repent.

—LUKE 5:32

"Is it Friday yet, Miss Pat?"

She waited for my answer, her large ebony eyes hopeful, cornrows and bronze skin unusually clean.

"No, honey, it's Wednesday."

"But I want it to be Friday so I can hear your Bible stories."

My heart thrilled at her words, echoed by so many children in this low-rent district.

I am the rare Caucasian living in this tenement area of mostly single mothers, abandoned or unwed, where drug deals often "go down." I recall the deep depression I suffered early after moving here and my bitter complaints to a close friend. "This wasn't my picture of retirement, forced to live in such a place due to finances. I have nothing in common with these people!"

"*These people?*" she repeated. "Jesus died for these people!"

God used her words to touch my heart and ultimately fill it with compassionate love for those around me—especially the children. I began holding after-school Bible classes in the clubhouse every Friday. My friend supplies me with beautiful Bible story books. Lives are changing here—especially mine.

✣ *We are most blessed when we serve Jesus where we are.*

— Pat Harris, as told to Kitty Chappell —

That's Not My Job

So then, let us aim for harmony in the church
and try to build each other up.

—ROMANS 14:19

*I*f only he would listen to me!"

For possibly the thousandth time, my husband's refusal to take my advice left me so frustrated I wanted to scream! I was convinced if he would just do things the way I knew he should, our life would run much more smoothly. Problem was, he didn't see it that way. Years of conflict between us resulted.

One day, as I read Romans 14, several verses stood out like a blinking neon sign. *"Accept him . . . without passing judgment."* Was I my husband's judge? *"To his own master he stands or falls . . ."* Was I my husband's master? *"The Lord is able to make him stand . . ."* I had tried everything to change him and it wasn't working. I'm not able—and it's not my job! My role is to bring peace to our marriage and lift my husband up in love. All my efforts are wasted when expended in the wrong area.

✻ *When we focus on doing our jobs and trust God to do His, everything works better.*

— Liz Collard —

The Touch of Sympathy

Finally, all of you should be of one mind. Sympathize with
each other. Love each other as brothers and sisters.

—1 PETER 3:8

*O*ur friends had been trying for months to get pregnant. And
suddenly they were. Then four months in, they lost the baby
they wanted so badly. We all gathered at the church for the funeral.
When I talked to them in the line, the mom, Dorine, wept, and
so did I.

"It's tough," I said.

"I didn't think it would be this hard," she answered.

I moved off to talk to her husband, Dan, a good friend. As I did,
I watched my wife talk to Dorine. I couldn't hear what they were
saying, but they shared a lot of hugging and tears.

Sympathy. It's so necessary in a grief situation. Sometimes we
struggle with what to do or say. It doesn't always come naturally.
But we simply need to share our friends' grief. When we really
sympathize, we show God's love. We don't parrot clichés or just
throw out a Bible verse here and there. We feel with them. That's
the kind of love God honors.

✳ *True love shows up and shares another's pain.*

— Brian Varney —

Brotherly Love

Supplement your faith with a generous provision of
moral excellence . . . knowledge . . . self-control . . .
patient endurance . . . godliness . . . and brotherly
affection with love for everyone.

—2 PETER 1:5–7

*I*t was the Saturday morning of the local Easter egg hunt. I
handed baskets to my two grandsons just as the man in charge
shouted, "Ready, set, *go!*"

The five-year-old zoomed off, scooping up eggs for his basket
while his little brother slowly let go of my hand and toddled across
the park.

When the whistle ended the hunt, both boys scampered toward
me and began counting their eggs. Soon, the older boy noticed the
three eggs in his brother's basket and began moving his own eggs
into the other basket until they were both half full.

After the man recognized a boy who had the most eggs, I looked
at my five-year-old and asked, "Do you know you found as many
eggs as he did?"

"It's okay," he smiled. "My brother needs me and I like to
help him."

A tear trickled down my cheek. My five-year-old grandson
just taught me a lesson about sacrificial love—the real meaning
of Easter.

✳ *Sharing what we have with others expresses God's love.*

— Betty J. Dalrymple —

Wrestling With God's Provision

Whatever is good and perfect comes down to us from
God our Father, who created all the lights in the heavens.
He never changes or casts a shifting shadow.

—James 1:17

"That's not what I want, God." The wrestling match had begun. I was tired of moving and I didn't want to look for new roommates, so I camped out in that corner.

My next move was to tell God that I didn't want two particular friends to be my roommates. After a few weeks of looking for options, I was miserable, but still I resisted and stubbornly wrestled with His provision.

Eventually they both moved in. Throughout the next year they blessed my life incredibly. So when they each eventually got married and moved out and I was left with the options of finding new roommates or moving again, it was hard, but I told God I'd trust Him this time rather than fight.

Again He provided. I moved to a new house with another great roommate. If I had planned it I probably would have done things differently, but in His unfailing love God provided exactly what I needed once again.

⁂ *Sometimes it is hard to accept God's provision, but He is unchanging and always lovingly cares for us.*

— Laura Chevalier —

Freed by Stern Words

An open rebuke
is better than hidden love!

—PROVERBS 27:5

The small group had spent endless hours listening to me retell the story of how I had been abandoned and betrayed by believers and people whom I had once considered close friends. At times I knew this new group of Christians must have been sick of hearing the retold saga, yet they lovingly encouraged me to vent, stating it was a part of the healing process.

My venting did subside with time, but it never fully diminished even though I had been with the group for nearly three years. One evening when I began my story again, a lady spoke up. "You need to get over this and move on!" She stunned the group with her blunt words and elevated voice.

While others were shocked by what they perceived as a calloused remark, I knew she was right. I saw her open and candid rebuke as a message from God.

That verbal kick in the pants freed me from my self-pity and encouraged me to get back on the road to recovery.

✳ *Sincere rebuke is medication for a sick soul.*

— Steven Thompson —

A Walk to the Library

For he has not ignored or belittled the suffering of the needy.
He has not turned his back on them,
but has listened to their cries for help.

—PSALM 22:24

*I*nstead of driving, I decided to walk to the library after lunch. An elderly man in front of me had stopped to look at a motorcycle parked on a front lawn.

"Hello," I said. "Be a good day to ride that bike."

That's all I said. The man started talking. Within minutes I learned that he and his terminally ill wife lived in a building next to the library. An aide was caring for his wife, and this allowed the husband a few minutes away from the apartment, but not from his problems.

"The hardest part," he said as tears flowed, "is that she understands everything I say to her, but she can't talk, can't even ask for a glass of water."

Usually I talk and want to fix things, but I heard a voice within me say, "Listen, just listen."

When we said good-bye at the library, I knew the One who understands our sorrows had arranged this encounter. I felt joy knowing God had used me. Since then, I'm a better listener.

❖ *Sometimes we love best when we just listen.*

— Deb Vellines —

The Special Coat

May he grant your heart's desires
and make all your plans succeed.

—PSALM 20:4

I strutted out of the store with the big fashionable box in my arms. I couldn't wait to get home and see what Daddy thought.

Wearing the coat, I danced into his workshop. I paraded in front of Daddy and spun around. "What do you think? Do you like the coat?"

Mom entered the shop and explained to Daddy that we had brought the coat home on approval, because it was more expensive than we had planned.

I watched Daddy's face with my sixteen-year-old eyes pleading for approval.

Oh, pleeeease, Daddy, pleeease.

He picked up a rag and methodically wiped his grimy fingers one by one. My heart raced waiting for his answer.

"I . . . think she needs to have that special coat," laughed my daddy.

I jumped up and down and hugged him. I loved him so.

This coat my daddy provided said to me, "She is worth it."

I felt special even without the coat, because of his action.

✣ *Our heavenly Father gives us the desires of our hearts because we're special to Him.*

— Bev Schwind —

The Love of Money

Don't love money; be satisfied with what you have.
—HEBREWS 13:5

*W*hen John D. Rockefeller was asked what he wanted, he said, "Just one more dollar." At the time, he was the richest man in the world.

In time, though, Rockefeller realized even his billions couldn't satisfy. He turned to doing good works, donating money to charity, and so on, to give back to those who had given so much to him. When he went out on the streets in his limousine, he would take packets of dimes to throw out of the car to the children running alongside. It was a small thing, but the kids loved it.

I once had a friend who thought about little more than money. He ended up divorced, his kids hated him, and all they wanted was for him to die so they could get their hands on his money. He finally died alone.

What if he had loved other things besides money? His family? His wife? Friends? People working for him? How different his life might have been.

✻ *Don't love money; love the people and the God you can give it to.*

— Joseph Compaine —

Love Is Patient and Kind

Love is patient and kind.

—1 CORINTHIANS 13:4

I can still see them sitting at the kitchen table, Mother with one hand extended, fingers spread wide apart, and Daddy carefully applying bright red polish to each nail.

Mother received a diagnosis of diabetes too late to stop the progression of damage to her eyes. In spite of multiple laser treatments, she eventually became legally blind.

Daddy, not a patient person by nature, not only treated her to a weekly manicure, he also took her for daily walks, gently holding her arm and guiding her steps. He frequently accompanied her to the store and patiently helped her select the perfect dress. And each morning he carefully applied her makeup before they left the house. He often applied rouge and lipstick a little too generously, but the end result was not as important as the act of love it represented.

Their unselfish love for one another raised the bar a notch higher, motivating me not only to verbalize my love for family and friends, but also to actively look for ways to demonstrate it.

✢ *Demonstrating patience and kindness to those around us in concrete ways blesses and enriches us as well.*

— Louise D. Flanders —

The Grumpy Professor

Remember your leaders who taught you the word
of God. Think of all the good that has come from
their lives, and follow the example of their faith.

—HEBREWS 13:7

*D*r. Bailey, psychology professor at my college, delighted
in embarrassing his students. I was often the brunt of his
jokes, but I determined to never let him get to me.

At the beginning of class, I had bravely asked him if he would
call me Ann instead of my first name, Elizabeth. Making a face,
he announced, "I'll call you whatever I want to call you."

I was the only student from that class who also signed up for his
second semester class. "Hello, Ann," he said as I walked in on the
first day of that semester. It was then that I realized how much I
had come to love this grizzly old bear that no one else could stand.

Right at the end of school, I learned that Dr. Bailey was battling
terminal cancer. He had talked with my father and told him how
much I had meant to him that year. It was evident then that God
had chosen me to love this grieving and grumpy professor.

✳ *God often shuts us in so that we have no choice but to love.*

— Ann Varnum —

My Rockin' Rollin' Daze

The Lord is my rock, my fortress, and my savior;
my God is my rock, in whom I find protection.
He is my shield, the power that saves me,
and my place of safety.

—Psalm 18:2

Not long after my divorce, a 5.5 magnitude California earthquake rocked and rolled our tiny apartment. I'd just had ankle surgery, and my plaster-encased leg prevented me from running to my preschool-age sons.

I yelled, "Come to me," and crawled toward my sons' bedroom. My terrified children teeter-tottered from their room into my arms.

A few days later, three-year-old Kyle let out a bloodcurdling scream. His tiny body quivered as he shrieked, "Ert kwake. Ert kwake." Leaves on a tree trembling from the wind had thrown Kyle into a state of anxiety.

I hugged Kyle and reassured, "It's okay. Mommy's here."

When unseen tectonic plates shifted underneath my marriage, uncontrollable anxieties shook my world. Like Kyle, I trembled, feeling emotionally traumatized. As I slept, I shivered, clinging to my Bible like my childhood teddy bear. I seized every chance to bury myself in God's promises. Jesus called, "Come to me. I'm your rock, your refuge, and your deliverer."

During my most terrifying, rockin' rollin' days, God held me close, reminding me, "It's okay, Scoti. I'm here."

We can always count on the Rock who is firm through all the earthquakes of life.

— Scoti Springfield Domeij —

God Is a Special-Ed Teacher

You, Lord, hear the desire of the afflicted;
you encourage them, and you listen to their cry.

—PSALM 10:17

*U*ou can do better than that," my teachers would tell me.
"You're too smart to get a B+," my parents would say.
Their intended encouragement backfired, and I felt dumb and incompetent.

Now I teach special-needs children: kids with emotional problems, learning differences, developmental delays. And I say to them, "Good job! You're getting there! You almost made it that time!"

I say, "I can see how hard you're working! What great effort!"

And they smile, feel successful, and try again.

That's how God speaks to me. He never says, "Here's the standard for people who've been Christians as long as you have, and you're not meeting it. What's wrong with you? He says, "You're making progress; you're going to make it! Good effort!"

He doesn't say, "I can't believe you just said that! How could you be so thoughtless? What's wrong with you, anyway?"

No, He accepts my repentant apology, wipes away my tears of shame, and sets me back on my feet with a hug to try again.

✤ *Because the Lord accepts and encourages us, we can accept and encourage others.*

— Elsi Dodge —

Knowing All the Answers

Anyone who claims to know all the answers
doesn't really know very much.

—I CORINTHIANS 8:2

*M*y wife sometimes calls me the "Answer Man" because I tend to know the answers to trivia questions, both biblical and otherwise. It's a nice nickname and I am thankful that my memory does retain a lot of the facts I learn, but I know the truth: I actually know so little. But I don't tell her that.

Our world focuses a lot on what we know. While theoretical knowledge, a retention of facts, and even experiential knowledge is good, knowledge only goes so far.

Knowing the answers is not what life is all about, although it can help. As Theodore Roosevelt, John Maxwell, and other leadership gurus have said, no one cares how much we know until they know how much we care.

Life is not about building up a library of knowledge in our brains. Whether the facts are useless trivia—which I excel in—or vital facts, knowledge alone doesn't change a whole lot. It's when we combine knowledge not only with passion, but with love, that we can have a great effect on others.

✻ *Knowing is not enough. Loving is the best part of knowing.*

— Joseph Compaine —

He Has My Collar!

With a strong hand, God grabs my shirt.
He grips me by the collar of my coat.

—Job 30:18

*Y*our daughter has schizophrenia; the next two years will be very difficult."

Words spoken by the doctor were tucked into my heart. As her illness progressed, I immersed myself in education. I devoured books about mental illness along with my Bible, devotionals, and other writings. Each breath was a prayer for my Kathy. In addition, I turned to my personal army of prayerful supporters. The diagnosis was shared, along with my grocery list of prayer requests:

- Kathy to accept her need for medication.
- Kathy to understand her diagnosis.
- Wisdom and understanding for me.

My life was reduced to a constant stream of meetings with doctors, therapists, and social workers sandwiched between caring for Kathy, my business, and our home. But in the midst of my pain, I felt loved. My wounds were bound by prayers, a casserole shared, and friends devoting their time to attend to our needs. The garment of love was draped around our shoulders, warming my soul. Each morning I prepared myself for the challenges by inhaling God's promise of His faithfulness.

�֍ *Thank you, dear Father, for the grace to see you in the midst of our busy daily existence.*

— Mona Rottinghaus —

Across Continents

Every time I think of you, I give thanks to my God.

—PHILIPPIANS 1:3

When I heard my friend Caroline's melodic voice and saw her face on my computer screen, I was as excited as a little child. It was our first Skype connection from my home in America to hers in Kenya.

"I can feel your love—all the way here!" she said. Right away we talked about things that really count.

"Faith is my theme this year. I want to trust God in everything." I watched her lips move and love shine from her eyes. She poured out her challenges.

"You have become my mentor. I can tell you anything," Caroline commented.

"And God drew us together in a remarkable friendship," I added.

I pondered my words. Caroline is thirty years younger than me, grew up in Africa, and met me on a plane nine years ago. When she studied in Denver, we visited by email, over the phone, and in person. When Caroline received her master's degree, my husband and I went to all her events, joining some of her family. Remarkable, indeed.

* *No matter ages or backgrounds, God's love woven into friendships can create something special.*

— Charlotte Adelsperger —

Come As a Little Child

When doubts filled my mind,
your comfort gave me renewed hope and cheer.

—PSALM 94:19

The day at work had been stressful, and I left the office feeling drained and badly in need of a hug.

Shortly after I arrived home, my phone rang. When I answered it, I heard a little voice on the other end of the line sob, "Grandma, I want to hold you."

My two-year-old grandson, David, had hurt himself and wouldn't be calmed until his mommy let him call Grandma.

Since we lived just five minutes apart, I jumped in the car and rushed right over to let my grandson *hold me*. While he did, I could feel the loving arms of God comforting me as I comforted little David. What bliss to be sandwiched in the hugs of two who love me so much. I felt the stresses of the day melt away. And David and I were both calmed.

✻ *Sometimes we just need to cry out, "God, I want to hold you!" and let His love comfort us.*

— Jan Christiansen —

I Make a Difference

Those who trust in the Lord will find new strength.

—ISAIAH 40:31

*B*rynie was a young man starting in the business world. I met him at a men's conference we were both attending. Even though I was much older, we seemed to click as friends.

He went to my church, so after the conference was over, I invited him out to lunch. We talked about his job.

Brynie said he was struggling because he was new at being a financial advisor. I encouraged him to persevere, because God was there to give him strength.

We continued having lunch periodically. And as time went by, he reported he was doing better. I kept encouraging him to work hard.

Last month when we met for lunch, Brynie handed me one of those trendy plastic rubber-band bracelets. It said on it, "I Make a Difference."

Brynie told me, "Because you stayed by my side and encouraged me so much, I am very successful now."

I am still wearing the bracelet everywhere.

※ *Giving others support shows them they can accomplish their goals.*

— Doug Bolton —

What Love Does

So you see, faith by itself isn't enough.
Unless it produces good deeds, it is dead and useless.

—JAMES 2:17

I only had a few errands to run after church before I could enjoy a restful Sunday afternoon. As I shifted my car into reverse, an awful shaking told me that this day was going to be anything but restful.

I prayed all the way to the repair shop, hoping it was something simple, not a huge headache with an even bigger repair bill. The mechanic explained the problem and my options. At best, it was a $500 repair. At worst, I'd need a $2,000 transmission.

For me, one of the more burdensome aspects of being a single woman is bearing life's responsibilities alone. As I stood there considering the situation, I felt the full weight.

I decided to call my uncle for advice. Well-versed in cars, he told me to take the car home. He volunteered to drive up the next day and make the repairs. I thanked him and apologized for having to bother him.

"It's never a bother, dear," he said. "That's what love does."

✻ *Love won't allow you to bear burdens alone.*

— Tina Givens —

Too Harried to Be Sacred

This is a sacred day before our Lord.

—NEHEMIAH 8:10

O ne harried day, I stopped for fast food and ran into an elderly man from my church. He pulled his son toward me.

"I want you to meet Pauline, she's a parish nurse," he told his son. Then he explained to me, "We're on our way back to the nursing home. My wife . . . is slipping away. If you could . . . it would be nice . . . come see her."

What did I get myself into? I groaned inwardly. *God, you know all the plans I had for today...* After all, I wasn't going to start the parish nurse position until the first of the year.

Another thought flashed through my mind. *Let's see if you really want to be a parish nurse.*

Okay, God, I'll go there and leave my uprooted schedule for you to handle, I responded to Him.

I went. I did nothing—sat, listened, watched the husband. He talked to his wife, kissed her, and wiped her face. He appreciated my visit so much.

✻ *When we show love, we make any day a sacred day.*

— Pauline Sheehan —

Protection in the Night

Show me your unfailing love in wonderful ways.

—Psalm 17:7

The shrill chirp jolted me awake.

"Hullo?" my husband mumbled. Then, "Thanks."

He jumped up and disappeared down the hallway.

Minutes later, he slid back into bed. "That was Kathy across the street. Our garage door was open."

The next morning I saw Kathy. "Vince says I shouldn't have called," she said.

"No, we're grateful. We've had stuff stolen before."

"At two o'clock I bolted awake. A little voice said, 'Fred and Martha's garage door is open!' I got up and made the call. The strange thing is, just minutes later, I heard a car drive down the street very slowly, like it was casing the neighborhood."

I got goose bumps. Clearly, Kathy's prompting and obedience saved us from another burglary.

I had prayed to be more alert to God's love in my life. His answer? To use our neighbor to protect us. How often does God demonstrate His love and we're oblivious, completely missing a divine kiss?

I thank God for all those times, even if it is two o'clock in the morning.

✣ *Be alert to God's love and protection which comes in many forms, at any time.*

— Martha Pope Gorris —

The Perfect Job

Trust in the Lord with all your heart;
do not depend on your own understanding.
Seek his will in all you do,
and he will show you which path to take.

—PROVERBS 3:5–6

*A*fter praying for the perfect job, I thought my prayers were answered—until I discovered I was the only Christian in an office filled with people who practiced immorality and profanity.

"What are you doing, Lord? This is not the 'perfect' place I prayed for. This is a sin pit!" I told Him.

I gave my notice at work but promised to stay until my replacement was found. And I searched for another job. Despite having numerous job interviews for positions I was well qualified for, I wasn't hired. Discouraged, I searched God's Word for an answer. It seemed every Scripture pointed to love, which fulfills the law, works no ill toward its neighbor, and reflects Christ.

I finally realized why God placed me there. It wasn't for me; it was for Him. My co-workers needed Jesus. When I yielded and asked God to fill my heart with love for each of them, He answered that prayer abundantly. Two years later, I wept when I moved to another city—and thanked God for giving me that perfect job.

✳ *We are happiest and most usable when we yield to Christ regardless of our circumstances.*

— Kitty Chappell —

Loving Others Through Prayer

The earnest prayer of a righteous person has great
power and produces wonderful results.

—JAMES 5:16

I hung up the phone and felt helpless. My friend was suffering after major surgery and there was no way for me to help. She was hundreds of miles away, and phone calls of encouragement just seemed so inadequate. I prayed for her on the phone as we talked, but I wished I could do more. If only I were closer, I could help her with her struggles and burdens in so many ways.

Then it hit me. Praying for her was not the only the way I could help—it was the best way. Physical help could be beneficial, but prayer was the greatest way to serve the one I cared about. Showing love through prayer made me an active participant in God's intervention in the comfort and healing of someone I loved.

I now understood that praying for those we love moves God and His angels to powerful and compassionate action.

✳ *Prayer can be the best way to show love toward those important to us.*

— Michael K. Farrar —

But What About Me?

And this same God who takes care of me will
supply all your needs from his glorious riches,
which have been given to us in Christ Jesus.

—PHILIPPIANS 4:19

I was jealous of the dog. My husband said the mutt we call Annie is the dog he always wanted. Every day he takes Annie for long walks through the woods while I stay home with my bum knee. Her daily needs are his priority.

"That's my girl," he tells her several times a day. I want to be his girl.

Recently my husband was looking for a car to replace the one I had. One day I found an eleven-year-old, one-owner, garage-kept vehicle that was the exact model, body shape, and color I wanted, and it only had 30,300 miles. My husband was astounded. He'd been looking for cars in good condition and in our price range for months and hadn't found anything. How could I have found that car?

Imagine my sense of awe when the thought came to me, *Why, I'm God's girl. He provided for me.* I know God cares for me. I'm no longer jealous of the dog.

✣ *No matter how we feel, God's care and love for us is constant.*

— Jean Davis —

Me? Feed My Enemy?

If your enemies are hungry, give them food to eat.
If they are thirsty, give them water to drink.

—PROVERBS 25:21

One night when I stepped outside our home in El Salvador, running footsteps approached behind me. A hand seized my wrist. I stopped struggling when I saw the pistol aimed at me.

"Give me money. Quick!"

I surrendered our money box. As the robber fled, he fired two shots back toward me.

After that, any noise made me jump. Whenever I'd hear footsteps behind me, I'd freeze. At night I lay awake.

When I heard of the robber's arrest, I remembered the words in the Bible about loving our enemies, and if our enemies hunger, feeding them.

"Me? I'm too scared," I argued. I tried to dismiss the idea but couldn't.

Finally I prayed, "Okay, Lord. I'll do it."

I started making donuts, and immediately my fears lessened. At the police station, I asked to see the man in custody. When I gave him the donuts, I felt more pity than fear.

That night I slept.

I still startle easily, but I'm at peace. My healing began the day I fed the man who robbed me.

✳ *God's love enables us to serve those who mistreat us.*

— Verda J. Glick —

You're Someone Special

But our bodies have many parts, and God has
put each part just where he wants it.

—1 CORINTHIANS 12:18

*M*y friend Frank wailed, "I'm just such a loser. I have nothing to give. All I do is take, and that gets me nowhere."

I felt for him. He was an alcoholic, and his wife, a member of our church, had asked me to pray for him many times. Besides praying for him, I'd befriended him. But this was the first time he was serious about faith. I asked, "What do you want, Frank?"

"I want God. But I don't think He wants me. There is nothing about me that is positive or good or desirable."

It was difficult persuading him that God actually loved him. Frank finally decided to accept Christ. I began to see the transformation in the way he felt about himself. After a while, he came to me and offered, "I can't do much, Clay, but I'm good at cleaning and fixing things. Do you need any of that? Can I help the church in that way?"

I told him yes, and pointed out that maybe he had the gift of helps.

He asked, "What's that?"

I explained how God gave all His people spiritual gifts and talents. He was so excited, he cried, "Maybe God can use me. Maybe He did love me enough to give me abilities! Maybe I do have something special for Him."

✤ *God gave us all gifts to serve, love, and give. What ones do you have?*

— Clay Taylor —

Love in Bloom

And if God cares so wonderfully for flowers that are
here today and thrown into the fire tomorrow, he will
certainly care for you. Why do you have so little faith?

—LUKE 12:28

Gingerly, I carried the little basket home from school. Inside it
nestled two little purple flowers. Violets for my mom. Mrs.
Dennison, my first-grade teacher, had told us all about May Day,
when people celebrate spring by giving flowers. I couldn't wait to
hand my basket to Mom.

Mom loved flowers, and it showed. In front of our house, her
rosebushes grew big, exuding perfume for a great part of the year.
The south and west sides of the house were lined with daffodils,
tulips, and hollyhocks. The north side boasted peony bushes. She
even had a huge, magenta azalea that just wasn't supposed to be
able to live year-round in northern Missouri. But it flourished for
my mom.

I have picked up the love of flowers and plants from my mom.
I love to wander around in the warm months examining how God
expressed His creativity in the plant world. As I see how He intri-
cately designed the different plants, caring for their smallest details,
I marvel. And I remember that I mean more to Him than all His
botanical beauties.

✽ *This season, each time we see pretty flowers, may it be a reminder
to us of how much our Father cares.*

— Jenni Davenport —

Keep My Heart Soft

If only you would listen to his voice today!
The Lord says, "Don't harden your
hearts as Israel did at Meribah,
as they did at Massah in the wilderness."

—PSALM 95:7–8

*H*e has such a soft heart."
I don't often hear this description, but my grandmother and parents used it. Anyone who demonstrated kindness, a forgiving spirit, and compassion received this honor and respect.

When I was a newlywed, this saying took on a special meaning. After a heated exchange with my husband, I retreated to the bathroom. Standing by the mirror, I raged at the injustice of his position. The Lord interrupted me right there. "Don't harden your heart against him."

His words shocked me out of my temper tantrum. This man prayed for, nurtured, and protected me. In the grand scheme of things, was my opinion so important that I'd shut him out?

Scriptures zipped through my mind, including the famous love chapter 1 Corinthians 13. I often prayed I'd have a soft heart toward God, but now I understood that required openness toward people as well. How could I have a heart open to God, who forgave me of so much, when I built walls against those dearest to me?

✣ *When I see Him, I want to hear, "You were willing and obedient. You have a soft heart."*

— Susan J. Reinhardt —

Honored by God

Believers who are poor have something to boast about, for God has honored them.

—JAMES 1:9

"If I told you I feel honored by God because I have no money, no great job, no nice possessions, you'd think me crazy," Mike said to me one day. "But I feel that way. I have a great ministry to children and teenagers. The kids in it love my family and me. And we see them grow and live for God every day. What could be better?"

Mike worked in an inner-city ministry that struggled to pay the bills every day of the week. But he always smiled when I sat down with him for coffee and a talk. He would probably never get a medal from the president. But he was a good man. And I could see why God made him feel honored.

After talking to him, I thought about the work I do. I'm not rich. I don't have great clothes or a fantastic house. But God has honored me too. Honor from God doesn't take the form of money or position or power. It's His showering His love on us and on those to whom we minister.

* *God honors those who love Him.*

— Karl Cumberland —

A Cure for That Relationship

Love never gives up, never loses faith, is always hopeful,
and endures through every circumstance.

—1 CORINTHIANS 13:7

*E*ver look at something through a magnifying glass? Things look distorted and larger than they are.

That's what I did with my son-in-law a few years ago—every flaw, every fault—and the more I viewed him through that magnifying glass, the bigger the flaws and faults got. Our relationship suffered and our dislike for each other upset my daughter. I knew something had to change, and it would probably have to be me. The timing could not have been better; the Scripture portion I was reading was 1 Corinthians 13.

The first thing I knew I needed to do was to get rid of the magnifying glass. I started focusing on the positive things about him, no matter how small, and I started voicing those positive things out loud.

By the time I was through, I realized he wasn't such a bad guy after all. My whole attitude toward him changed and I became friendly and complimentary, which in turn changed his attitude toward me and ultimately spilled over into peace for my daughter.

�֍ *Change your focus and you just might change your relationship.*

— Diane Petree —

Anxious Heart—Healed Heart

He heals the brokenhearted
and bandages their wounds.

—PSALM 147:3

*J*ust two years ago, our five-year-old granddaughter, Ethne, lost her other grandmother. Recently, we buried her daddy. "Oh, Lord, it's too much! She's so young. What can I do to comfort her and make sure that this suffering doesn't unravel her tender faith?" I cried.

About a week after Ethne's daddy went to heaven, I took her swimming.

"Grammy," she said simply, "Jesus is with us right now." She spread her arms wide.

I smiled. "Yes, He is." I pictured us floating in God's unending love.

"And," she added, "Daddy is with Jesus. . . ."

I nodded.

"That means Daddy is right here with us too, because he is with Jesus."

"That's true and wonderful!" I knew I'd received a treasure. "I've never thought of it that way before." I squinted at her as she splashed in the water. "Who told you that?"

Ethne paused for a moment. Then, with a pure and special light in her eyes she answered, "Jesus told me."

I had no doubt that He had, and that stilled my anxious heart.

✽ *We are not responsible or able to mend a broken heart; only the love of the Lord can do that.*

— Sue Cameron —

Pressed Buttons

"Don't sin by letting anger control you." Don't let
the sun go down while you are still angry.

—EPHESIANS 4:26

*M*y roommate, Kit, had done it again. She'd pushed my buttons until my adrenaline surged. I tried to ignore her antics, but time and again she got firmly under my skin.

One day I suddenly realized that I so often felt angry around Kit because this is what she intended. She was an angry, insecure person at that stage in her life and was taking it out on me. She was adroit at finding my Achilles' heel and shooting arrows into it, then hoping I would go down to her level.

When I realized she was probing my weaknesses, I didn't feel like such a failure for having to go to God again and again to ask for strength to love her.

In life, we occasionally encounter people who, for whatever reason, enjoy trying to aggravate us and seeing if we will respond in kind. It's okay to feel angry, but we need to give it to God as soon as possible so as not to become resentful or bitter.

✻ *The Bible doesn't say it's a sin to be angry, just not to respond in sinful ways or let it control us.*

— Julie Durham —

God's Love Teaches Us Endurance

We can rejoice, too, when we run into problems and trials,
for we know that they help us develop endurance.

—ROMANS 5:3

*R*unning a mile was the worst requirement of the college gym program. I never did well at this. I just couldn't get enough air, and then I ended up walking half of the mile. Several guys encouraged me, but it didn't help much. I always finished last and got an F for the performance.

One afternoon as we prepared for the run, a guy I knew was also a Christian sat down next to me. "Hey," he said. "I see you really struggle with this."

"I have a lung problem," I explained. Later I learned that half my right lung didn't work.

"So that's it."

"Yeah. I don't know what to do about it."

We both stared off into space. "The important thing is that you keep on going. You don't quit."

"I usually get an F."

"Not in God's way of looking at it. Endurance is important to Him, I think."

I went into the run feeling better, feeling like this guy with his encouragement had shown me love—his and God's. That day I tried a little harder.

✳ *God shows love in many ways, especially through the encouragement of other Christians.*

— Richard Holland —

Mission Made Possible

For nothing is impossible with God.

—LUKE 1:37

*M*y friend had always been calm in any crisis, compassionate but firm with her students. But a darkness loomed over her, filled with the unspeakable shame of childhood sexual abuse.

As she began telling me of the torture and molestation she endured, I sometimes grew overwhelmed. Tempted to cut and run, I constantly prayed, "Lord, this is your work. Help me to just listen and prove the truths of your loving acceptance."

With each detail, I assured her of God's love and my love. "Nothing you say can change that."

"Some things are too awful to tell you," she said with head bowed, her voice almost inaudible. "You probably couldn't take it."

Finally, late one night, she told me her darkest secret. Though it made me sick to hear what she'd experienced, God flooded me with His tender love. I wrapped my arms around her and said again, "I love you and God loves you."

From then on, she started to cast off the shame and feel God's love and peace.

✢ *When you're helping someone through a seemingly impossible burden, God's love will strengthen and heal you both.*

— Beverly Abear —

The Meal We Don't Serve

"The Lord knows I shouldn't have done that . . ." he said
to his men. "The Lord forbid that I . . . attack the Lord's
anointed one, for the Lord himself has chosen him."

—1 SAMUEL 24:6

*W*hat do you have for Sunday afternoon dinner?

While growing up, I was often served "roasted pastor."
Over the dinner table after church, someone would ask, "What did
you think of the pastor's sermon?" Someone else would give an
opinion, and eventually the pastor was cooked!

We were hyper-critical on Sundays. And when you're focusing
on mentally dissecting the leader's words, it's hard for the Holy
Spirit to get through the fog of criticism to your own heart.

At some point, I read this Scripture—and became good friends
with people in ministry. I saw that they weren't perfect but were
people God called to do their best to help others grow spiritually.
I learned my role was to respect their call, listen to their insights,
and let the Holy Spirit work in my life—and theirs.

In our family now, we still talk about sermons and other teach-
ings of leaders, but the questions revolve around "What did God
teach you through this?" instead of "What did you think?"

✢ *As we show love and respect for God's servants, we show it for Him.*

— Julie Durham —

When I Needed Help

Our help is from the Lord,
who made heaven and earth.

—PSALM 124:8

I stood over my five-year-old daughter, Sara, as she lay in the hospital bed gasping and laboring for every breath she took. She had aspirated streptococcus into her lungs and was very ill. The doctors were unsure of her recovery.

I was afraid and angry because death could come and steal her breath away in the night, and I could do nothing to stop it. I needed peace as much as Sara needed to be healed. I felt helpless, and her condition seemed hopeless. My wife and Sara were both looking to me for answers, but I had nothing for them.

God brought me to my knees in the hospital chapel that night as I prayed for Him to spare Sara's life and give me peace if He took her. I realized that God's love is greater than life and death. His love reaches beyond the beyond. As a calm swept over me, I could face the future with hope, for help was simply a prayer away. Sara made a full recovery.

✣ *In the midst of the unknown and even death, God is our only hope, and He is always ready to help.*

— Vince Byrd —

Welcome Home, Aunt Dorothy!

Jesus repeated the question: "Simon son
of John, do you love me?"
"Yes, Lord," Peter said, "you know I love you."
"Then take care of my sheep," Jesus said.

—JOHN 21:16

*B*aa!" I heard one of Jesus's lost sheep calling to me. It was my
Aunt Dorothy after her husband of fifty years passed away. She
really was lost, having no children of her own and nowhere to go.

The more my husband and I thought it over, the more we knew
we should take her in. It helped that Aunt Dorothy was so easy to
get along with, but it was still a little scary knowing she would be
with us *all* the time! I have to admit, I was sorry to see my living
room furnishings given away or stored, and the guest bathroom
taken over with pharmaceuticals.

Then I thought about Jesus's command to Peter. He said three
times to take care of His sheep if we love Him!

It's been nearly four months, and what a blessing Aunt Dorothy
is. She is a sweet, always cheerful presence in our home, and a godly
example of faith through difficult times. I don't know who received
the bigger blessing here, Aunt Dorothy or our family.

✻ *Following God's commands always leads to blessing.*

— Sarah Bergman —

My Christian Burqa

Above all, clothe yourselves with love, which
binds us all together in perfect harmony.

—COLOSSIANS 3:14

*R*ecently I've lost a lot of weight, which has necessitated my buying a series of transition clothing.

As my mind was set on new clothes, I was pleased to discover that the Bible offers fashion advice, along with everything else. Colossians 3:12–14 describes how a Christian can be dressed for success.

So I've been asking the Lord every morning to dress me for the day. I ask Him to swaddle me with humility, so that every time I move, I'm reminded that He's God and I'm not. I ask for compassion and kindness, gentleness and patience, forbearance and forgiveness.

And last, over all that, I put on God's agape love. That is sort of like wearing a Christian burqa, I've decided. Love covers me so completely that people will see Jesus, not me. And everything I see and hear, do and say, feel and think, is filtered through my loving Lord.

✛ *Be dressed for success . . . in God's love!*

— Elsi Dodge —

Like Mother, Like Daughter

Everyone who makes up proverbs will say
of you, "Like mother, like daughter."
—EZEKIEL 16:44

As my daughter and I planned her younger sister's baby shower, we tossed around various party ideas such as food and decorations. We set a day and time. Neither of us discussed our gifts.

I planned to sew a baby dress using fabric from my old prom dress and a vintage pattern that once belonged to my husband's grandmother. I'd also purchased a special bonnet.

One night, my eldest phoned full of excitement over her day of shopping. She had purchased fabric and a vintage pattern to make a baby dress and bonnet. My comment was, "You are so like your mother!"

It is true—I see myself in both of my daughters. I generally see the parts that make me happy because both are wonderful young women. Sometimes I see similarities in the not-so-good things, and believe me, I can pick them out and trace them back to myself in a heartbeat.

✳ *Are you leaving a loving example for your children to emulate?*

— Sandra McGarrity —

Holiness Topped With Love

Let us cleanse ourselves from everything that can
defile our body or spirit. And let us work toward
complete holiness because we fear God.

—2 CORINTHIANS 7:1

When I first became a Christian, my mother became an implacable enemy. She didn't like my conservative brand of Christianity because she'd grown up in a conservative home and always hated it.

As a result, we argued constantly. Every good thing I did was put down. Every bad thing I used to do—drugs, drinking, womanizing—she said I should go back to. "I preferred you that way."

I didn't know what to do. But some Christian friends who mentored me said, "Just love her. Let her see the greatest change in you as real love—toward her and her friends and everyone else."

I stopped arguing and fighting and simmered down the gospel wars. I wrote a note to one of her dying friends. I praised her to others. I let her know I loved her with numerous hugs, kisses, and statements. In time, she softened. We became a loving mother and son again, and life began to work.

And in time, God made sure she understood and accepted the Gospel. That was the best thing of all.

✳ *When we strive to live holy lives, not everyone will like it. But as we make sure we add love to holiness, the combination is often unbeatable.*

— Don Richards —

Surely You Repay

Unfailing love, O Lord, is yours.
Surely you repay all people
according to what they have done.

—Psalm 62:12

This Friday we'll have a pizza party for the kids to celebrate great behavior," my daughter's teacher announced.

While my daughter cheered at the news, I sympathized with the teacher. I knew they had no classroom budget for pizza and pop. The money for the children's party was doubtless coming out of her own pocket.

"Pay for part of it," a voice inside me nudged. "Show her you appreciate her and care by paying for the drinks."

While paying for drinks wasn't much, it's still a lot when you wonder how you're going to pay the bills. My husband and I were self-employed and the recession had hit us hard. I'd just finished my last major contract. We were in big trouble.

But I obediently sent money to the teacher.

That night my husband went to a meeting and at the last minute took some product to sell. Usually he didn't make sales at that meeting, but he decided to take the materials just in case.

You guessed it; the materials sold. He brought home ten times the amount I'd given the teacher.

* *When we sacrifice to show that we care, God often repays what we've given.*

— Jenni Davenport —

Ask, Seek, Knock

Keep on asking, and you will receive what you ask for.
Keep on seeking, and you will find.
Keep on knocking, and the door will be opened to you.

—MATTHEW 7:7

My husband and I run an inner-city ministry. One day when out and about, I noticed a young girl with a baby sitting outside a market. The Holy Spirit prompted me to talk with her. We chatted for some time. I asked her if she needed anything, and she said her baby needed a stroller.

Later that week I ran into a friend who had a lovely stroller that she was getting rid of.

I phoned the young girl to arrange a meeting. She arrived, baby in arms. As we walked, I paused and said, "The morning I met you, I asked God to use me that day in some amazing way."

The young mother stopped. She had tears in her eyes and said, "The morning I met you, I asked God for help." We embraced each other and shared the warm, tender, all-powerful love of God. He is so faithful.

⁂ *His love works extraordinarily through the ordinary.*

— Tracey Dale-Akamine —

Mining for a Heart of Gold

Therefore, accept each other just as Christ has
accepted you so that God will be given glory.

—ROMANS 15:7

My friend Andy was approaching me at the conference when
he suddenly got a horrified expression and dashed into an
unused conference room.

I grinned as I realized what was happening. He'd noticed that
Ilene was making a beeline straight for him. Andy was one of the
most respected leaders in our field. And Ilene was one of the most
obnoxious. She continually promoted herself, bragged, and tried
to push her way among those she considered important. Andy
was one of the kindest souls I'd ever known, but he just clearly
couldn't deal with Ilene.

I greeted Ilene with the grin still on my face. For the first few
years I'd known her, I reacted like Andy—avoiding her at all costs.
But then somehow I began to get to really know her. I learned that
beneath her bragging was a heart of gold. I learned to explore that
heart more and focus on it when her words began to turn me off.
Now I'd gotten to the stage where I could chat with Ilene and give
her the praise and respect that she so desperately sought.

✳ *Sometimes when we mine a person's life, we find a heart of gold
beyond the crusty exterior.*

— Janet Graham —

Useless Talk

For there are many rebellious people who
engage in useless talk and deceive others.

—TITUS 1:10

I watched in horror as the two men, my friends, argued about
political issues going on in the world. In the end, because
neither could convince the other of his position, they resorted to
name-calling. Such words as *racist, bigot, idiot,* and worse came
out. I was amazed that two friends could be so violent with each
other. Why did they do this?

I broke in and said, "Look, I can see wisdom in both of your
positions. But descending into this kind of tactic is foolish, and it
will hurt your friendship."

"Yeah, now Farmer's gonna hit us with religion if we don't
watch out," one announced to the other.

I smiled. "If you want to know something about the Bible or
Jesus or God, I'll speak up. But I'm not going to call you infidels,
although you probably are."

We all laughed again. "Come on," I said, "Go vote for your
beliefs and positions, but don't resort to nastiness. Look, how
about a Coke?"

We all sat down to our sodas and moved on to more agreeable
topics.

✣ *You love when you show the better way.*

— Gene Farmer —

More Than Enough

For your love for me is very great.
You have rescued me from the depths of death.

—PSALM 86:13

I fell on the bed crying, "God help me! Am I ever going to be loved by my husband? All we seem to do is fight."

Feeling frustrated and hurt, I poured out my complaint before the Lord.

A small voice whispered from deep within, "Probably not, but I will be more than enough for you." God's answer was not what I expected.

I asked, "Excuse me, but did I hear you correctly?"

The stillness in my spirit assured me: God had spoken. I had never been so conscious of God's presence. All I could do was lie on the bed and worship Him, because I knew He was with me. The sweetness of His love overwhelmed me, as He quieted all my fears.

For thirty-five years, God's amazing grace has made it possible for my husband and me to live at peace with each other. He has given me great love for my husband, and God's love has sustained me at the times when my husband's could not. The Lord has been more than enough.

✻ *Nothing and no one can satisfy your soul like the love of the Lord.*

— Marty Prudhomme —

I Gave!

If I gave everything I have to the poor and even
sacrificed my body, I could boast about it; but if I
didn't love others, I would have gained nothing.

—1 CORINTHIANS 13:3

I gave up house and car, family and friends. I sacrificed my
comfortable home in the States to live on the mission field
with people whose culture was so different from my own.

I gave clothes and shoes, money and food. I did without so they
could have what they needed.

"Do you love them?"

*Look what I have done, Lord. They eat in my home and use
my telephone.*

"Do you love them?"

Why, I pray with them and take them to ladies' meetings.

"Do you love them?"

Before the day the Lord confronted me, I thought I was doing
everything He wanted me to do. But now I got on my knees and
asked the Lord to help me love them the way He loved them, and
care for them the way He cared for them. He transformed my life
that day. I chose to love. He gave me His love for these people.

Twenty years later when I left, my friend said, "You may have
palagi (a foreigner's) skin, but you have a Samoan heart."

Thank you, Lord.

✻ *God can help you love and not just give.*

— Francine Duckworth —

Meet My Friend

Inside the Tent of Meeting, the Lord would speak to
Moses face to face, as one speaks to his friend.

—EXODUS 33:11

*M*y children weren't very old when they began coming home from Sunday school with pictures and crafts that included the words *Jesus is my friend*.

Way before Jesus was born, God proclaimed himself to be a friend to people. After He helped Adam and Eve find their Eden resort, He actually walked and chatted with them every day. I don't imagine they discussed lofty theological concepts. I doubt that Adam and Eve were rocket scientists—in fact, they were probably the original rubes—but apparently, God just liked being with them and talking about everyday stuff.

Moses was another person that God liked to chat with as if Moses were His buddy.

Sometimes it's hard for us to imagine, but God wants to be our friend too. He doesn't just tolerate our company; He enjoys us. He likes not just being our advisor, but our companion. We don't have to be brainy or understand all the concepts He set in place in the world. We don't have to meet certain expectations. We can just be His friend.

✳ *Enjoy God on a personal level—and let Him enjoy you!*

— Jeanette Gardner Littleton —

The Forgiveness Test

If someone says, "I love God," but hates a Christian
brother or sister, that person is a liar.

—1 JOHN 4:20

*M*y first thought was, *Not on your life!* He'd lied to me, cheated me, and now he was calling and asking for help.

I told my mom all the gory details of betrayal, and she responded with a simple question: "Did you forgive him?"

"I've forgiven him, but that doesn't mean I have to help him."

"If he'd never hurt you, would you help him?"

"In a second."

She smirked. "Interesting."

"How's that?"

"Because my pastor just preached about how to know if you've really forgiven someone."

"Really? I'm listening."

"You know you've forgiven someone when you can show them love and treat them as though the offense never happened. If you've really forgiven this guy, you should help him as though he never wronged you."

I didn't like the sound of that, but it was right. I realized I hadn't forgiven, and overcoming my lack of forgiveness was tough. With God's help, I tossed my bad attitude aside, called him back, and agreed to help. In the end, it became a deeply liberating spiritual experience.

✳ *Showing true love through forgiveness is liberating and fulfilling.*

— Bobby Lewis —

Love Made the Difference

To acquire wisdom is to love oneself.

—PROVERBS 19:8

*S*arah was a single mom who rented an apartment next to mine when I lived in San Diego. She received no support for her baby girl, Megan, so I gladly helped them when I could.

One afternoon, Sarah called to say she had just been offered a well-paying job. I was elated, until she explained it was a modeling job that required her to pose naked. I felt heartsick about the step she intended to take and the possible future impact on Megan and her.

"I know what you're thinking, but I need the money," Sarah said defensively and hung up. I immediately prayed for this young mother I had come to love and whom God loved. The next day, she phoned back to tell me she had rejected the offer.

I moved from San Diego but saw Sarah and Megan two years later, happy and well. Sarah's fiancé was with her also.

"Thank you," she said, "for loving me enough to make me think about the future. It made all the difference."

❊ *God's love working through you can bring change in a soul.*

— Jessica Talbot —

Financial Famine and Heaven's Cents

Once I was young, and now I am old.
Yet I have never seen the godly abandoned
or their children begging for bread.

—Psalm 37:25

*P*lease don't make me wait until my last penny is gone," I begged God after a quick peek at my bank statement. As an independent contractor, I was ineligible to receive unemployment benefits. Several agencies expressed interest in my services, but their bureaucratic processes moved far too slow. Would their employment date and my first paycheck come after bills exhausted my bank account? Would my house head into foreclosure?

After every positive interview my spirit soared, then nosedived when I received no formal offer.

All I wanted? Emotional and financial relief. All God wanted was my complete trust in Him.

To build my faith, I kept a daily blessings journal, recording how God provided for me every day. God filled my journal with His faithfulness. For money found while cleaning my garage, to a friend giving me $20, to a neighbor making dinner for me, I praised God.

Then in one day, *Jehovah-Jireh,* the Lord my Provider, inundated me with three checks, a long-awaited refund, and an email announcing, "You're hired."

God's provision sustained me during financial famine, reminding me of His amazing trustworthiness.

✳ *Though famines may come, God sustains us.*

— Scoti Springfield Domeij —

Two Best Men

The man who loves wisdom brings joy to his father.
—PROVERBS 29:3

When my son Brendan was getting married, my wife and I were reviewing candidates from a long list of groomsmen, trying to guess the one he would choose for best man. He had a number of close friends, and we were worried one or more might be hurt when he made his selection. When he called and told us he would like his grandpa and me to share the role, I was overwhelmed. This is something you do for your close buddy.

Then I realized that was exactly what he was trying to communicate. With his grandpa as my role model, I had my triumphs and failures as a parent. But as we stood together watching his adorable bride coming up the aisle, I realized he had honored us both in the highest possible way. No matter how young or old our parents and grandparents may be, let's think of creative ways to honor them. After all, Exodus 20:12 says it's the only commandment from God that comes with a promise: "Then you will live a long, full life."

✳ *Love is letting others know the good your parents have done.*

— James Stuart Bell —

The Sacrifice of Silence

If you claim to be religious but don't control your tongue,
you are fooling yourself, and your religion is worthless.

—JAMES 1:26

*A*ren't you coming, Mom?"

"No, honey, I'll wait here." Mom turned up the car heater. "You go ahead."

My brother Danny and I hurried to Grandma's door, our ears stinging from the cold, our eyes blurred with tears. We'd just come from Daddy's funeral, which Grandma was too sick to attend.

Grandma lamented the loss of Daddy and her other son, who'd died earlier. She offered no comfort for us children, only cold self-pity. She still had six children left. We'd said good-bye to our only daddy.

As a teenager, I asked Mom why she'd not gone in to see Grandma with us that day.

"Your grandma hated me and blamed me for the alcoholism that killed your daddy. I knew she'd not welcome me in her home."

"Yet you never spoke a word against her all these years."

"I didn't want to poison your memories of her or your daddy by passing along the bitterness. I cared more for your happiness than my own justification."

As I hugged Mom, my heart filled with joyous warmth. So this was love.

✻ *When speaking might cause pain, love chooses to remain silent.*

— Jeanette Levellie —

The Presence of Love

When three of Job's friends heard of the tragedy he
had suffered, they got together and traveled from
their homes to comfort and console him.

—JOB 2:11

*I*t's okay, Grandpa."
Little Elizabeth wasn't talking much since she wasn't three
yet, but she had that phrase down pat. And she already knew one
of her chief jobs in life was to help and love my dad, who'd had a
stroke several years earlier and was losing his capabilities to move.

Of course Dad was dealing with the depression that can come
as your body stops working right. But each time Grandpa sat in
his chair crying, little Elizabeth pulled her yellow plastic chair up
against Grandpa's burgundy recliner, right between his legs, facing him. She'd babble gentle words to him so quietly, the rest of
us in the room couldn't hear her. But we could tell by the tone in
her sweet high voice, the nods of her curly blond head, and gentle
pats that she was encouraging Grandpa.

After a couple of minutes, she'd go get a Kleenex, hand it to
him, and go back to her post. Though his mind may be confused
and his body was rebelling, his spirits were revived by a loving,
sympathetic heart.

❧ *Sometimes love just keeps a grieving person company.*

— Jeanette Gardner Littleton —

Investing in Love

You will always harvest what you plant.

—GALATIANS 6:7

I found her on the porch one summer morning, hair matted, thin, and eyes clouded. I recognized that someone had
discarded the half-grown pup and warned my wife that if she fed
the dog, it would stay.

My good-hearted wife fed the starved dog anyway, and soon
Apples became a part of our family. We built a pen, got a doghouse,
and nurtured her back to health. Our children groomed, walked,
and played with her, and she blessed our lives for fourteen years.

Why had our family fallen in love with this discarded mutt? It
resulted from investing time, energy, and resources in providing
for Apples.

Often we feel that love results from others caring or providing for us, but our deepest emotional ties usually result from our
investment in others.

When someone says they've quit loving another, I often sense
that the lack of love results from failing to invest in the life of that
individual. When we invest patience and kindness and dispel our
anger and judgments in relationships, we then find an emotional
bond springs forth.

✴ *Like most business transactions, love has to be invested in before
we will discover a payoff.*

— Steven Thompson —

The Blessing of Friends

God has made everything beautiful for its own time.

—ECCLESIASTES 3:11

There are certainly prettier gardens than mine in the world. It's scraggly in places where plants are just getting established, and it's a little lopsided in areas too. But if you look closer, you'll notice something else.

Under each cluster of plants is a hand-painted sign. The signs read *Melissa, Karen, JoAnn, Denise, Jane, Paula, Sandra, Cheryl,* and more. This is my *Girlfriend Garden.* You see, each plant in it began as a clipping from a friend's yard. So my garden isn't just made up of flowers I love, but also the plants my friends think are special—plants they've tended and grown themselves and are now sharing with me.

When I stop to admire my garden, I'm overwhelmed by the blessing of good friends. I visualize the yard each plant came from and the friend who dug it up to share it with me. What a lavish blessing from God our friends are!

❖ *Friends and flowers are two of God's most extravagant blessings. Nurture both.*

— Mimi Greenwood Knight —

The Look of God's Love

The one who looks at me is seeing the one who sent me.

—JOHN 12:45 NIV

*B*radley walks into my office and stands, rocking back and forth. He sticks his tongue out, sputtering and making his motor sound. I stop working.

"Hi, Bradley! I'm glad you came to see me."

Bradley has profound mental retardation, yet he communicates his needs quite well to the staff. "Ahhhhh!" he says loudly, greeting me.

He stands next to me and reaches for my hand. His touch is gentle, his palm slightly rough. He stops rocking and sputtering. Turning his head, he tips his chin up slightly and looks at me. His eyes reach into me, showing that we are of the same spirit. I feel as if Jesus is standing before me, sharing His love with just a look.

Bradley's giving me the greatest gift he has to offer—his look. I feel incredibly blessed. His look reassures me that God has chosen me to serve people with disabilities.

I haven't done anything to deserve Bradley's gift—or God's unending love. But I am grateful for both.

✣ *May we be open to seeing God in the most unlikely places and people.*

— Mary Beth Oostenbrug —

The One Who Wants to Help

Suddenly, a man with leprosy approached him and
knelt before him. "Lord," the man said, "if you are
willing, you can heal me and make me clean."
Jesus reached out and touched him. "I am willing," he said.
"Be healed!" And instantly the leprosy disappeared.

—MATTHEW 8:2–3

*B*ut Mommy, I'm afraid to ask Daddy for help," my little one said, burying her head in my leg. "He's busy on his computer and might get mad."

Mentally I had to concur with my daughter. Her father certainly didn't like to be disturbed from his work on the computer. I could understand her hesitancy.

The leper in Matthew didn't have that hesitation. When he came to Jesus, I imagine the crowds parted quickly! But this leper was desperate enough to brave people's anger to get close to Jesus. Once there, he came straight to the point: "If you want to, you can make me well again."

Jesus didn't say, "Let me think about it." Or, "Just a minute."

Instead He instantly said, "I want you to be healed." Not only that, but Jesus actually touched this man—a medical pariah of society who was probably oozing and gross.

What needs do you have? If you'll battle through the circumstances to reach Jesus, He will meet them—not only *will*, but *wants to*. He's eager for you to feel His healing, loving, empowering touch.

✻ *Jesus wants to meet our needs with His healing touch.*

— Jenni Davenport —

Boldly Loved

Love each other. Just as I have loved you,
you should love each other.

—JOHN 13:34

The day after my husband died, I was frantically preparing for our son's arrival from an overseas deployment when a church member stopped by.

"Brenda, I can't visit right now," I explained, "Dan's coming and . . ."

Pushing past me, she said, "You have tons to do, right? That's why I came."

Without hesitating, Brenda started washing a sink full of dirty dishes. Next, she made my beds with fresh linens. Then she asked, "Where's your vacuum?"

When I told her I had to leave to pick up my son at the airport, she announced, "I won't let you make that long drive alone."

Within minutes, she had another church member waiting out front to take me.

"Now, go with Judy," Brenda insisted, wrapping me in a hug, "and don't worry. I'll take care of the housework."

When my son and I arrived home, exhausted and grieving, we were greeted by an immaculate house, flowers on the table, and a blessing still lingering in the air . . . the comfort of being loved.

✳ *Love boldly. Let people know they're not struggling alone.*

— Laura L. Bradford —

Sharing One Man's Dream

Respect everyone, and love your Christian brothers and sisters.

—1 Peter 2:17

A stranger approached at the bookstore as I was signing copies of the book I'd written. He wore a ragged wool coat, soiled shirt, and tattered jeans. Thick, scratched glasses hugged his weathered cheeks. With stammering speech, he talked about the glory of writing and extended a roll of cherished, stained pages pulled from his coat pocket with rough and dirty fingers.

"I am a writer too!" he proclaimed.

I read his crumpled poems carefully and he relished my genuine interest. I couldn't tell whether his plans to publish were reality or a dream never realized, but I grasped his hand and shook it heartily after listening.

"It's been a pleasure meeting you," I said. And I meant it.

He smiled widely, revealing tarnished teeth. With a tear in his eye, he thanked me profusely as if I had done some remarkable feat. I nearly cried, wondering if anyone ever makes eye contact with him or knows his dreams. In an unexpected moment, I got to be my Lord's hands and heart to a man who was probably homeless but only wanted to share his dream.

✺ *It matters how you treat all people because all people matter.*

— Brenda Black —

Caring in Secret No Longer

Dear children, let's not merely say that we love each
other; let us show the truth by our actions.

—1 JOHN 3:18

*B*uddy and I sat outside the sanctuary. Inside, teenagers sang
praise songs, but outside, Buddy was sullen. He hadn't been
his boisterous self all week at camp.

"What's wrong?" I asked.

"You don't really care," he replied.

"Not true," I said. "I've cared about you for a long time."

Buddy stared at his hands. "I don't believe you."

Why should he? When Buddy had been a sixth-grader, he dis-
rupted Sunday school each week with his unruly behavior. One day
after I scolded him, he said, "Everyone's always yelling at me . . .
at school, at home, and at church."

That's when God spoke to my heart. He told me to send Buddy
anonymous notes, praising him when he did something right. So
that's what I secretly did for the next three years.

When I told Buddy about the notes I'd sent him, his eyes widened as he realized it was true. It was a turning point for both of
us. He told me about his parents' pending divorce and I could
finally help him.

✻ *God has cared about you and me for a long time, at least two
thousand years.*

— Pam Zollman —

Only Love Will Work

And let the peace that comes from Christ rule in your hearts.
For as members of one body you are called to live in peace.

—COLOSSIANS 3:15

I don't want you to marry that girl!"

Ann, my future mother-in-law, didn't mince words. With stark awareness, I knew I was not the wife she envisioned for her only son. Although our wedding day proceeded with a tentative truce, her frequent, disapproving comments throughout our first year acted as the proverbial salt on my wounded heart.

One night as Ron and I knelt to pray, the pain of her rejection overwhelmed me.

"I really hate your mother!" I cried.

Ron embraced me as I "uploaded" all my anger to the Lord. Then he gently asked, "Now what?"

I knew. In a whisper I prayed, "Lord, change my heart for Ann. Help me love her."

On her birthday that year, I baked a heart-shaped cake. Wistfully she said, "No one has ever made a cake for me before."

Suddenly, His love washed over me, and my heart found the freedom to love her.

I thank the Lord yet today, for He changed my heart and brought love's harmony to Ann's heart and mine.

✻ *God's love freely working in us never fails to embrace others, help-*
ing them love too.

— Jane Owen —

Send Out a Blessing

Bless those who persecute you. Don't curse
them; pray that God will bless them.

—ROMANS 12:14

*T*he young man looked downright sinister. He had come into
our little chapel on the boardwalk with some questions, but
they were mostly hostile. Halfway through a conversation, he began
cursing at me.

"I don't want to hear any more about your storybook Bible,"
he shouted, every other word an abusive swear word.

I tried to be gentle, listening and responding only when he indicated he would hear me. But certain things really tripped his
switch. "Jesus" was one of them. Whenever I mentioned the Savior's
name, he went ballistic.

"He's a liar and a charlatan," he sneered. "You're an idiot if
you believe in Him."

Finally, it came time for him to move on. I said, "Bless you, my
friend. I hope you find God's love some day."

He made an obscene gesture.

Even mild persecution or scorn like that can hurt. But giving a
blessing is a way to show love, even if a person doesn't seem very
receptive.

✳ *Bless and love others even when you think your words fall on deaf
ears; you never know how God will use it.*

— Jerry Constance —

Big Wheel Brother

Your love has given me much joy and comfort, my brother, for
your kindness has often refreshed the hearts of God's people.

—Philemon 1:7

My brother, Scott, has been a joy since the day he was born.
At least, that's what my parents said. I saw him as the red-
headed monster who wanted to ride my Big Wheel.

Until we moved to Spain.

Suddenly, he was the only kid on the block who spoke English
and liked baseball more than soccer. Then all the kids in our neighborhood started getting sick.

Meningitis.

Epidemic.

The doctor who diagnosed Scott did not speak English, but
one shake of his head and my parents knew. Before the nurse took
him away, Scott opened his eyes and said, "Mom?" He squeezed
her hand.

"Yes, son. I'm here."

"I hope Emily doesn't get this." Then his little body collapsed
into convulsions.

For weeks, I was not allowed to go near Scott. I promised God
that I would let Scott ride my Big Wheel if He'd just heal my brother.

He did.

And Scott didn't even want that Big Wheel anymore.

✣ *Selfless love can transform sibling rivalry.*

— Emily Osburne —

Love Moves Mountains

A friend is always loyal,
and a brother is born to help in time of need.

—PROVERBS 17:17

"Go away . . . I'm busy," snapped Jack.

"I'm sorry. I'll come back later," I replied with a sigh.

Jack was a real curmudgeon. No one in the office liked him, but I kept trying to be nice to him.

From that day on, I continued to be polite but kept my distance. It seemed the wiser choice given Jack's penchant for brushing people off.

After having a difficult time selling our house with my husband very ill, I was dreading the move we were about to make.

"How will I get everything moved with just myself and a sick husband to do it?" I asked myself in despair.

The morning of the move, our doorbell rang. There on the front steps stood Jack and a whole army of helpers. Jack, it seems, used his curmudgeonly ways to round up the whole office to help us. In a little over three hours, we had everything moved.

✱ *Some curmudgeons are angels in disguise.*

— Christine Trollinger —

Pool Boys and Pure Lives

How can a young person stay pure?
By obeying your word.

—PSALM 119:9

*O*h, look. I've shocked the innocent newlywed," Jill said with a derisive laugh.

I blushed. I was on the church staff and was in the church kitchen with a group of moms. We were fixing treats for vacation Bible school when Jill, who was a decade older than me and long married, made a rather suggestive comment about her pool boy—years before *Desperate Housewives* came on TV, and less than a year after I'd gotten married.

The moment passed. But over the years, when it's fluttered into my mind occasionally, I've thought of Psalm 119:9. Only it's not just the young person who needs to keep his or her ways pure, but the older person too!

Fortunately the Bible not only tells us to be pure, but it also gives us hundreds of tips on how to maintain that close relationship with God. As we seek to live pure lives for Him in an impure world, we experience more and more of His love and presence.

✳ *A person who loves God maintains a pure life by reading, studying, and following God's Word.*

— Jenni Davenport —

Learning Obedience

Even though Jesus was God's Son, he learned
obedience from the things he suffered.

—HEBREWS 5:8

*T*his is really tough to get," I said to my seminary roommate.
"I feel like I'm in way over my head."

"You have to study here," he said. "It's not a walk in the park."

"Study. Right."

Over the days and weeks, I spent hours trying to parse Hebrew
verbs, work through arcane passages of the Bible, and understand
flights of theology that left me firmly on the ground.

One night, my roommate came home late from a date. I was
still up. At my desk. Poring over texts, writing a paper. He walked
over and took a look.

"Good stuff," he said. "You're doing well."

"I don't think so," I said. "But I'm doing what God wants, I
guess."

"You're learning obedience, like Jesus did. Doing the things you
may not much like but that please God."

I had to laugh. "Is that what I'm doing?"

He said, "Yeah. It's an important thing. There are many times in
life when God calls us to obey Him. Even when we're not sure where
He's going or what He's doing. That's when we really please Him."

I didn't much like the thought, but in my heart, I knew it was
true.

✳ *If you want to show your best love for God, obey Him.*

— Karl Cumberland —

Room for One More

He comforts us in all our troubles so that
we can comfort others. . . .

—2 CORINTHIANS 1:4

I was deeply depressed as a teen. Both my parents worked late into the night; I baby-sat my toddler brother and endured abuse from an older brother; and my sister, the sunshine in my life, married and moved away. I often contemplated suicide and attempted it twice. My salvation through those years was Edith, a friend's fun-loving mother who "adopted" me and showered me with affection. She is undoubtedly one of the gifts God planted in my life even before I knew He loved me.

Years later, my sixteen-year-old son told me about a friend who'd been assaulted and continually threatened by a male relative. Besides that, excruciating back pain plagued her, and her family wouldn't get her medical attention.

When he asked, "Can she come here?" I remembered Edith. While my brain said, *No way we can manage that,* I knew the power a caring surrogate could exert. So I said yes.

While her time with us was measured in weeks, not years, we gave her a chance at healing and helped her family through a tough decision-making process.

✣ *God cloaks us with His love so we're able to offer the same to others.*

— Mary Kay Moody —

He Only Has Eyes for You

If a man owns a hundred sheep, and one of them
wanders away, will he not leave the ninety-nine on the
hills and go to look for the one that wandered off?

—MATTHEW 18:12 NIV

*E*ach year my husband, Steve, and I attend a convention for his work. The opening night of the convention features a reception for about four hundred members and spouses. My husband is much more the social butterfly than I am, so one year I asked him to go early and I would meet him there.

Arriving late, I realized I might have difficulties finding him in the crowd. As I stepped through the door, my eyes scanned the ballroom. In the midst of all the people, I spotted him.

By the time I found him, Steve was already looking at me. He had found me first. It was as if no one else were in the entire room.

The same is true of God and you. Even though there are more than six billion people in the world, it's as if He only has eyes for you. In Matthew, Jesus says that one lost sheep is more important to Him than a crowd. God loves people, and He loves them individually.

✳ *God loves you—as a person and as a unique individual.*

— Susan Campbell —

Dreams of the Heart

Hope deferred makes the heart sick,
but a dream fulfilled is a tree of life.

—PROVERBS 13:12

*W*ait, Mom, there's one more present."

My twenty-one-year-old son handed me a computer-generated card sporting a picture of us in my daughter's Miata convertible.

I opened the card. A car key! My daughter, ready to start a family and in need of a more practical car, and my husband, eager to make me smile, conspired with my father to make my dream of owning this particular car come true.

"Thank you," I mumbled through tears of joy. I looked up into the eyes of my precious family, realizing they heard the cries of my heart and plotted this surprise together, no matter how impractical.

Nine years have passed, but each time I drive that car, I reflect on my family's sensitivity to my fragile tomboy dreams of adventure locked in an aging body. When the wind tugs at my hair and I smell the scent of fresh-mown hay, I reflect on God's gifts and thank Him that I'm never too old to enjoy them.

✣ *A family's example of sacrificial love points us to the much greater unconditional love of God.*

— Linda Jett —

Love Never Lets Go

We know how dearly God loves us, because he has given
us the Holy Spirit to fill our hearts with his love.

—ROMANS 5:5

*S*end him to a boys' home," family members demanded. I
stood firm.

No! A mother does not give up on her son!

Yes, he arrived as a troubled child at four months old when
my husband and I adopted him. He wouldn't eat and was a stiff
baby—wouldn't relax in our arms. As he grew, he agitated kids
and adults. One offended church worker said, "He is the worst
child I've ever had."

He made our dogs yelp and threw rocks at children. He burned
his sister's treasured dried flowers. His school recommended him
for a behaviorally disordered class.

Sure I cried over him. I yelled at him at times. But the minute we
adopted him, God showered—more like pelted—my heart with
His love for this precious new life. It was a love that refused to die
through many long years of turmoil.

Today, my son, a responsible adult, calls his growing-up years
his "dark days," and ends our phone calls with, "Love ya."

✳ *When God's love saturates our hearts, we can stand firm for others.*

— Peggy Halter Morris —

Enter the Holy Place

And so, dear brothers and sisters, we can boldly enter
heaven's Most Holy Place because of the blood of Jesus.

—HEBREWS 10:19

I just don't see what's so great about prayer. It's just talk. I
guess you're talking to God. But God's everywhere, right?"
Matt, a member of our small group, said.

Steve, the leader, responded, "Suppose you need something so
incredible that you have to go to someone great and powerful to
get it. Think the president. Or a king. How would you tell him
about your need?"

"I guess I'd have to go to Washington, D.C. To the White House.
To his office. I guess I'd be very reverent and present my best argument and hope he would say yes," Matt answered.

"Good," said Steve. "Now think of it this way. The place where
God was in the land of Israel was in the temple, in the Most Holy
Place, where the Ark of the Covenant and other things were. Only
the high priest could go in there. But because of what Jesus did,
when you're praying, you enter the Holy Place and stand, or kneel,
before God's throne. Every time you pray. Think of it that way."

"That changes everything," Matt said.

✳ *The love of God is so great that when you pray, He lets you come
into His most Holy Place to talk to Him.*

— Richard Holland —

The Weight of Guilt

So if the Son sets you free, you are truly free.

—JOHN 8:36

*H*e was barely twenty, but guilt weighed him down as if he were eighty. Hunched and shuffling, the metal bracelet on his ankle confirmed that this man knew agony.

I had just finished telling the group of inmates my painful story of childhood sexual abuse. He urgently approached me as if I alone could relieve his burden. A wounded child himself, he had raped his neighbor and was serving his sentence. Tortured with remorse, he desperately wanted to apologize to the young girl and her family. But a restraining order forced him to wear his guilt like an anchor.

Though I relived my own traumatic assaults through his tearful confession, God's love overpowered my anger and confusion. I heard myself say, "I'll be your victim. Tell me what you need to tell her."

He sobbed with regret as his apology pierced my wounded heart.

Two broken hearts collided. God showed me how to forgive him. We prayed. He smiled and simply said, "Thank you." The weight of his guilt was gone: God's love set us both free.

✻ *One courageous act of obedience can release people from bondage through God's love and the miracle of forgiveness.*

— Tricia Propson —

Lawn-Care Blessing

When you see these things, your heart will rejoice.
You will flourish like the grass!
Everyone will see the Lord's hand of blessing on his servants.

—ISAIAH 66:14

The large corner lot that drew my husband and me to our home now looked more like a jungle than a residential lawn. How was I going to take care of my nine-month-old son and cut the lawn since my husband's sudden death?

All at once, the rumbling sound of a lawn mower filled my ears. I ran to the front door. A college-aged neighbor who owned a small landscaping business was mowing my lawn. He had been working across the street the day my husband died and knew what had happened.

I stepped onto the porch. "Thank you so much. I would like to pay you, but . . ."

"I don't want any money. And I'll cut your grass for the rest of the summer."

I blinked back tears. "I don't know what to say."

"Don't say anything. I want to do this."

Years later, I still think about that unexpected lawn-care blessing. God knew my needs and provided before I could even ask.

✳ *In what way can you show God's love and be a blessing in someone's life today?*

— Susan Kelly Skitt —

The Father Who Cares

And you saw how the Lord your God cared for
you all along the way as you traveled through the
wilderness, just as a father cares for his child.

—DEUTERONOMY 1:31

*B*abe, I checked your oil and it looks okay," Dad said as he shut
the front door behind him. "Your windshield fluid was getting
low, so I added some. And I think I'll go put some air in your tires."

He barely heard my thanks as he turned around and went out
the door again. I kept chatting with Mom until he returned.

Nearly every time I drove across town to visit my parents, Dad
checked my car's vitals. He also made sure I always had tools, an
emergency kit in my trunk, and a full tank of gas. And if the car
needed to go into the shop, Dad took it while I was at work.

Maintaining my car was just one of the ways Dad took care
of me. He helped with my little fix-up house, took care of my
pets when I was gone, even frequently checked to make sure I had
enough money.

Because my father showed such loving care for me, it's easier
for me to have faith in the Father who's promised to care for me.

✳ *God is the ultimate good Father.*

— Jeanette Gardner Littleton —

God's Love Changes Things

But to you who are willing to listen, I say, love your
enemies! Do good to those who hate you.

—LUKE 6:27

On my first day of work as an office supervisor, the staff I
was to supervise let me know my presence was unwelcome.
They had expected one of their own to be promoted to the position
and resented an outsider being awarded the job. In retaliation, the
workers banded together to stonewall me at every turn.

Baffled and frustrated, I asked God how to work in this hostile
environment, since I did not want to resign. The answer came from
the Sermon on the Mount—be salt and light and win the people
through love.

Patiently and consistently, I sought every opportunity to assist,
praise, deal fairly, and encourage each one to stretch his or her
skills and talents.

When my final day of work arrived, a surprise awaited me. The
staff had ordered a large cake on which was written, "Good-bye.
We will miss you very much!" And beside the cake were personal
messages of thanks from each staff member. God had completely
transformed our office through the presence of love.

✢ *There is no greater power than the love of God working in us.*

— Jessica Talbot —

Hugs—Pass Them On!

Instead, be kind to each other, tenderhearted, forgiving one another, just as God through Christ has forgiven you.

—Ephesians 4:32

When she was living with us, I noticed that my octogenarian mother had a definite need for touch. She tried fulfilling it by trying to get her grandson, my son, to hug her. At his independent stage, he was not interested. Mom persisted, but he, just as adamantly, refused. He'd say, "I'm all out of hugs, Grammie."

I thought of a solution to this dilemma. Surprising him with a tight squeeze, I exclaimed, "Now you have a hug; I just gave you one. You can give one to Grammie." Developing a crooked little grin, he thought it over, and then ran to give her an embrace. We all got in on the act and felt better about each other. Touching can be contagious!

The elderly can easily fade into the background when they're uninvolved or have trouble with sight or hearing. Expressing kindness to the aged will make more sense when we find ourselves on the other side of the rocking chair.

✳ *A gentle hug for older folks—and anyone else—makes them feel like the treasures they are.*

— Dianna Brumfield —

He Will Lift You Up

So humble yourselves under the mighty power of God,
and at the right time he will lift you up in honor.

—1 PETER 5:6

I always loved the movie *Chariots of Fire* and the story of
Eric Liddell, the sprinter from Scotland who ran in the 1924
Olympics. He won a medal for his efforts, and many said his run
was the "jewel of the games that year." Some great quotes came
out of that movie.

One of them happened when he explained to his sister why
he had to run. Because the qualifying heats for his best event, the
100-meter sprint, were held on a Sunday, he refused to participate.
But he still wanted to run. He told his sister, "When I run, I feel
[God's] pleasure."

When he finally ran in the 400-meter race, an event he did not
excel at, one of the contestants passed him a little piece of paper.
On it was written, "He who honors me, I will honor" (see 1 Samuel
2:30).

Liddell went on to win. God honored him as he had honored
God.

✳ *God's honor comes to those who truly love Him.*

— Brian Varney —

Life Is a Beach

The Lord himself watches over you!
The Lord stands beside you as your protective shade.

—PSALM 121:5

When the going gets rough, I mentally go to the beach. Nearly every summer, my husband's family gathers for a week on the Outer Banks of North Carolina. I love feeling warm sand, watching sand crabs scurry, and listening to ocean waves.

The first year, I wondered why the family lugged so much gear—especially a huge, clunky umbrella—from the house to the beach. But I quickly learned how hot the sand becomes to walk on, and how quickly a flaming summer sun roasts skin. I gratefully ran for that protective shade. At other times, the umbrella shielded us from stinging sand the wind spat at us. The umbrella protected us from harsh realities of life on the beach.

Do you ever feel like your life is a dance on broiling sand? Or that you're being burned or stung by the elements? Let God and His love be your shade, your protection from the harsh realities of the elements of life.

✣ *Protective coverings are meant to be taken advantage of.*

— Julie Durham —

Easy to Pray for

> May your Kingdom come soon.
> May your will be done on earth,
> as it is in heaven.
>
> —MATTHEW 6:10

I tried to pray, but the words got stuck in my throat.

The tears fell, but I finally got the words out.

"Lord, you know that person has hurt someone I love! How can I pray a blessing? Help me to pray and love!"

Do you have people on your prayer list who are easy to pray for? You love them so much that the prayers flow from your mouth to God's ears with ease. You pray for their health, spirit, family, specific needs, and everything that concerns them. Because you love them so deeply, words come easily.

Then there are others whom you struggle to pray for. It is hard. The prayer doesn't come easily.

You find you don't really want to pray for them, but pray you must. Why? Because prayer is the key to loving people. You can't continue to pray and not love. Pray and then pray some more! Then leave the results to God.

✣ *Love helps those that are hard to pray for turn into people who are easy to pray for.*

— Donna Collins Tinsley —

Get Up and Go

So Peter went over the side of the boat and
walked on the water toward Jesus.

—MATTHEW 14:29

My brother-in-law and I watched his young son run down a sloped, gravel driveway. Suddenly the child tripped and landed on his knees and hands. In that shocked instant before the boy's crying could begin, David called out, "That's all right. Go ahead. Get up. You'll be okay."

Puzzled, I told David, "That hurt." He agreed and went right on loudly encouraging my nephew. Shortly, the youngster stood and walked back up the driveway. He was fine—only a little blood, and he wasn't crying. My brother-in-law was right. His son did not need comforting love. He did need encouragement to get up and go on.

I still use David's example of problem-solving love with children and with adults. Since this event, I tend to give more encouragement than sympathy. I also remember the Lord's words and actions when Peter tried to walk on water. Jesus caught him and kept him from falling into the water. Then he said, "You of little faith, why did you doubt?"

In other words, "Go ahead. Get up. You'll be okay."

✣ *Love limited to sympathy interferes in the process of overcoming problems.*

— Virginia Colclasure —

Living in a Jaguar

But if there are any poor Israelites in your towns when
you arrive in the land the Lord your God is giving you,
do not be hard-hearted or tightfisted toward them.

—Deuteronomy 15:7

A young teddy bear of a man sat on a blanket in the cold
night air. Three cats and two dogs climbed over his lap,
and a green parakeet sat on his head. I handed him my last fifty
bucks. "I think God wants you to have this."

"You're silly to give him your money," my friend responded.
"He probably drives a fancy car." She chided me into the night and
pointed a finger when someone told us the man drove a Jaguar.

"See!" she said. "I told you so."

The next day, I saw that Jaguar. It was broken down and rusted
and smelled of wet animals. It hadn't moved from the spot where
it sat in many years. As I walked by it, the young man opened the
door and with a big smile said, "I remember you."

For the next twenty minutes I talked of God's love with the
mentally challenged young man, all the while thinking that if he
were my son, I sure would be glad if someone took time to care.

✣ *Giving is about letting go and trusting God, even when others don't
understand.*

— Sandy Cathcart —

Postal Requirement

Treat them like native-born Israelites, and love them as
you love yourself. Remember that you were once foreigners
living in the land of Egypt. I am the Lord your God.

—LEVITICUS 19:34

There she stood waiting until I spoke—a fashionably dressed
Sudanese woman with tears welling her eyes. Brightly I
greeted her. "Hello, Ashol!"

In barely understandable English, this wife of a former ambassador to Lebanon exclaimed, "I need help!"

"Ashol, I'm glad to assist you," I replied to my newest Christian friend.

She explained, "I've tried to pay bills for three days—the postman won't pick up; I got call—my electricity and phone being shut off."

She extended two addressed envelopes. The corners were bare.

"Oh, Ashol, you need stamps." I reached into my purse, handed her one, and affixed the other one myself. On next glance, I realized she had placed her stamp in the center of the envelope. Knowing she was still near tears, pen in hand, I quickly drew an arrow from the stamp to the upper right hand corner of the envelope.

While I walked with her the half block to the post office, Ashol smiled broadly. "God blessed me today with your care and friendship."

✢ *Even the smallest actions of a friend can make a big difference.*

— Zeta Davidson —

Broken Hearts

So the Lord was sorry he had ever made
them. . . . It broke his heart.

—GENESIS 6:6

I love the peace of a quiet house. It's still nice after my thirteen-
year-old son gets home from school.

But the moment my seven-year-old girl walks in, the spats begin.
It's not just her or him. It's both of them. No matter how I try to
regain that peace, it just doesn't happen; the kids are home and
sibling rivalry is in full swing. And at those moments, it's really
hard not to think, *Why did I ever have kids?*

When I read this verse it suddenly struck me: God "was sorry he
had ever made them. It broke his heart."

Wow! This verse reminds me that when our kids make a mess
of things, God knows how we feel. So what did God do? He didn't
give up on humans. He found the salvageable element and began
working with it.

Depending on our kids' ages, we can only do so much when
they've tangled their lives. But we can follow God's example and
give our kids—and other mess-makers in our lives—another chance;
we can believe in them and keep working with them.

❋ *When your kids, or others, break your heart, go to God—He knows
how you feel!*

— Janet Graham —

Discipline With a Purpose

If God doesn't discipline you as he does all of
his children, it means that you are illegitimate
and are not really his children at all.

—HEBREWS 12:8

*I*n some situations, it seems like it's just one problem after
another," my friend Brian told me as we sat sipping coffee in
his office. "Some days I just want to scream. And you know—the
problems get bigger and worse. When I first started this business,
they were little things. Now? Sheesh!"

"Did you ever think that God might be disciplining you?"

"I've done something wrong?"

"Not necessarily," I said. "Discipline doesn't just mean punishment. It could be that you are in God's training program. Out there
in the future are some things that may be so big you'd run the op-
posite direction if you knew about them now. But He's disciplining
you, training you, sending you the smaller things so you'll be ready
when you get the really big things."

"You're kidding," he replied.

"No, that's how God works. Study the life of Jesus. See how
God did it with Him. He didn't face the cross the first day. He was
in the process of being prepared."

✢ *God disciplines us because He loves us, not just when we do wrong,
but to prepare us for the days ahead.*

— Karl Cumberland —

You Let Me Dance

But Peter said, "I don't have any silver or gold for
you. But I'll give you what I have. In the name of
Jesus Christ the Nazarene, get up and walk!"

—ACTS 3:6

I'd been trained as a social worker, so what was I doing working in a financial organization? How could I fit into this world
and make a difference?

The answer came one morning when my friend at work, Gina,
gave me a beautifully wrapped gift. Inside was a snow globe music
box containing a ballerina. I shook the globe, and snow fell gently
around the ballerina to the music of *Swan Lake*.

The thoughtful gift touched me, but why did Gina think of me
when she bought it?

"This is how you make me feel," Gina explained. "When we work
together, you listen and encourage me to be myself. You never try
to change me." She paused, then whispered, "You let me dance."

In that moment, I realized God never expected me to give what
I didn't possess or couldn't do. He only wanted me to pass along
those gifts He showered on me—gifts like love, encouragement,
comfort, or a listening ear.

✳ *Giving only what we've been given—God's love—lets others dance
their own Swan Lake.*

— Gloria Ashby —

Spiritual Intercession

For God has not given us a spirit of fear.

—2 TIMOTHY 1:7

*S*omething's wrong with Janet," I said to myself as I climbed out of bed on a summer night at the campground where my husband and I worked. We lived a hundred miles away from our grown daughter, Janet. She hadn't called, but I knew something was not right.

I dressed and paced under the stars, begging God to protect my daughter from unknown danger. Finally, finding peace, I returned to bed.

Early in the morning, the phone rang. Someone had attacked Janet the night before, but she was able to get away unharmed. I prayed with her, thankful I had been awakened to intercede.

She reminded me that years earlier, I had put Bible verses in her lunches to memorize. As she struggled through what had happened, she was strengthened by 2 Timothy 1:7, "For God has not given us a spirit of fear."

"Mom," she said, "I remembered that Scripture, and it helps me not to be afraid now."

✻ *God's love intercedes for us even as a mother intercedes for her child.*

— Pat Miller —

To Forgive a Thief

But if you refuse to forgive others, your
Father will not forgive your sins.

—MATTHEW 6:15

While we lived in the Republic of Panama, my husband was attacked by a robber wielding a knife. Though wounded, my husband resisted until the man escaped into a nearby housing complex. In a rare act, local residents turned the thief over to the police.

We had been robbed before in other developing countries, and I had personally found stealing to be a particularly difficult offense to forgive. Nevertheless, God gently nudged me to avoid judging by my own cultural standards and to start loving as Jesus loved. This violent incident was my toughest challenge.

When the young Panamanian was sentenced to a year in jail, I learned that God had transformed me. Instead of taking satisfaction in the man's fate, I felt sad and grieved for his future. My husband and I forgave him and sincerely prayed he would survive the harsh jail conditions and turn his life around.

Even though we were robbed again in Panama, the spirit of anger was no longer there. God's love had shown me how to forgive a thief.

✶ *Only by God's divine love can we truly forgive from the heart.*

— Jessica Talbot —

Love for a Lifetime

Three things will last forever—faith, hope, and
love—and the greatest of these is love.

—1 CORINTHIANS 13:13

*R*ay signed out of the visitors' logbook and offered me a weak
smile. His teary eyes met mine as I reassured him that his
presence comforted his precious wife of fifty-eight years. His daily
visit ended, and he trudged out the locked door of the dementia
facility where I worked.

Day after day, Genevieve wrestles a wheelchair to get in and out
of her car and come see her husband, formerly an oral surgeon,
who now depends on others to feed him. Genevieve's shoulders
slump with fatigue, and still she lovingly stands by her man.

Bert huffs and puffs after walking from the assisted living center
next door. Weakened by emphysema, he exerts heroic effort on the
daily trek to visit his wife. An hour later, he returns to the lobby
and rests a moment, his face drawn in grief after leaving the love
of his life behind.

Ray, Genevieve, and Bert will return tomorrow, even though their
spouses have forgotten their names. No wonder 1 Corinthians 13,
the love chapter of the Bible, proclaims that of faith, hope, and
love, "the greatest of these is love."

✳ *May our love for others endure, no matter the cost.*

— Nora Peacock —

Blackberries and Borders

A hot-tempered person starts fights;
a cool-tempered person stops them.

—PROVERBS 15:18

*Y*our neighbor stopped by." My son-in-law paused. "She says she's going to sue you."

I froze in disbelief. "What?"

My daughter explained, "She's tired of the blackberries growing through the fence. We have until this weekend to clear them away, otherwise she'll sue."

I fought my own anger and tried to understand her frustration. With a house and yard still under construction and a husband working six days a week, we hadn't tended the blackberries as we should have.

Not being a gardener, I wasn't sure what to do. As the weekend approached, the blackberry vines stayed as they were, weaving their way through the fence, taunting my neighbor.

I decided to head to the store for an herbicide, but my daughter dug out the yard clippers and attacked the fiendish bush instead.

I glanced out to see she wasn't alone. My neighbor stood on the other side of the chain-link fence chatting with her, and she was smiling!

My daughter's calm action defused the situation and endeared her to my neighbor, healing our relationship.

✼ *A loving response can turn an angry neighbor into a new friend.*

— Cheryl Secomb —

Grumblers and Complainers

These people are grumblers and complainers,
living only to satisfy their desires.

—JUDE 16

I tried to help Sarah walk with the Lord, but she was a tough case.

"Another lousy sermon," she said as we walked out of the auditorium.

"It wasn't one of his best."

"I haven't even heard one of his best," she said, pulling on her coat. "And the singing is getting to me. Why do we have to stand and sing song after stupid song? Can't they do something else?"

I wasn't sure what to tell her. "You know, Sarah, there are verses in the Bible that warn against complaining all the time."

"I don't complain all the time."

"Quite frankly, yes, you do. I'm sorry. You never have anything good to say about anyone or anything related to church. I think you need an attitude check."

She frowned. "I really do, don't I?"

"Look, every time you're tempted to complain, think of five good things. What are five good things you can think of about the service tonight?"

It took a while, but gradually Sarah stopped complaining. Then it was amazing how quickly she began to learn and grow through the very church she'd complained so much about.

✻ *It's too easy to complain. A heart of love finds the good, and, if necessary, helps change the bad things.*

— Zach Davidson —

Love and Freedom

He is so rich in kindness and grace that he purchased our
freedom with the blood of his Son and forgave our sins.

—EPHESIANS 1:7

Boom! Snap! Bang!
I stood behind my husband, my chin resting on his shoulder as we watched the glorious fireworks display. Pretty soon, I could feel my husband giggling from the very core of his being.

The Fourth of July is one of my favorite holidays, and not just because it's the only time I've heard my husband laugh like a school-boy. I've always liked American history and have been touched by the courage of our forefathers. For me, it's a day to celebrate my national heritage and thank God for the freedom my ancestors fought for.

There's another day of freedom I like to celebrate every year. It's the anniversary of the day nearly forty years ago when I found spiritual freedom. On that day, I learned that God loved me so much that He sent His Son to give His life so I could find freedom from my sins.

As I take time out to celebrate what God did for me so long ago—and in the years since—it's a great reminder of His love.

✣ *Have you celebrated your anniversary of spiritual freedom—of the time you learned how much God loves you?*

— Janet Graham —

Happily Ever After

For your kingdom is an everlasting kingdom.
You rule throughout all generations.
The Lord always keeps his promises;
he is gracious in all he does.

—PSALM 145:13

*A*unt Susie, come listen to my story."
I looked at my five-year-old niece, her pixie face and blue eyes begging me to sit on the living room floor. Grinning, I sat next to her on the carpet. "Okay, Sarah. Tell me your story."

"There are three kingdoms." Sarah pointed to brown colored stones from her rock collection. "This is Woody Wrangle," she announced. "This is Rocky Road," she said about the small pile of gray rocks. "And this is the North Pole, where the snow people live." She pointed to the white pebbles she had gathered during a family vacation. She continued weaving her fantastic tale.

Marveling at her creativity, I thought about how my dad would tell adventure stories to his children and grandchildren. It seemed my brother's child had inherited the storytelling gene! However, the most important stories my dad would tell were true stories from the Bible. He taught us God's story of love and redemption—a kingdom story that has a happily-ever-after ending because of Jesus.

✳ *To whom are you telling the true story of God's everlasting love?*

— Susan Kelly Skitt —

A Bit of Marital Advice

You husbands must give honor to your wives. Treat
your wife with understanding as you live together.

—1 PETER 3:7

*W*hen my husband and I met in college and married just six
months later, we didn't have much time to find out how
to be a married couple. We learned along the way. However, there
is one tidbit of advice we received that has meant more to us than
anything else.

My dad was a preacher, and he married us. I remember hearing
him tell my husband, "Kiss her when you're going out or coming
in."

When we married, most of the wives were homemakers, so the
man did most of the "going out and coming in." However, all
these years later, we still remember the good-bye kiss when one of
us leaves to do something, or when we come back home. It also
helps us to remember my precious dad and his homespun wisdom.

Even though we're now a couple of senior citizens, it always
brings a smile and a happy memory when my husband comes toward me, puckers up for a kiss, jingles his car keys, and announces,
"I'm going out!"

�֝ *Lord, help us to be thankful for our helpmates, and to show them
our love.*

— Juanita Nobles —

Ray of Sunshine

Never let loyalty and kindness leave you!
Tie them around your neck as a reminder.
Write them deep within your heart.

—PROVERBS 3:3

A dull monotony weighed on my spirit as I stared at the road. Was it really that important for me to visit my mother every day at the nursing home? I'd been doing this for a year—the same drive each afternoon, then sitting beside her bed for an hour. She was getting so forgetful now and slept most of the time anyway. Would she know if I skipped a day?

"God," I prayed. "There are so many other worthwhile things for me to do. Is this how you want me to spend my time? Two hours every day going to see my mother?"

A few minutes later, when I entered Mother's room at the home, I saw her pale face light up with a smile. "Oh, Linda, when I see you walk in here, you're like a ray of sunshine to me."

Later, as I drove home, tears rimmed my eyes. All doubts dissolved. I'd heard God's answer. What else could I do that would so easily bring someone that much happiness?

✶ *Time sacrificed in love warms a lonely heart.*

— Linda W. Rooks —

Words of Love

Your words have supported those who were falling;
you encouraged those with shaky knees.

—JOB 4:4

I met Katie at a conference when she and her husband sat next
to me at a round table. She was simple and plainly dressed,
but I felt compelled to tell her, a total stranger, that she was pretty.

Katie responded like a starving child who'd been handed a loaf
of bread. Soon I noticed how her husband treated her. He yanked
a pen from her hand; he growled a response when she asked him a
question. Later, when we took a break for dessert, Katie followed
me around like a lost puppy.

After the conference, Katie asked for my address. We corre-
sponded for a few months. She wrote pages and pages about her
struggles, her broken dreams, and the hopes and dreams she had
for the future.

Since then, I've tried to obey God's prompting to compliment
other strangers, like the young woman working the drive-thru window at McDonald's. It feels awkward at the time, but I realize it's
not my words but Jesus's message to them.

✻ *We never know how our words will bring hope and encouragement*
to a total stranger.

— Rebecca Stuhlmiller —

A Good Example

As a result, you have become an example
to all the believers in Greece—
throughout both Macedonia and Achaia.

—1 THESSALONIANS 1:7

The teen was desperate. "I can't go home. My dad will kill me. He hates me. I don't know what to do."

I knew a little about this young man. He'd been coming to our youth meetings for a while. But now he seemed terrified. "What did you do?" I asked gently.

"I stole money. I trashed my room. I sprayed paint on his truck." He looked down, weeping. "I didn't mean it; I was just so mad."

"What if I talk to him for you?"

"Now? He's too mad."

"Okay," I said. "How about you come to my house for the night. Things will look better in the morning. Then we'll go see him together. Does that sound like a plan?"

He looked up at me, astonished. "You would do that?"

"Sure. Now let's go."

On the way out, one of the youth leaders caught me. "That was great, James. You showed him a real example."

Your example is a witness—of God's love and yours.

— James Hopkins —

Reaching Out

They share freely and give generously to those in need.
Their good deeds will be remembered forever.
They will have influence and honor.

—PSALM 112:9

*I*t had been a long and tiring day at work, and I longed to get home, have a hot bath, and make dinner. The traffic was dense so I decided to take a shortcut through a narrow lane. I came upon some huts where a woman and child were eating what looked like stale bread.

After I got home, I called a friend, Reena, and we took some food to them, as well as clean clothes, bars of soap, and rice, flour, and vegetables.

"These people need mosquito nets. And thick plastic sheets to cover the tops of their huts from the rain," Reena said.

"There are so many with so many needs . . . how many can we help?" I voiced my concern.

That weekend we returned with some mosquito nets.

I was wondering if our offerings made any difference, but my friend pointed out, "Better something than nothing."

❊ *We can't meet all the needs, but we can meet some of them.*

— Sudha Khristmukti —

Waiting on God's Promises

The Lord . . . did exactly what he had promised.

—Genesis 21:1

"Mommy, you promised we could go to the park. When? Let's go!"

My son isn't patient when I've promised to do something. He wants my promises fulfilled immediately. So sometimes he learns about waiting.

Abraham was one of those in the Bible who had to wait. God had promised him a son, but years passed and he and Sarah were still childless.

Finally, Abraham tried to force God's promises to come true—he impregnated his wife's maid, planning that he and his wife could raise the child.

What a mess that ended up to be! When God's promises did come true, and Abraham's legitimate, promised son was born, a legendary clash began—one that some theologians believe was the beginning of the Arab and Israeli conflict today.

Waiting on God is tough. But it's necessary to keep believing He'll do what He promises, and since He loves us, His timing is perfect.

✳ *When we're waiting on God, we have to trust that His timing is perfect!*

— Jenni Davenport —

Deflated, But Not Defeated

Here on earth you will have many trials and sorrows.
But take heart, because I have overcome the world.

—JOHN 16:33

*D*eb sent me a balloon the day my last child finished high
school. Two months later, it still hovered, tied to the cow-
shaped clock in the kitchen.

Lonely with my last kid gone, I decided to clean house, starting
with the deflating balloon. At the wastebasket, its string slipped
from my hand. The balloon floated into our ceiling fan, which
started beating it to death. I leaped to retrieve it from another
punch, but it escaped, jumping back into the fan, only to receive
another beating. I stopped the fan to save the balloon's life. Sighing,
I gave it a new home in the sunroom, tied to a chair, where it could
spend its last days rising and falling and looking out into the woods.

I called Deb, who was recovering from a heartbreaking divorce.
"Remember that balloon you sent me? Well, it turns out it's a fighter
like you are! Looks like you both get another chance."

Thanks to the persistent balloon, we shared a laugh, grateful
for a unique lesson in courage.

✳ *If we're drowning in self-pity, we may miss a chance to encourage
others.*

— Kristi Paxton —

A Love Overwhelming

Dear children, let's not merely say that we love each
other; let us show the truth by our actions.

—1 JOHN 3:18

*T*he pile of packages the woman carried overwhelmed her.
My middle-school son stood next to me in the checkout line,
but he didn't see the weary woman slowly progress down the long
walkway toward an open register. Thirty yards separated her from
the finish line, but from the looks of the tottering tower, I doubted
she'd make it.

Empathizing, I nudged my son and nodded my head in the
woman's direction.

"Why don't you go help her? She looks like she's having a hard
time."

The moment he recognized her predicament, he jumped to work,
squeezing past the people behind us and making quick headway
toward the over-burdened woman. Within seconds, he'd taken some
of her packages and led her toward the closest checkout line.

As we left the store a few minutes later, my son's face beamed.
I reminded him: Often in showing God's love, we experience the
overwhelming fullness of it for ourselves.

✣ *As we intentionally extend God's love to others, we find our own
need met with the overflow.*

— Michele Cushatt —

Rainstorm Reprieve

If you can help your neighbor now, don't say,
"Come back tomorrow, and then I'll help you."
—Proverbs 3:28

Chills wracked my body as I completed my last errand. Maneuvering my vehicle through the rivulets of water that cascaded down the street, I couldn't wait to get home and into dry clothes.

Trudging through the fat raindrops that pelted the sidewalk, her worn coat wrapped close around her hunched body, a woman fought against the biting wind.

I pulled over and opened the passenger door. "Need a ride home?" I asked. When I waved her inside, she hesitated, and then accepted the invitation.

Tears spilled down her cheeks as she shook her head. "I have bills to pay. The electric company. The gas company. My landlord. If I don't pay him today, he'll kick me out."

I drove her to the appropriate places and helped her inside each building before taking her home.

She uttered few words, but her parting grin spoke volumes.

I arrived home late, cold and soaking wet, but God's smile warmed my heart with a glow as bright as a crackling fire.

✳ *Don't be afraid to get wet, for God's warmth prevails even on rainy days.*

— Patti Shene —

When God Calls

If you help the poor, you are lending to the Lord—
and he will repay you!

—Proverbs 19:17

I rarely had cash, and I couldn't wait to spend it on something amazing. But an idea popped into my head. What if I gave it to the needy? At first the idea annoyed me, but I soon realized what I needed to do—send my first check to support a teen in Ethiopia.

Four months and a couple of hundred dollars later, I found myself wondering if I could still provide for this teen and if it was worth it. I prayed, and all I felt in return was that I should trust God. So I sent another check in the mail.

Soon after, I received a note from my Ethiopian friend. He said, "How are you doing, whom I love and respect? I am doing well. I just passed on to the eighth grade. I am so happy! I am ready to continue my education well."

That is what God did with my faithfulness. Nothing can compare with the knowledge that I am changing this teen's life!

✻ *When God calls us to give, the outcome of obeying is always worth more than the gift itself.*

— Jonathan D. Miller —

Never Invisible to God

Thereafter, Hagar used another name to refer to the Lord, who had spoken to her. She said, "You are the God who sees me."

—Genesis 16:13

A devastated woman slumped in the chair in my office at a domestic violence agency. As our counseling session neared its end for the day, she tried to convey how empty and alone she felt. She said she had no friends. Her husband was charming—everyone liked him but tolerated her because they were a package deal. Sometimes she even wondered if her own children cared about her.

"I like you," I said, looking directly at her.

She raised her head then shook it. "You're paid to like me."

I held her gaze. "No, I'm paid to listen to you. I like you because you're likeable."

She watched me a moment, then looked out the window.

I hoped she'd take in my words, that our weeks of working together would convince her I spoke the truth. But I knew that women whose husbands repeatedly beat them and treated them like objects usually grew into the role of object, not person.

She blinked back tears. "Thank you," she whispered.

✷ *Who needs to hear today that they are not invisible or unimportant to God?*

— Mary Kay Moody —

Love Leads the Way

And why worry about a speck in your friend's
eye when you have a log in your own?

—LUKE 6:41

*M*y family was driving me to distraction with bad tempers
and disappointing attitudes.

My usually mild husband was struggling at work. He took his
frustration out by yelling at the sports teams on television and
behaving aggressively.

My normally placid oldest child decided that he would enjoy
provoking his younger brother—and ignored my pleas to stop.

My youngest was expressing his dislike of swimming lessons by
throwing tantrums. His teacher had been on the phone, advising
me of the latest antics.

I thought I would turn to my Bible to find some words of wisdom to share with them—to make them see the errors of their
ways. However, the message that leaped from its pages spoke to
me instead.

I read Jesus's words about judging others and looking at myself
first. I read about blessing others, not cursing them—and I decided
I needed to examine my own heart.

Then I prayed, and not only did I begin to feel love for my family
again, but they began to change too.

✳ *The ones we love often don't need our judgment—they need our
prayers.*

— Dianne Fraser —

A Different Way to Worship

For ever since the world was created, people have seen the
earth and sky. Through everything God made, they can
clearly see his invisible qualities—his eternal power and divine
nature. So they have no excuse for not knowing God.

—ROMANS 1:20

As I read about John the Baptist in Matthew 3:4, I wondered
why the Bible specified what the man wore and ate. Was
he the first back-to-nature kind of guy? He certainly seemed to
make good use of the resources God put on the earth.

I started thinking about our natural resources. I've never considered myself an environmentalist, but I certainly believe in recycling. I'm concerned about many of the pollution issues that concern most Americans; I try to do my part in little ways by clustering my driving errands, cleaning up around me, and conserving energy.

If a Christian believes this earth is not our final home, that heaven is, why bother? I see these steps not just as common sense and helping preserve the earth for my children and their children. As I take time out to look at nature, I see it as God's fascinating creation. In a sense, I worship Him by practicing good stewardship with this world He's given us.

✳ *The earth is a loving God's gift to us, and we show our love for His work by practicing good stewardship.*

— Janet Graham —

God the Gardener

For everything there is a season,
a time for every activity under heaven.

—ECCLESIASTES 3:1

My dad was a gardener. But we didn't plant any seeds in South Louisiana during the year after Hurricane Katrina struck. What was left of our world after the hurricane was so ugly that the thought of gardening—the thought that we had any power to make the world around us pretty again—was inconceivable.

But God had a surprise for us. We didn't sow any seeds. But He did. The experts say the sunflowers that popped up randomly all over South Louisiana were the result of seeds that may have been in the soil for twenty years or more. As the storm unearthed hundreds of trees in our area, the seeds were awakened and bloomed.

Then, just like a rainbow after a thunderstorm, they delighted us by popping up in the hundreds—in the thousands—amidst the rubble, reminding us that God had not forgotten us. His mercy is new every morning, and life would be beautiful and bountiful again.

✢ *Our lives consist of different seasons. Through them all, God's love and mercy never changes.*

— Mimi Greenwood Knight —

The King of Compassion

When the Lord saw her, his heart overflowed
with compassion. "Don't cry!" he said.

—LUKE 7:13

*H*ey, man," a stranger approached my husband as he pumped gas. "I need to buy a can of oil for my car so I can go see my sick dad, and I forgot my wallet."

I looked around and saw no empty car—only a wine store across the street.

My husband didn't look for corroboration as he opened his wallet. I was glad I was the one working in downtown Chicago instead of my husband. He would have never survived the panhandlers. God's given Mark a gift of compassion, and many hard-luck stories—whether financial appeals or excuses from our kids—get the benefit of his doubt. His heart just overflows with compassion. Kinda like Jesus, I guess.

Compassion was a main element of Jesus's life. Day after day, He was bombarded by people who had needs. Jesus never expressed frustration with all the people and their problems. Instead, Jesus truly felt their pain, responded with love, and used His abilities to help them.

✳ *When we have needs, we can turn to the One whose compassion is unending.*

— Jenni Davenport —

Faith Gives Us Righteousness

But people are counted as righteous, not because of
their work, but because of their faith in God.

—ROMANS 4:5

*T*he man sat on the park bench carving away at a stick in his
hand. I sat down next to him. After watching, I said, "That's
quite an interesting figure you have there on your stick."

"Just passing the time," he said. He showed it to me. It was a
face of some sort. He was good at it.

We talked about different things. Later, I found out he was a
Christian. I asked him what the greatest thing about being a Christian was for him. He said, "You know, I was a pretty bad sinner
most of my life. Still am. But the idea that God made me righteous
by faith because of His love for me amazes me every day."

"How come?" I asked, wondering where this came from.

"To be considered perfect? To be looked at as a good person
by God with the things I done? It shocks me down to my toes."

I kept thinking about it. God's love was such that He not only
gave me a new life, but a new character. He saw me as good, righteous, worth knowing. That was a real encouragement. I realized
God has done much more than save me. He made me fit for eternity,
and heaven, all at once.

✻ *God's love not only transforms us day by day, but He made us
perfect from the day we believed. What a gift!*

— Joseph Compaine —

Deere Love

When people do what is right, it shows that they
are righteous, even as Christ is righteous.

—1 John 3:7

I'm thinking this week about our first neighbor, Polly. We were
newlyweds, and Polly had just lost her husband. We found
her at our door with cookies in hand. As we sat around the table
eating them, Polly filled us in on all the news of the neighborhood.

The next time my husband saw Polly, she was trying to start her
lawn mower. Thinking she needed some manpower, Paul drove his
mower to her yard and gave hers a few cranks. When it didn't start,
he mowed her half acre of grass with his John Deere.

That night he said, "Polly just lost her husband and her mower
doesn't work. I think God wants us to help her." That summer of
helping our neighbor stretched into twenty-five more. All three of
our children loved mowing, so there was always someone to help.
This week as I told my daughter about Polly's death, guess what
she remembered? The mowing.

"Yes," I said, "mowing was our way of 'loving our neighbor
as ourselves.'"

✳ *Love will always find a way of expressing itself.*

— Linda Beach —

Let It Go!

In that day the wolf and the lamb will live together;
the leopard will lie down with the baby goat.
The calf and the yearling will be safe with the lion,
and a little child will lead them all.

—ISAIAH 11:6

*M*om! Dana and Kristen went to the mall without me! And it was my idea in the first place." My pre-teen daughter tried to stem the tears brimming in her eyes.

My jaw clenched. It wasn't the first time they'd done this. No one hurts my girl and gets away with it!

The next day they knocked on the front door. "Is Lindsay home?" they asked, sweet smiles on their angelic faces.

"Lindsay!" I hollered, and left them standing there as I turned and marched into the kitchen. The three of them spoke quietly in the foyer for a while before Lindsay came to ask, "Can Dana and Kristen stay for lunch?"

"After what they did?" I retorted heatedly. "No!"

"Mom, they're sorry, and well . . . if I can let it go . . . can't you?"

How do you like that? There I sat, holding a grudge while Lindsay's actions reflected the heart of God.

"Of course," I replied sheepishly, cheeks pink with embarrassment. "The girls are welcome to join us."

✢ *Sometimes we learn from our children instead of the other way around.*

— Susan A. Karas —

Genuine Religion

Pure and genuine religion in the sight of God the Father
means caring for orphans and widows in their distress.

—JAMES 1:27

*M*y youngest daughter, Caitie, is of that generation that wants everything to be genuine and asks uncomfortable questions. She came home from her Christian school with tear-filled eyes because of a video about orphan boys in a war-torn African country. The other students seemed to show no response. She asked, "So what does true Christianity look like?"

On a mission trip to Costa Rica, she answered her own question. Children in a mountain village were suffering disease because of a lack of clean water. There was limited time to put in a septic system. She crouched with a heavy pickax in an eight-foot hole in the hundred-degree heat, refusing to take breaks as she whispered to herself, "It's for the children."

As Caitie told me this story, I thought of the words of Jesus: "When you did it to one of the least of these my brothers and sisters, you were doing it to me!" (Matthew 25:40).

✻ *True Christianity does more than feel empathy for those in need. True Christianity meets that need.*

— James Stuart Bell —

Never Alone, No Matter What!

For I will be with you as I was with Moses.
I will not fail you or abandon you.

—JOSHUA 1:5

*N*ine-year-old Daryn shrieked in fury. Social Services was moving him. Again. He'd felt safe in his current home, he liked being in my class, and he was about to lose it all. No wonder his fear came out in anger.

In an empty conference room, I held him close, trying to protect myself from his flailing feet and hands, while he screamed threats and obscenities.

As he tired, the spaces between his shouts became longer, and I started inserting my own comments: "Some kids . . . who know they're leaving my class . . . decide to make me mad . . . so I won't like them anymore."

Daryn froze. "Does it work?"

"Nope! I still love them forever."

He collapsed into me, sobbing. I rocked him until he quieted and put him on the bus with a hug. I never saw Daryn again. But I hope and pray he remembers that his teacher loved him, no matter what.

✣ *In trouble, in joy, in sorrow, or in danger . . . we are not alone.*

— Elsi Dodge —

All Because of Food

Blessed are those who are generous,
because they feed the poor.

—PROVERBS 22:9

My husband started a new church and a bicycle shop at the same time. One day Gary called me from the shop. "I've just hired Jim, and we're hungry. Is lunch ready?"

I didn't know what to expect, but the young man in filthy bib overalls with a wild mop of hair shocked me. While Jim washed his hands, Gary whispered, "He's homeless and a recovering drug addict."

"How can you trust him? I'll fix food today, but no more."

Even as I said it, I knew Gary would bring Jim in for lunch every day, and I realized that I had an attitude problem. Soon Jim not only ate lunch with us, but he joined us for dinner every night. Within a month he showed up at church—no one cared about his ragged clothing. Before long, Jim accepted Christ as His Savior.

Gary's faith in Jim and one meal helped change my heart toward recovering addicts and the homeless. God helped me grow in grace and mercy all because of food.

※ *A hand stretched out to the poor is rewarded with beautiful friendships.*

— Kat Crawford —

Becoming a "Why"s Mother

And now a word to you fathers. Don't make your children
angry by the way you treat them. Rather, bring them up
with the discipline and instruction approved by the Lord.

—EPHESIANS 6:4

*W*hen you have to tell your child no, don't just say, 'Because
I said so,'" my spiritual mentor instructed. "Instead, explain why."

After I had kids, I started to see the wisdom of her words. When
I just say no without reason to something my kids think is a logical request (and kids think every request is logical!), I've seen their
eyes fill with clouds of anger and rebellion. They assume I'm just
being mean and they become surly.

On the other hand, when I give the reason, they start to understand—even if they may not agree with or like my answer. They
trust me more and start understanding my perspective. Best of all,
they start evaluating whether their requests are really a good idea.
They even obey quicker because they realize I have good reasons.
And hopefully they start to trust God better when He says no.

No's happen, but whether dealing with our kids or other people
in our lives, let's make them as painless as possible to save needless
frustration.

✶ *Love takes the extra time and trouble to give others the courtesy
of an explanation.*

— Janet Graham —

I Am Distinctly God's

O Lord, if you heal me, I will be truly healed;
if you save me, I will be truly saved.
My praises are for you alone!
—JEREMIAH 17:14

*I*n the fifteenth century, the Japanese did not throw away broken ceramic objects. They mended them with a technique known as *kintsugi*, or golden joinery. Skilled kintsugi artisans sprinkled powdered gold on sticky lacquer holding broken seams together. These golden seams are distinctly Japanese. Enhanced by the master artisan's touch, a broken pot that normally would have been tossed actually became lovelier, more precious, and more valuable than before.

When everything I valued was shattered, I saw myself as I really am. Broken. Vulnerable. Helpless. Busted relationships, discarded promises, and destroyed expectations extinguished my hope that I could be restored. Hard times tested my fragile heart, sensitizing it to others—also broken, crushed, and flung away like useless debris. How can I thank God enough for picking up each piece and patching together my life and heart better than before? I am not disposable to God. I'm precious and valuable.

�֍ *The restorative touch of our wounded healer, Jesus, highlights our brokenness, letting others know we're distinctly God's.*

— Scoti Springfield Domeij —

Doing What God Has Commanded

Love means doing what God has commanded us,
and he has commanded us to love one another,
just as you heard from the beginning.

—2 JOHN 6

*H*ave you ever thought of God's new commandments?" I asked the group one night as we studied the Bible.

"What do you mean?" someone said.

"Well, there are the Ten Commandments in the Old Testament. Most are repeated in the New Testament, so they're still in force. Then there are the Great Commandments that Jesus gave in the New Testament—to love God with all your heart, soul, mind, and might, and to love your neighbor as yourself. But are there others?"

Everyone seemed flummoxed. But then someone said, "To share our stuff when there's a need."

"Exactly. What else?"

"To be devoted to each other. Never take revenge, but leave it to God."

"Sure."

"Preaching the Word in season and out of season."

"Good," I said. "In fact, most of the New Testament is God's commands to us. We should learn them and obey them in the power of the Spirit."

✣ *When we truly love God, we live His commandments almost without thinking about them.*

— Zach Davidson —

Life Lessons in Grace

May our Lord Jesus Christ himself and God our Father,
who loved us and by his grace gave us eternal comfort and
a wonderful hope, comfort you and strengthen you.

—2 THESSALONIANS 2:16–17

I heard the screaming far down the hallway. Hysterical and high-pitched, it was a tongue I didn't recognize. With loud cries of pain, an aide yelled over the din, "Someone get Noreen! Now!"

I poked my head out to see Noreen bolt from the nurses' station to the baths. Pushing the aides aside, she stroked the thinning hair of a woman strapped into a wheelchair, and spoke softly in German. The flailing gradually subsided until the woman doubled over, shaking.

As Noreen reassured her in broken German, the woman rubbed the tattoo on her arm and sobbed.

"No showers," Noreen barked at the aides. "Only sponge baths in her room."

Startled, I imagined the horrors of World War II this woman relived in her memories. As Noreen wheeled her away, the woman rocked and hummed, joined by Noreen's soft voice. "Jesus loves me, this I know . . ." Noreen demonstrated a love and grace rarely seen in that nursing home.

✻ *Love understands the baggage, fears, and tears another person may carry inside.*

— Sandy Heuckroth —

Loved for Being Me

But God showed his great love for us by sending
Christ to die for us while we were still sinners.

—ROMANS 5:8

As a child, I learned God loves unconditionally. Years later my children showed me what that meant.

After months of outpatient and finally inpatient treatment for clinical depression, doctors called for a family conference about my returning home. The depression kept me from functioning as a wife and mother, and I was afraid I'd fail again.

"Are you ready for your mom to come home?" one of the doctors asked the children, ages ten and eleven. They jumped up and down and shouted, "Yes!"

"Is that because she cooks your favorite food?" Both heads shook back and forth.

"And all the fun places she takes you? Is that why you want her at home?" Again the answer was no.

I had not done anything for them for a long time.

"Well, why do you want her to come home, if she doesn't do the things you like?"

"Because," they said as they ran over to hug me. "We just love her."

Then each one grabbed a hand and said, "Come on, Mommy. Let's go home."

❊ *God loves us, not because of what we have done; He just loves us.*

— Elizabeth W. Peterson —

Late for Kim Again

Don't look out only for your own interests,
but take an interest in others, too.

—Philippians 2:4

*O*nly ten minutes late today," I congratulated myself as I hurried along the campus sidewalk. "I'm getting better."

I could see my friend Kim—cheerful, punctual Kim—waiting on the corner.

"Sorry I'm late. Ready to go?"

But Kim was neither cheerful nor ready.

"Katie, when you're late, it makes me feel like you don't care about me; that I'm not important."

I was humbled and horrified. I had always thought of lateness as the result of poorly estimating how long things take, not the result of being selfish and inconsiderate. But Kim was right. Was sleeping ten more minutes or reading just one more email really more important than my friend?

I began to see punctuality as an expression of love. Would I love others as God commanded, putting their interests above my own? Or would I love myself first? That conversation changed me. Now every time I'm tempted to do just one more thing when I know I should be leaving, Kim's words echo in my heart, and I choose to love.

✣ *Love starts with doing unto others as you would have them do unto you.*

— Katie Robles —

Dinner With Billy Bob

Do not seek revenge or bear a grudge against a fellow
Israelite, but love your neighbor as yourself.

—Leviticus 19:18

*W*hen my pastor challenged our congregation to have a neighbor over for dinner, I winced. Our closest neighbor was Billy Bob, a trucker whose foul language competed with a barking dog chained among spare tires.

I made the phone call, anticipating an excuse. Hadn't a football game prevented Bob from pulling me out of a snowbank the winter before? To my shock, he accepted the invitation. Over marinated venison, Bob spoke to my husband for the first time since his son had snuck into our garage and driven a tractor through its walls ten years ago. When he left I felt relieved, both at having broken the ice with our estranged neighbor, and for getting the outreach "over with."

The next morning Billy Bob called. Would we like to come for dinner that evening? I steadied myself to keep from fainting and chirped, "What shall I bring?"

We ate in Billy Bob's garage on lawn chairs. He gave my kids a new kite. And when a snowstorm buried our driveway that winter, he plowed us out.

✣ *What relationships do we squander by not esteeming the Billy Bobs in our lives?*

— Faith Bogdan —

Ultimate Betrayal, Ultimate Love

It is beyond my power to do this . . . but God can.
—GENESIS 41:16

We'd been close, like sisters. Together with our husbands, we shared many adventures—travel, business, tennis, double dates—even attended the same church; our children were friends.

Then the painful discovery, the double betrayal: my friend became my enemy, the other woman. Their affair had lasted two years.

The day came when she and I stood alone together in a room—the first time since the discovery. I had no words, just resentment. *How could she?*

Then, God did a miracle.

When our eyes met, my heart melted. Instantly, He flooded my soul with the most profound love and compassion for her; mercy and forgiveness washed over me like fresh rain.

"How can you look at me," she asked, "with such a loving smile . . . twinkling eyes . . . after what I've done! You seem so . . . so radiant!"

"Whatever you see on my face is what God has just put into my heart. My heart can't love like this. But His can, through me."

We hugged. "He loves you. And so do I."

God transformed two hearts that day.

❖ *Never underestimate the power of God's love; it can soften the hardest of hearts—in the twinkling of an eye!*

— Sara King —

The Height of Security

No power in the sky above or in the earth below—indeed,
nothing in all creation will ever be able to separate us from
the love of God that is revealed in Christ Jesus our Lord.

—ROMANS 8:39

I faced my fears one hot summer day on a cable car, but not
of the San Francisco variety. My son Sam, a college junior,
my husband, and I took an impromptu tour of Pittsburgh and
ended up at the Duquesne Incline. It is a cable car that climbs a
steep hill like a ski lift.

The car has wooden seats and large windows affording a pan-
oramic view of the city. Because of my fear of heights, I avoided
such rides in the past.

At first I sat in the back and didn't look out.

But on the way down, thanks to my son, I faced the view with
a new perspective on Pittsburgh, and my fears.

I told Sam I could ride the incline because he was sitting next
to me.

How much more, though, should I remember that God is sitting next to me at all times. And He is in me. My fears pale in
comparison to His eternal provision.

✢ *Nothing can separate us from Him—high or low!*

— Kristianne Ovenshine —

A Strong Grip

With all these things in mind, dear brothers and sisters,
stand firm and keep a strong grip on the teaching we
passed on to you both in person and by letter.

—2 THESSALONIANS 2:15

*M*y friend had been through a rough time. He lost his job
at a church, and a second one in a Christian school. He
struggled with finances for several years, but his wife had a good
job, and she kept them together.

Then suddenly, she died of a heart attack. I really wondered if
this would put him under. When things settled down, I called him.
"How're you doing?"

"It's tough," he said. "But I'm holding on tight."

"Tight?"

"To God. His Word. Memories. Prayer. They've all become much
more important to me in ways I never expected."

We talked more and I realized he was in the best situation possible. Holding tightly to God, the Bible, prayer, and things like
love and compassion are what survival is all about in this life. I
knew he would stumble through this time somehow and emerge
okay at the end. Why? Because I knew the same God who gripped
him gripped me.

✳ *There's no one better to hold on to than God. He'll love you through
everything.*

— Sam Donato —

Imperfect Hands, Perfect Heart

If you have two shirts, give one to the poor. If you
have food, share it with those who are hungry.

—LUKE 3:11

*W*e were on our way to the building site with food for the
men working on a mission chapel in Haiti. As always, when
we took food to the men, we were immediately surrounded by a
group of children. They had hungry eyes and outstretched hands
but smiles on their faces.

We had anticipated this so had brought extra cookies with us.
Of course, we didn't have enough. There were always too few
cookies and too many children.

As I held out the last cookie, my eyes were drawn to a hand that
appeared to have an extra pinky finger. I put the cookie in that hand
and then stood back to see whom it belonged to. He was about
eight and had a smaller boy with him.

I could tell they were both hungry. The boy I had given the cookie
to looked at it, then at the smaller boy. Carefully he broke the cookie
into two even pieces and shared it with the one who had none.

✻ *An imperfect world is no excuse for an unloving heart.*

— Brenda J. Young —

Staying Power

Don't ask me to leave you and turn back. Wherever you
go, I will go; wherever you live, I will live. Your people
will be my people, and your God will be my God.

—RUTH 1:16

*J*ohn's wife, Ella, was forgetting things. It distressed her that she couldn't remember the name of her hometown, so she spent some time with her medical dictionary and diagnosed herself.

"I have Alzheimer's," she announced, and she was right.

For ten years after that, John took good care of Ella. During her last few years he hired a caregiver, for he no longer had the physical strength he once had.

We missed John in church, but Sunday was the caregiver's day off, and he wouldn't leave his wife. I felt awkward the first time I took dinner over. Ella sat in the living room, not understanding a word John and I were saying, her eyes staring into space.

"She's elsewhere. I just hope she's comfortable," John said.

After Ella died, John rejoined the volunteer fire department. Spring came into his life after his long wintertime vigil. I'm grateful I knew John during that time. For through watching his example, I learned that love doesn't just mean celebrating the easy times with someone, but also being committed through the tough times of life.

✳ *"For better or for worse" is easier said than done.*

— Sarajane Giere —

From Duckling to Swan

Anyone who welcomes a little child like this on my behalf
welcomes me, and anyone who welcomes me welcomes
not only me but also my Father who sent me.

—MARK 9:37

*W*hile leading the dance ministry at my church, I met a young lady who was twelve years old and experiencing the awkwardness and invisibility that all preteens have. She wanted to join the dance ministry, and I said, "Welcome!"

Remembering my own preteen days, I made the effort to reach out to her outside of the ministry, to be a listening big sister when she needed one, and to be a friend on days when she had many and on days when she had none. I worked with her on her dancing and saw her awkwardness turn into grace and poise and confidence. Now she, in turn, is an example to the younger students at my studio of what it is like to reach out to those who feel invisible.

You see, when we allow God's love to shine from us, we have the blessing and joy of seeing the awkward duckling turn into the beautiful swan.

✻ *Allowing God's love to shine from us means that we learn to look at and love on the hearts of others!*

— Kirsten B. Kline —

Just the Way You Are!

No one has ever seen God. But if we love each other, God
lives in us, and his love is brought to full expression in us.

—1 JOHN 4:12

*H*ey, you teenagers, what do you know about spray tanning?"
All conversation stopped.

"Nana! Why would *you* want to know about that?" seventeen-
year-old Nate questioned. "That's what the school girls did before
prom."

"I'm going on a cruise and I want to look good in my swimming
suit," I explained. "And a friend suggested spray tanning."

"Nana, I don't think you'd like doing that," fifteen-year-old
Amanda advised.

All eight grandchildren had an opinion and tried to share it at the
same time. Chaos reigned. Then one small voice pleaded, "Don't
get sprayed, Nana. I love you just the way you are!"

"Yeah, that's right," the rest of the grandchildren chorused.

Two weeks later, I put on my swimming suit, looked in the mirror, and smiled as I remembered little Lily's words. My husband
donned his suit, looked in the mirror, and said, "Wow! Who's that
old man in his bathing suit?"

"Don't say that, dear," I said. "Remember, God and I love you
just the way you are."

�֍ *The innocent love of a child reflects God's unconditional love for us.*

— Betty J. Dalrymple —

Love Is Faithful

The Lord leads with unfailing love and faithfulness
all who keep his covenant and obey his demands.

—PSALM 25:10

*A*t my new job as desk ward secretary, one older charge
nurse took an instant dislike to me when she found out I
was "religious." Even when I did my job well, there were no thanks.
Judy only sniffed with impatience and spoke sharply to me.

The more I prayed about the situation, the more tension grew.
Things came to a head one evening when there was an emergency.
As soon as the crisis was over, Judy told everyone how incompetent
and useless I was. Blinking back tears, I apologized even though I
wasn't at fault. Back home I broke down, telling the Lord that there
was nothing more that I could do. He replied, "Just be faithful."

The next evening I gave Judy the biggest smile I could muster
up. To my shock, Judy smiled back. While we never became close
friends, we ended up with a great working relationship.

�֑ *Love is faithful in the face of difficult circumstances.*

— Dorcas Annette Walker —

"It's Not Fair!"

I thank Christ Jesus our Lord, who has given me strength to do his work. He considered me trustworthy and appointed me to serve him.

—1 Timothy 1:12

It wasn't fair! I'd been assigned the lowliest, least pleasant job on my church's Saturday workday list—deep-cleaning the bathrooms. And not just the women's side either. Those yucky men's stalls were included in my job assignment. Plus I had to endure the overpowering smell of the chemicals in the cleaning supplies. I didn't care if I *was* the pastor's wife. I felt irritated and resentful.

As I begrudgingly headed for the bathroom, supplies in tow, I heard the Spirit's gentle chiding. "Your spirit isn't pleasing to me, Pat. You need an attitude change. You have forgotten that God loves a cheerful giver—in your case, time donated in His name means you need to cheerfully complete this least desired task."

"Thank you, God, for reminding me whom I serve." I scrubbed those bathrooms until they sparkled that day. I went home amazed at how satisfying volunteering for God with a cheerful spirit could be. Even when it includes cleaning the bathrooms.

May God teach us to enjoy serving others as a sign of our love for Him.

— Pat Stockett Johnston —

Called to Cross the Aisle

Don't forget to show hospitality to strangers, for some who
have done this have entertained angels without realizing it!

—HEBREWS 13:2

*S*hy. Another word for uncomfortable. I'm always shy about
approaching people I don't know. But now I understand—
love is uncomfortable sometimes.

From what seemed like a block away in the huge discount store, I
saw Dad in the vegetable section, bent almost double, his magnifying glass pressed against the cans on the bottom shelf. From across
the aisle, a young woman approached him. They exchanged a few
words, then she stooped, picked up a can, and handed it to Dad.
I was close enough to hear him thank her.

"I really appreciate it! I need the kind without salt, but I'm lucky
if I just get green beans instead of peas."

God took care of Dad. Again and again, He sent people to him
who didn't hesitate to approach an elderly man with poor eyesight.
God's tender love for Dad, yes; but also, I realized, His tender love
for me, expressed in the generous actions of people I didn't know.

I'm still shy, but now when God calls me to cross the aisle, I go.

✳ *Sometimes love is as close as opening our eyes.*

— Kathleen Brown —

Ties of Love

I led Israel along with my ropes of kindness and love.

—Hosea 11:4

After thirty-five years together, our marriage was on the rocks. Deeds had been done that could not be undone. Harsh and hurtful words had been exchanged. I was convinced there would be no path back from the hard road of experiences we'd left in the wake of our relationship. Separation was inevitable and I steeled myself for it. But God had other plans.

One evening when I returned from work, there was a piece of white paper taped to the living room wall. It said, "I love you, I love you, I love you," in diminishing fonts. Another sheet with the same words was taped to the bathroom mirror. A third hung on the wall over the bed. Soon, I answered a knock on the door. My husband met me there, dressed in his best suit, and said, "Let's go out. Let's start over."

The gesture was the beginning of a reconciliation that solidified our marriage, making it stronger than ever at forty-one years until my husband's death some time later.

✻ *Through love, God paves the way to reconciliation.*

— Deb Wuethrich —

Words That Still Speak

Let everything you say be good and helpful, so that your
words will be an encouragement to those who hear them.

—EPHESIANS 4:29

*I*t was one of those chilling calls that make you tremble in the
middle of the night.

"Pastor, it's Dolly," the man said to my husband. "The paramedics are taking her to the hospital and it doesn't look good."

My husband jumped out of bed and hurried to the hospital, but
when he arrived, Dolly had already passed.

Dolly was a beautiful person. She lived to love and encourage
others, and faithfully picked up folks for church in the van every
Sunday morning.

I was unable to attend Dolly's funeral because I was recovering
from major surgery. When our mail arrived that day, I was shocked
to find a get-well card she'd written on the morning of her death
to cheer me. Little did she know when she wrote and mailed those
words that they'd be some of her last.

During the time of her funeral, I sat home crying like a baby
in my recliner, holding her precious words close to my chest. She
closed with, "I miss you. I love you. Get well soon."

✳ *None of us have the promise of tomorrow. We only have right now
to speak life-giving, encouraging words to show our love.*

— Peggy Morris —

Never Forgotten

See, I have written your name on the palms of my hands.

—ISAIAH 49:16

We were waiting in a cafeteria line at one of the Smithsonian museums in Washington, D.C. My two-year-old son held on to my hand. Suddenly, he turned around and let go to get closer to his grandpa. But as he turned around, away from his daddy and me, he panicked. He couldn't see us anymore. Though his grandpa and grandma were right there, he thought his parents had deserted him. The funny thing was—we had never moved.

Sometimes we as Christians forget that God is constant. We turn away and panic because we think we've been left on our own. We think God has forgotten us just when our need is the greatest. But God never moves. In fact, God has gone a step beyond being there for us. God has inscribed us, written us onto His hands. Not just our name or identity, but all of us. No matter where we are in life's journey, we remain in the hands of God.

❊ *Isn't it wonderful to know that God loves us and treasures us more than we can begin to love Him?*

— Susan Lyttek —

Our Priceless Inheritance

We have a priceless inheritance—an inheritance
that is kept in heaven for you, pure and undefiled,
beyond the reach of change and decay.

—1 PETER 1:4

We talked about heaven and our inheritance in the Bible study. People were excited.

"You know," one lady said, "I think I'm going to spend the first hundred years just trying all the different kinds of ice cream. And I'll never get fat."

That made us laugh.

Another said, "I think seeing my grandparents again will be important for me. I've missed them so much."

I jumped in with, "Meeting people like Paul, Peter, Adam and Eve, and of course, Jesus. That will be incredible."

We talked more, and I said, "But what about your inheritance, the things God will give you?"

"I don't know," one said. "I don't think it's stuff or material. It's more like joy, love, and goodness."

"And righteousness. Being perfect," another said. "That's what I want."

It was an exciting thought. That will be an amazing day.

✳ *When we look forward to heaven, it shouldn't be material items that draw us, but love, joy, peace, and other intangibles.*

— Patrick Mitchell —

Need More Love?

God is love, and all who live in love live
in God, and God lives in them.

—1 JOHN 4:16

*E*very detail of the women's luncheon was painstakingly tied to the theme: *love.* I sat at a table, staring at the red heart-shaped centerpiece, wondering when it would end.

But then the speaker made a statement that struck me to the core. She said we can't drum up love in ourselves—we can only be filled with it. Apart from the source, the flow is cut off. If we struggle to love others, the real problem may be our lack of *God,* not our lack of love.

I thought about how many times I had missed morning devotions lately, the weekends when we chose to sleep in and skip church. It was true. I had wandered from my Lord. Was it any wonder I was impatient with my children, critical of my husband, annoyed by others? I vowed to reconnect to my Source. How sweet it was when God's love flowed through me again!

✳ *If we need more love, we need more God—because God is love.*

— Liz Collard —

In the Company of Sinners

The Pharisee stood by himself and prayed this prayer:
"I thank you, God, that I am not a sinner like everyone
else. For I don't cheat, I don't sin, and I don't commit
adultery. I'm certainly not like that tax collector!"

—LUKE 18:11

*M*y husband, Ken, and I met Rocky and Roxanne at a marina
in Durban, South Africa, and quickly learned they were
no ordinary couple. Rocky was a drug dealer and Roxanne ran a
prostitution ring.

During a strong gale, Rocky's sailboat broke loose, and it was
Ken who rescued their yacht. When Rocky insisted on rewarding us,
we eventually agreed to have dinner with them sometime. Secretly,
I dreaded the idea of eating with criminals.

Months passed and we sailed to Cape Town where, to our as-
tonishment, Rocky and Roxanne appeared one day. They had come
to keep their promise of dinner together.

As we ate, I sensed their yearning for acceptance but recognized
the barrier their life choices posed. Suddenly I was overwhelmed
by God's compassion for them and felt ashamed of my pharisaic
attitude. For two hours, the four of us talked about important life
issues, and I regretted it was the only opportunity to share God's
love. Soon after that one evening meal, Rocky was shot dead by
a rival.

�֍ *As sinners, we must be willing to associate with other sinners before
we can show God's love to them.*

— Jessica Talbot —

Full of Mercy and Good Fruit

But the wisdom from above is first of all pure. It is
also peace loving, gentle at all times, and willing to
yield to others. It is full of mercy and good deeds.
It shows no favoritism and is always sincere.

—JAMES 3:17

I lived on a quiet street and enjoyed a good relationship with my neighbor. We shared produce from our gardens and tips about growing peonies. When I learned that she had lied to me about a community issue, however, our interactions became strained. Working in my yard one day, I seemed to feel her eyes watching me.

I wanted to shoot angry looks her way, make her sorry for her deceitfulness. But I had been sharing Christ with my neighbor; I needed to demonstrate His love. Struggling with my emotions, I remembered a song my children had learned in vacation Bible school. It was an adaptation of 1 Corinthians 13: "Love is patient; love is kind . . . Love is not easily angered; it keeps no record of wrong."

Singing the song to myself, I waved and smiled and kept pruning the shrubs.

Months later, my neighbor approached my car as I pulled to a stop in the driveway. "I got baptized this weekend," she said. "I thought you'd like to know."

✢ *God's love makes our witness effective.*

— Sherry Poff —

Nights of Deep Sighs

Give your burdens to the Lord,
and he will take care of you.
He will not permit the godly to slip and fall.

—PSALM 55:22

I don't know what to do," my friend Debbie wails.

I listen on the other end of the phone line and squint at the clock. It reads 3:00 a.m. After twenty-five years of marriage, Debbie's husband suddenly walked out on her.

"Why is this happening?" Debbie continues. "I'm so lonely."

"I don't know why," I say, "but I know God will be faithful."

"I can't stand this emptiness," Debbie cries.

A shiver of empathy rolls across my back as I think of my husband asleep in the next room. Debbie keeps talking, but now her words make little to no sense, more sobs and sighs than syllables. I open my Bible to the book of Psalms and start reading. Night after night, week after week, we repeat this process. I have no answers, but the soft love of God pours through the phone.

Today, years later, Debbie still loves the sound of my voice, because to her it is the sound of God's comfort in her time of need.

✢ *Often His Word is far better than our words.*

— Sandy Cathcart —

Small Blessings

But the Holy Spirit produces this kind of fruit in our
lives: love, joy, peace, patience, kindness, goodness,
faithfulness, gentleness, and self-control.

—GALATIANS 5:22–23

*A*s usual, it was late Sunday night and I had just started my laundry. With all of the time spent practicing softball and studying, laundry was simply the last thing on my to-do list.

Because of the loud noise the dryers made, in between loads I jogged back and forth from my dorm room, studying for a test. On my fourth trip back to the laundry room, I found my clothes already neatly folded and organized. Petting my freshly cleaned sweatpants in shock, my fingertips ruffled a piece of paper loose from the pant leg. I opened it, chuckling at the small smiley face looking back at me.

Instantly, I picked up a sweater from a stranger's pile of clothes next to mine and began to fold.

Since that time, I've asked the Lord to help me appreciate the small blessings He has given through those around me. I've asked Him to help me not only be thankful for those He has placed in my life, but also to be a blessing in their lives.

✳ *Often little blessings bring big benefits.*

— Caitlin M. Vukorpa —

When It's More Blessed to Receive

I don't say this because I want a gift from you. Rather,
I want you to receive a reward for your kindness.

—PHILIPPIANS 4:17

I think you might have hurt your dad's feelings," my husband,
Mark, told me one night after we'd gone out to dinner with
my dad and his girlfriend, our kids in tow.

"What did I do?" I asked.

"Well, your dad wanted to pay for the meal, but you insisted
on picking up the check," Mark explained. "I think that hurts his
feelings and his pride."

"But he's on a fixed income," I said. "And besides, there are five
of us and only two of them—well, four of us," I amended, realizing
that our toddler usually ate from my plate.

"Yes, but your dad wants to. It's a gift of love. You need to learn
to receive."

Mark hit a nail on the head there. It's always been easier for me
to be the person to treat another—instead of being the one treated.
But I'm learning when we deny another person the opportunity to
give, we often end up depriving them of a blessing.

✲ *Sometimes the best way to exchange love is to graciously receive
a gift.*

— Jeanette Gardner Littleton —

Crunchy Love Notes

Imitate God, therefore, in everything you do, because
you are his dear children. Live a life filled with love,
following the example of Christ. He loved us and offered
himself as a sacrifice for us, a pleasing aroma to God.

—EPHESIANS 5:1–2

*L*ook!" My granddaughter smiled as she held up a folded
potato chip from her bag. She teased a minute before passing it over to me.

"You learned well, sweet girl," I replied, reaching out to receive
her love offering.

This granddaughter had watched her grandfather smile and
give me folded potato chips for most of her five years. She quickly
caught on that sometimes even little things mean a lot.

I love folded potato chips—you know the ones where both ends
stuck together as they sizzled in the hot grease?

Folded potato chips are just one love our family shares. Other
families may have a secret handshake, a special signal to show their
love, or a word that only they understand.

How often during the day do I see a little thing God sends just
to say "I love you"? It could be a beautiful flower, a soft breeze, a
clear blue sky. Or it could be a folded potato chip delivered through
the hand of a loved one!

✽ *There is no end to the small expressions of God's love.*

— Linda Gilden —

A Little Prayer Warrior

Finally, dear brothers and sisters, we ask you to pray
for us. Pray that the Lord's message will spread
rapidly and be honored wherever it goes.

—2 THESSALONIANS 3:1

I pray for you every night!" These were the words penned to me by an eight-year-old girl. She had sent her note as part of a care package from several members of my church. I taped her letter on the wall in my bedroom in the remote northern region of Kenya, where I lived. Every day as I prepared to go out into the community, which was dominated by Islam, I would read her note and find encouragement.

It is a humbling thing to find out that someone so young whom you barely know is praying for you and your ministry regularly. It changes your heart. It makes you want to get out of bed and face each day, whatever may come. It keeps you going back to serve those who are hard to love. It reminds you that you are there to love. The prayers of that little one made a difference in my ministry, and they reminded me that I was loved too!

✣ *Writing a note or praying a prayer for someone is a powerful expression of love.*

— Laura Chevalier —

Rejoicing in the Lord

But let the godly rejoice.
Let them be glad in God's presence.
Let them be filled with joy.
—Psalm 68:3

The last time I went to the grocery store, I caused a small riot. I saw two old friends in separate checkout lines. After approaching and embracing Elsa, I pointed in Joanie's direction, walked over to Joanie, and pointed back at Elsa. That's all I did: point, walk, point.

You should have heard the squeals of delight at the end of the checkout counters once the two friends had paid for their groceries. They hadn't seen each other in months. There was hugging and rejoicing and praising God. People pushing grocery carts around our celebration looked back at us as they passed.

Elsa, ninety-four, had recently fallen and was hospitalized for twenty-one days.

"They said I'd probably never be able to live by myself again," she said, leaning on the grocery cart.

Of all people, Joanie, age ninety, understood. She'd had two falls resulting in broken bones and two hospitalizations herself.

It was good to catch up with old friends. That reunion came about because I "just happened" to stop by the store for Tic-Tacs.

* *To be instruments of God's love, sometimes all we have to do is show up.*

— Jean Davis —

Love or Money?

You will always have the poor among you,
but you will not always have me.

—JOHN 12:8

*T*he wedding was not lavish, but given the background of the young couple's parents, it was more elaborate than the normal wedding. It was beautiful and it was also especially Christ-honoring.

"The money they spent should have been used to help orphans," one of my friends snapped.

Immediately I thought of the story in John 12 when the woman poured her perfume over Jesus's head. Jesus's treasurer suggested the perfume should have been sold and the money given to the poor.

But Jesus didn't agree. The most giving of men, He knew it was more important for this woman to show her love than for the money to be used in any other way.

There are many times when we should sacrifice our resources for humanitarian causes and Christian ministries. But there are also times when we should use our resources to celebrate the people we love—whether through a wedding, a graduation, a birthday party or other celebration, or a nice gift.

✣ *Sometimes the best use of resources is a gift or event that says, "I care."*

— Jeanette Gardner Littleton —

End-of-Life Love

All praise to God, the Father of our Lord Jesus Christ. God
is our merciful Father and the source of all comfort.

—2 CORINTHIANS 1:3

*H*e was only twenty years old and his heart was breaking.
He had just admitted his grandmother to the hospice
inpatient unit where I worked. Her death was imminent when she
arrived.

He was her only family. His dad had left him with her years
earlier and had never returned. She had been his whole life. And
he had been hers.

When she got sick, he took a leave of absence from work to
stay home and take care of her. His girlfriend was helping him and
supporting him as much as she knew how.

He was frightened. He had never seen anyone die and he didn't
know what to expect. But putting his own pain and fear aside, his
first loving words to me were, "I don't want her to hurt or be afraid."

That was my goal too, and within an hour we had her peaceful.

Then I turned my attention to him. He needed a shoulder to
cry on and mine was available.

�֍ *To say "I care" or "I love you" to someone means nothing unless
you can feel that person's pain too.*

— Brenda J. Young —

Radiating God's Love

So all of us who have had that veil removed can see
and reflect the glory of the Lord. And the Lord—
who is the Spirit—makes us more and more like him
as we are changed into his glorious image.

—2 CORINTHIANS 3:18

*T*hat must be the house."

My mother's uncertainty about leaving me, her fourteen-year-old daughter, at the home of strangers, even for a Bible meeting, showed in her voice.

While I longed to grow in my new Christian faith, I felt an overwhelming shyness about entering a new situation. For several minutes I sat in the car, searching for a familiar face. Just then a young man approached us.

He knocked on the glass. "Can I help you ladies?"

We both gasped, not from fear, but amazement!

Like a visible halo, the Holy Spirit shone around the young man's face. It was as if Christ himself stood there! God's love radiated from his eyes, entering our hearts and calming our fears and doubts. In an instant, my fears and my mother's doubts evaporated.

"Is this the right house for Student Life?" I managed to ask.

"Yes."

Completely at peace, I accompanied him inside, ready for the next new experience in my walk with Christ.

✳ *Those who love God can't help but reflect His love to others.*

— Tammy L. Hensel —

No Job Too Small

And the King will say, "I tell you the truth, when you did it to one of the least of these my brothers and sisters, you were doing it to me!"

—Matthew 25:40

You won't want to clean for others when you're older," my mother told me long ago.

But now, years later, that's exactly what I'm doing.

With long, tedious hours of sweeping, scrubbing, washing, vacuuming, dusting, and sanitizing, my cleaning business isn't glamorous by any means. But it's given me unique opportunities to step into the lives of others and become the hands and feet of Jesus to lonely seniors, weary parents, and busy teachers.

For example, I've met Mrs. Spencer, discouraged and struggling with cancer. While I'm on my knees scrubbing her floors, we often have deep, meaningful visits that bring a smile to her face.

Then there is Mr. Bennett, a grieving widower. While I clean his house, he reminisces about his wife with me—sometimes through laughter, sometimes through tears. Cleaning for him has allowed me to walk through the grieving process with him as a friend and see Jesus's thankful eyes shine out through his.

Cleaning other people's messes can be difficult at times. And it's true; I don't always feel like doing it. But God has shown me that no job is insignificant when done in His name.

When we serve others, it's often as if we're serving God directly.

— Angela Deal —

Abundantly, Freely

See how very much our Father loves us, for he calls
us his children, and that is what we are!

—1 JOHN 3:1

*T*he day I married my husband and became an instant mom to
two little boys, I walked down the aisle with visions of *Brady
Bunch* bliss. Little did I know that within months I'd be demoted
from beloved mother figure to wicked stepmom.

Living in a blended family is not always easy. In fact, it's often
complicated and overwhelming. Underneath the day-to-day challenges sits the fear that the stepchildren you love as your own will
never truly love you in return.

During a particularly difficult time, I grew discouraged in my
stepmom role and poured out my complaint to God: *I give so
much, God, with very little in return. It's so unfair!*

I know, He whispered to my soul, thick with the tender compassion of someone who knows what it's like to love so much and
receive so little in return.

Being a parent—step or otherwise—requires abundant love without any guarantee of payback. Thank heavens we have a Father
who has loved us in the same way!

✤ *To love as God loves is to do so abundantly, freely.*

— Michele Cushatt —

The Art of Love Giving

Some people are always greedy for more,
but the godly love to give!

—PROVERBS 21:26

*B*efore we go home, I want to get a little gift for each of my children," my friend told me while we were shopping. "Tomorrow is my birthday."

I thought this odd and asked, "Why are you buying them something on your birthday? Shouldn't they be giving you the gifts? After all, it is your birthday."

"I know, but it's just one way I have of letting them know I love them. This is a tradition I have followed since my first baby was born."

That evening, I thought about her unusual tradition of giving gifts on her birthday. I could not help but think of all the gifts God my Father has given to me: peace, family, friends, and the greatest of all gifts, His Son. These constant gifts are His way of letting me know how much He loves me.

✽ *Sometimes loving means giving.*

— Carol Russell —

Friendship With the World

Don't you realize that friendship with the
world makes you an enemy of God?

—JAMES 4:4

My friend told me how his beginning to smoke, drink, and swear had opened up doors with his friends who weren't Christians. "Now they listen to me talk about the Gospel. They ask questions."

"Don't you think these compromises are going to turn around and eat you alive?" I asked. "Has anyone become a committed Christian because of this change in your life?"

"No, but they're close."

"How do you know? How do you know they're not just seeing how far you'll go?"

"I hadn't thought of that."

But I knew his friends had. One day he came to me and said, "One of them accepted Christ."

"Is it real?"

"Don't know. He doesn't want to come to church."

I only nodded. It would take a lot more than smoking a cigarette to get the attention of these people; I knew that.

I've tried to work with the world's ways of doing things, meeting some people in the middle. It rarely works. And they end up compromised Christians with little commitment or concern for the truth. God just tells us not to do it.

⁂ *Love obeys God and reaches out in purity.*

— Patrick Mitchell —

Loving Last Words

Worry weighs a person down;
an encouraging word cheers a person up.

—PROVERBS 12:25

I want to tell you the last words your right ear will ever hear on earth," my husband said. He bent over my hospital gurney and leaned close to that ear. "I love you. I want to live the rest of my life with you."

I was the one with cancer, yet he was implying he would die first! Ken continued, "I honor you for being a woman of God."

Those reassuring words calmed me and made me feel loved. In a few minutes I would be taken to a five-hour surgery to remove my ear and hearing on that side, along with the rare cancer tumors growing there. I still couldn't believe I had ear cancer. No support groups existed for that, but Ken had supported me with his words.

Even though that surgery thirteen years ago left me with a disability, Ken's loving words gave me the hope I needed to dispel worry and fear. I will cherish them as long as I live.

✴ *Loving words have the power to banish fear and overlook defects.*

— Marcia K. Hornok —

Loving Aunt Jane

Perfect love expels all fear.

—1 JOHN 4:18

*I*t's about time!" Aunt Jane said. "I'll be late for my doctor's appointment."

"I'm sorry," I fumbled. Aunt Jane was always so ferocious that she terrified me. "The traffic was bad."

As I drove her downtown, I followed detour signs through a heavy construction area.

Aunt Jane couldn't see the signs, but she knew the way. When I turned an unfamiliar corner, she yelled, "What's wrong with you? Can't you do anything right?"

My stomach lurched.

Lord, help! I prayed silently. *Please give me your love and take away my fear.*

Aunt Jane never said another word.

Later, we shared a lunch of soup and scones. As we ate, she talked about her happy childhood in Scotland with her brother, my father. She revealed a side of her I had never seen before—frail, vulnerable, and human.

As I put on my coat, I felt real love for this little auntie—God's love. I slipped an arm around her and said, "I love you."

Her faded blue eyes filled with tears as she hugged me back. "I love you too," she said.

✣ *Fear cannot stand in the face of true love.*

— Agnes Lawless Elkins —

Kindness in a Crowd

Never let loyalty and kindness leave you!
Tie them around your neck as a reminder.
Write them deep within your heart.

—PROVERBS 3:3

*H*undreds of teachers, cooks, bus drivers, principals, and district employees gathered in the gymnasium. The room buzzed with conversations about the upcoming school year. I never felt as alone as I did on that first day of the district-wide teacher's meeting. I wondered where to sit and who to talk to.

During lunch, I stared into the crowd. Again, I wondered where to sit. Then I heard a voice say, "So, you're our new reading teacher from Pike County?" I turned around and saw two women looking at me.

"Yes, I am. How did you know?"

"Mrs. Rose told us about you." After a few minutes of small talk, one of the women asked, "Would you like to eat with us?"

Just before eating, my new friends bowed their heads and asked the blessing on our food. Then they asked the Lord to keep His hand upon my family as we looked for a new home. And every day, for the remainder of the school year, I ate lunch with my new friends.

�֍ *Always be willing to step out of the crowd to make a new friend.*

— Jeannie Fields-Dotson —

A Love That Confronts

But when Peter came to Antioch, I had to oppose him
to his face, for what he did was very wrong.

—GALATIANS 2:11

I hate confrontation. My heart pounds, my lip sweats, my ears ring, and I cannot sleep in anticipation of it. But sometimes confrontation is God's way of demonstrating His love toward us.

Early in my career I worked with a young man named Reed. I thought we were "buds," so I used to joke around and tease him. Sometimes I would call him a jerk or some other guy name.

One afternoon, Reed called to set up a meeting. He sat quietly across from me in my office and said matter-of-factly that I'd offended him by calling him a jerk and demanded an apology.

I quickly offered one, and after prayer together he shared some intimate details of why this so offended him. That confrontational meeting resulted in a loving friendship that lasts to this day.

Often the very thing we shun is the very thing we need to demonstrate God's love in someone else's life. Confrontation isn't welcomed, but it can be the tilling of a soil that reaps a great harvest afterward.

✻ *To say nothing takes nothing and means nothing; to speak the truth in love takes supernatural strength.*

— Jim Zabloski —

A Forgiving Prod

Make allowance for each other's faults, and forgive
anyone who offends you. Remember, the Lord
forgave you, so you must forgive others.

—COLOSSIANS 3:13

*D*iagnosed with esophageal cancer, my dad had three months
to live when my twenty-four-year-old daughter, Lindsay,
offered me this challenge: "Mom, I'm concerned Granddaddy's
going to die and leave you with regrets."

She used a kind and gentle voice. Compassion filled her eyes.
"You're a great mom. And he's been a great dad to you. I could
hold things against you too, but I choose to remember all the good
times. I don't want to see you regret his passing."

I marveled as I took her wise advice to heart. She was right. My
dad *was* great, a prayerful, godly believer who held my genuine
respect. There were odd-and-end things between us. No spoken
angst, but various incidents had hurt me throughout the years.
Normal stuff, maybe. But painful nonetheless.

God led Lindsay to challenge me that day. For as I prayed, I
could tell Daddy was also praying. Together, he and I resolved
everything that could have lingered past the mournful day he died.
Forgiveness is freeing.

✳ *Children can't go through life without any wounds from their par-*
ents, but they can choose to forgive.

— Pamela Dowd —

When Love Shines Through

But anyone who does not love does not
know God, for God is love.

—1 JOHN 4:8

*K*athy worked as if employed by God. Trustworthy and dependable, she was a shining light in a sometimes loveless, contentious, and biting environment.

She reported to the most difficult of all managers, Sam. Kathy recognized an underlying sadness in her boss and prayed for him daily. Soon Sam confided in her and asked her opinion on decisions, something he had never done.

One day he asked her what church she attended. He admitted to believing in God as a child, but as an adult nothing had gone right for him. Beginning with his failed marriage, he blamed God for all of his shortcomings. Love had evaded him for a long time, but he saw it in her and wanted that feeling back.

They prayed together there in the office and he began attending her church.

The entire office noticed the changes in Sam's attitude and demeanor. They suspected he and his assistant had fallen in love. The truth was, they had. Both were in love with Jesus.

✳ *Are you Jesus in the flesh, a shining light to others?*

— Georgeanne Falstrom —

An Open Door

Look! I stand at the door and knock. If you hear
my voice and open the door, I will come in, and
we will share a meal together as friends.

—REVELATION 3:20

*T*he peaceful night was pierced by a loud pounding on our church door. My husband and I were in the lobby to let people who had signed up to pray for an hour come in and leave safely through the night. As I opened the door, a strange woman who looked like she was on the verge of death—but was in fact on crack cocaine—fell into my arms sobbing. Her arms gripped me for dear life.

"Thank God someone was here! I was about to kill myself!"

I thought of my prayer half an hour earlier: "Father, if there's someone who is walking by the church and needs you, just send him or her to the door."

I never would have opened the door if God hadn't prepared me.

"You've come to the right place. We've been praying for you."

It's been several years with some serious ups and downs since Robin banged on the door. She lives a clean life for the first time in twenty-five years . . . and now opens the door to many others who need God's hand of love reaching out from the darkness!

✵ *When we find an open door, we should hold it open for someone else to find!*

— Eva Juliuson —

I Choose Love

My heart is torn within me,
and my compassion overflows.
No, I will not unleash my fierce anger.

—HOSEA 11:8–9

I'm not sure I can do this," I said, turning to my husband beside me. We sat in our parked car, shrouded in darkness as the restaurant's lights illuminated a young woman and children sitting at a table, framed in the window before us. "How can I go in there and pretend everything's okay? What about loyalty to our son?"

Dave took my hand and squeezed it. "You once loved her and accepted her as your daughter. Do you hate her now that she divorced our son?"

Tears filled my eyes and I shook my head. Dave was right. Harboring anger only prolonged the bitterness. It was time to stop picking at the scab and allow my heart to heal.

"Grandma! Grandpa!" the kids yelled as we entered the restaurant and approached their table.

Their mother, a hesitant smile on her face, stood as we drew near. "It's good to see you. Been a long time."

I smiled. "Thanks for letting us know you were in the area." I lifted my hand to touch her shoulder, but she wrapped me in a hug instead.

✳ *Loving others sometimes requires a love far greater and purer than our own.*

— Dawn Lilly —

"I Still Love You"

And I am convinced that nothing can ever separate us from
God's love. Neither death nor life, neither angels nor demons,
neither our fears for today nor our worries about tomorrow—
not even the powers of hell can separate us from God's love.

—ROMANS 8:38

*I*t started as an emotional and mental breakdown. I could
sob or become agitated by the slightest provocation, and I
felt physically ill.

Doctors' visits couldn't determine any specific physical problem. The condition stabilized in a few weeks; still, it took all my resources to retain my job, which was needed to keep our family of six financially afloat. I surrendered all other obligations including my church activities.

Lying in bed sobbing one evening, I inwardly evaluated my existence. I barely met our family's financial needs, I'd suffered a job setback, our car and house were sub-standard compared to others, I was ashamed of my radical behavior, and now I'd vacated my church activities. One by one I confessed my failures to God, including how I had failed Him.

In that moment of silence, my heart and mind received His answer: "I still love you." That unexpected reply to my personal evaluation not only surprised me; it started my recovery and has since reminded me that God's love isn't based on my earthly performance.

✻ *God's love is rooted in who we are, not in what we do.*

— Steven Thompson —

Lay Down Your Life

We know what real love is because Jesus gave up his life for us.
So we also ought to give up our lives for our brothers and sisters.

—1 JOHN 3:16

Ground Zero, 2002. At the bottom of that lifeless pit, I encountered a young man who traveled to New York on 9/11 and stayed to help wherever he was needed. He left his job, his family, and his life to serve.

I asked him what he would do now that his work was done. With tears in his eyes, he said, "Well ma'am, I am doing the only thing I can, I'm joining the army."

This selfless man was ready and able to do the job I couldn't. He was willing to lay down his life to defend America and protect my children in a war against evil.

He didn't hesitate. He didn't waver. He knew what he was called to do. He knew love.

As a middle-aged housewife and mother, I couldn't go to war, but I could support those who did. For the next six years, I organized gift drives for soldiers. Pouring God's love into every package, I never forgot the commitment of that young man to lay down his life.

✳ *Laying down your life looks different for everyone, but God's love in you will always look the same.*

— Tricia Propson —

"What Can I Do?"

Therefore, whenever we have the opportunity, we should do good to everyone—especially to those in the family of faith.

—GALATIANS 6:10

"What can I do to help you succeed?"

I looked into the kind blue eyes of the older man in front of me. His attitude was poised, as if ready to spring to action at my response.

Wes was a seasoned editor in the organization where I worked. I didn't know him well, but word of my dilemma had spread quickly among my colleagues. A year earlier I'd been promoted to a new position within the company. Now I'd suddenly learned that because of belt-tightening, that job was ending in three months and no other jobs were available.

I searched for open doors, but God seemed to tell me that self-employment was in my future. As I haltingly confessed this to Wes, he did spring into action. He gave me contract work. He paved my way with some associates. He asked probing questions to help me fashion my business plan.

But most of all, he believed in me. "You can do it, kid," he said again and again.

Nearly twenty years later, I'm still self-employed. And I'm still inspired by Wes's loving support.

⁂ *Want to show someone your love? Let him or her know you believe in them.*

— Jeanette Gardner Littleton —

Saying "I'm Sorry"

Live in harmony and peace. Then the God
of love and peace will be with you.

—2 CORINTHIANS 13:11

*E*agerly I unwrapped the birthday gift from my parents to find a musical figurine—my first. I wound the porcelain base and watched the figure revolve. It was a casting of a young couple sitting on the grass, heavy with the colors of the decade—avocado and brown. On the front of the figurine were printed the words *Love means never having to say you're sorry,* and it played the beautiful theme from *Love Story.*

I'd never seen the movie, but I was certainly familiar with that phrase. It adorned bumper stickers, plaques, posters, everything.

Since those days, I've grown up, gotten married, and had children. And I've learned that the mantra of the '60s, "Love means never having to say you're sorry," may sound romantic, but it just isn't true. I've learned that when I do something wrong and *don't* say I'm sorry, hard feelings build, relationships are hindered, and my soul becomes a bit more stubborn and hardened.

Because I love others, I apologize when I've committed a faux pas or sin. *Because* I love others, I admit it when I've been wrong and ask for forgiveness.

✻ *For some of us, love means often having to say we're sorry!*

— Julie Durham —

Seek Him First and Foremost

The one thing I ask of the Lord—
the thing I seek most—
is to live in the house of the Lord all the days of my life,
delighting in the Lord's perfections.

—Psalm 27:4

When my girls were three and four, the younger one woke up first one morning. I snuggled with her for a while, then sat her down with a cartoon while I went out to putter in the garden.

A few minutes later, my older daughter woke up and stumbled out of her bedroom half asleep. I heard her sister tell her, "She's outside." She hadn't asked where I was, hadn't called my name, but instinctively they both knew the first thing to do once your eyes open is connect with Mama.

It struck me: That's how I want to be with my heavenly Father. When my eyes open, I want to reach out and connect with Him before my feet even hit the floor. Before I pour that first cup of coffee, I want to praise Him. Before I reach for the morning paper, I want to thank Him for the day He's about to send my way. The best days are always the ones when I do.

Try putting God first today.

— Mimi Greenwood Knight —

We're a Temple

Don't you realize that all of you together are the temple
of God and that the Spirit of God lives in you?
—1 Corinthians 3:16

*H*ave you ever thought of yourself as a temple of God?
Recently, my wife got angry at me about something and
yelled a little. I stopped her and said, "Do you know who I am?"

She stared at me. "My husband?"

"No, I am the temple of God."

She stared a little longer, then laughed. "I guess that's because
you're a Christian."

"Correct."

"So I'm one too?"

"Right. But I said it first. So it only really counts with me."
She laughed.

It's a powerful truth. We are temples where God lives and enjoys us, leads us, speaks to us, loves us. God wants us to love each
other, because He put His stamp of love on each of us through
living in us. Now I tell myself to remember, when I cross paths with
another Christian, I'm seeing someone in whom God dwells, and
he deserves all the respect, love, and consideration I give to God.

✳ *Since you are a temple of God, you should love like one too.*

— Mark Littleton —

One Size Doesn't Fit All

We who are strong must be considerate of those who are sensitive
about things like this. We must not just please ourselves.

—ROMANS 15:1

*B*ut Mommy, I *want* you!" Elizabeth cried out.

I sighed. Sometimes it seems no matter how much love and
affection I pour on my youngest child, it's never enough.

Lord, she seems so needy, I told God. *Her brother seems happy
and secure with much less attention.*

But her brother is a completely different person than she is, He
answered.

I stopped in my tracks as some of my Christian education training from years earlier flashed through my mind. In communicating
with people, I had learned, it's not enough for us to present our
message. The real measure of successful communication is finding
we've presented our message in such a way that the person receiving
the message understands what we're communicating.

The same was true in this situation. While I felt the love I was
communicating to Elizabeth was adequate, she wasn't receiving
my message. If I truly wanted her to feel loved, I needed to keep
pouring the love on to meet her individual needs.

Love is not one size fits all; different people have different love
needs.

✳ *Loving wisely means not just looking at what we're giving, but
looking at what our loved ones need.*

— Janet Graham —

Looking Beyond the Packaging

May the Lord make your love for one another and for all
people grow and overflow, just as our love for you overflows.

—1 THESSALONIANS 3:12

I was twenty-three years old when I had my right leg amputated as a result of circulatory problems from an auto-immune disease. Chemotherapy I'd received during this illness caused me to lose my hair, and the massive steroids sent my body ballooning from a size eight to a size twenty-two.

I didn't recognize my reflection in the mirror, and I certainly didn't expect Ken, the man I'd dated during the previous two years, to be able to love the new me.

When I finally allowed him to visit, it was to release him from our committed relationship. Instead of looking relieved, Ken appeared hurt and confused.

"Why, what have I done?" he asked.

"Look at me!" I cried. "I'm no longer the same person."

Ken took my hand. "Oh, yes, you are. The packaging has changed a little, but inside is still the woman I love."

After accepting Ken's unconditional love, all that remained was for me to accept myself—altered package and all.

✳ *Through His love, God helps us learn to love ourselves.*

— Kathleen M. Muldoon —

Wrapped in a Holy Embrace

And anyone who welcomes a little child like
this on my behalf is welcoming me.
—MATTHEW 18:5

*I*t was love at first sight. As we sat next to each other at church,
her *I-know-something-you-don't-know* smile radiated sweet
innocence. Her mother returned my inquiring glance, giving me
unspoken permission to interact with her charming daughter.

One gentle touch from me was all it took. My newfound young
friend climbed up in my lap and rested her head on my shoulder.
Her legs curled to her chest while she sucked her thumb. For half
an hour, I held this precious teenager—going on two. Tears dripped
down my cheeks as I sensed the arms of Jesus enfolding the two of
us. The warmth of His loving embrace so touched the deepest needs
of my heart that I scarce dared to move, lest this holy moment end.

While I may never understand why children suffer disabilities,
one Down syndrome child let me in on her very special secret. Listen
close and maybe you'll hear her too: *Jesus loves me, this I know!*

✳ *No matter our limitations, God has a great purpose for our lives.*

— Nora Peacock —

Through the Eyes of Love

God is love, and all who live in love live
in God, and God lives in them.

—1 JOHN 4:16

*E*verybody, just look at Nicole!" Mr. Hansen, our high school
choir teacher, gazed up with admiration at the backdrop on
the stage where Nicole and five other students were painting scenery.
"Look at how steady her hand is."

"There goes Mr. Hansen again," Jennifer whispered. She rolled
her eyes, but we all knew she was speaking affectionately. Not
only was Mr. Hansen an excellent teacher, but he showed his love
for children by discovering their hidden qualities or abilities and
encouraging them.

During my four years in high school music, Mr. Hansen saw
through my timid, awkward exterior and recognized my vocal
talent. He encouraged me to continue studying at a conservatory
of music.

For forty years, God poured out His love for children through
Mr. Hansen. His loving example inspired me to become a music
teacher so that I could do the same for the next generation of shy,
awkward teens.

✣ *Seeing and inspiring the best in others requires God's vision.*

— Dena Netherton —

A Lesson of Love

When you refused to help the least of these my
brothers and sisters, you were refusing to help me.

—MATTHEW 25:45

I had been teaching a sixth-grade Bible class. My theme for
the two-week course was giving your life for Christ. I used
the examples of many of Jesus's disciples and others who were
martyred for doing God's will. I soon began to imagine how I
would give my life for Christ if such circumstances arose.

During this period of time, a conflict arose with an extended
family member. I went to great extremes to get my way in the dis-
pute, which ultimately hurt the other person's feelings.

After the incident, I again began to meditate on my willingness
to die for the Lord when He challenged me with this thought: "You
say you would die for me, and yet you wouldn't give up your rights
or desires for one of your own family members."

That day I learned an important lesson about loving God. Few
of us will ever be martyred for Christ, but often we are asked to
love Jesus by performing acts of kindness for others that might
inconvenience us.

✳ *The truest test of our love for God is often found in our willingness
to surrender our rights and desires.*

— Steven Thompson —

Grace in an East Asian Apartment

Live in harmony with each other. Don't be too proud to enjoy the company of ordinary people. And don't think you know it all!

—Romans 12:16

The mold beneath the plastic-covered window held my gaze. My East Asian friend had warned me before I went to visit her that her home was humble, but I was unprepared for the tiny, dank apartment we had entered.

Offering an apologetic explanation, she said it was a former utility room that had been converted into a living space. I knew that it had taken courage to open her home to me, so I prayed for God's grace to cover our week together.

She shared her small mattress with me each night, and each morning we folded it back into a simple, spring-less sofa to make room for a picnic breakfast on the floor. As we said grace, thanking God for food and friendship and a love for each other that spanned continents and cultures, I was aware of His presence with us.

My friend's humble hospitality blessed my heart, and my willingness to enter her life ministered to her. There is no doubt that our love for each other deepened that week.

⁕ *Opening our lives to others takes courage but can yield bountiful love.*

— Laura Chevalier —

Still Praying After All These Years

You don't have what you want because you don't ask God for it.

—JAMES 4:2

I'm empty, Lord," I confessed after twenty years of a challenging marriage that was coming to an end. "I know I should keep praying for Pete, but I'm numb inside."

Ask me to fill your heart with love for Pete.

"Oh, Lord. Just thinking of loving is exhausting." But I asked, and He filled.

A few years later, after being served with divorce papers, I figured I no longer needed to pray so much for Pete, and it was odd to feel affection for him. But I guess the Lord's love doesn't just fade away with different circumstances. That strong, steady love removed anger and bitterness, and inspired earnest prayers for Pete's health, his job, and most of all his salvation.

I wouldn't let anyone say anything disrespectful about him, including my very loyal and outspoken mom, so she got on board with me.

"Every morning I still pray for Pete," she said to me a few days ago. A mother-in-law praying for the man who divorced her daughter?

God's love is perfect.

✳ *It's not cheating to ask God to take over when we run out.*

— Ramona Nicks —

Helping the Next One

Love does no wrong to others, so love fulfills
the requirements of God's law.

—ROMANS 13:10

*M*y husband and I decided to climb Old Rag Mountain with our son Erik's Boy Scout troop. From his reports the previous year, we knew it would be challenging, but nothing prepared us for the vertical climbs, leaps of faith, and places where only teamwork would allow you to continue.

At one such place, Erik's friend Tyler stationed himself. A strong and athletic young man, he could easily have been one of the first to reach the top. Instead, he anchored in a niche in the rock and offered a hand to those below him.

When I had passed his station and thanked him, he simply smiled, nodded, and then offered his hand to the person below me on the trail. His hand up had given me the lift I required; now he had a mission for the next person in need.

Later on in the trail, we used Tyler's example to help other climbers. And helping each other, we all made it to the top.

✳ *Let's always remember that most of the Ten Commandments boil down to one—to love our neighbors as ourselves.*

— Susan Lyttek —

Standing With a Friend

Moses' arms soon became so tired he could no
longer hold them up. So Aaron and Hur . . . stood
on each side of Moses, holding up his hands.

—EXODUS 17:12

*M*om had Alzheimer's. Early on, I realized I needed help caring for her, but I was unbelievably stubborn.

When my husband gathered information about support groups, I refused to attend. My stomach churned at the thought of sitting in a roomful of people talking about the same challenges I faced every day.

But he persevered, and then my friend Judy joined the effort. They were so persistent that I finally began to weaken. The grace that eventually melted my resistance was the shocking postscript Judy tacked onto each plea: "Please give it a try. *I'll go with you.*"

Who would volunteer for that? Who would offer to sit and listen to the stories I knew would be shared?

But Judy did. So we went. And I experienced the relief that comes from sharing. The strength that comes from knowing you're not alone.

Now I help others in Alzheimer's support groups. I can stand beside them because of those who stood beside me—God, and a friend.

✳ *Love helps us hold each other up.*

— Kathleen Brown —

Relying on God Only

In fact, we expected to die. But as a result, we stopped relying on ourselves and learned to rely only on God, who raises the dead.

—2 CORINTHIANS 1:9

*M*y ten-year-old daughter and her friend wandered over to me during the softball game.

"Where's Anisha?" I asked. They were supposed to watch my four-year-old while I played softball. I'd watched the girls from my position at second base and when I was in the dugout. But I couldn't keep my eyes on them while I batted.

"She wouldn't obey me," her older sister, Leslie, said.

"So you gave up?"

Leslie shifted her feet. "We didn't think she'd go off on her own."

I went to find my daughter. As I walked around the giant community area where people cooked meals, played games, and partied, I realized this was the perfect place for an abduction.

"Please, God," I prayed, "Don't let this turn out badly."

Other people joined me. We finally found Anisha eating a hot dog with some picnickers. I was thankful and learned not to count on my older daughter to watch her sister.

I also learned that I needed to rely on God for everything, to keep in touch with Him, and to cry out to Him for His love and care whenever my family or I needed it.

✻ *Little or big, rely on God. He will come through.*

— Clay Taylor —

The Touch of Compassion

The Lord is close to the brokenhearted.

—PSALM 34:18

I sat in the Sunday school class surrounded by unfamiliar faces. Disheartening circumstances had forced my family to seek a new church. Still wounded and raw, I was struggling to keep my composure. The teacher kept asking questions about the lesson. All was quiet.

I had taught Bible classes for years, so I finally spoke up. As the words came out of my mouth, the tears flowed from my eyes. It was as if a dam had broken and my heart was releasing the pain. The room was filled with silence. Frustrated and embarrassed that I had exposed my brokenness, I bowed my head and clutched my hands together.

Suddenly I felt a hand gently cover mine. I looked up to see the lady sitting beside me with tears in her eyes. The compassion that flowed from her at that moment was overwhelming. I could literally feel God's love pouring into me through her touch. His presence seemed to envelope me. The healing had begun in a simple gesture by a stranger.

✣ *Father, enable us to see with your gentle eyes the one who may need a touch of your love today.*

— Lori Wickline —

Special in Someone's Eyes

Can a mother forget her nursing child?
Can she feel no love for the child she has borne?
But even if that were possible,
I would not forget you!

—ISAIAH 49:15

*W*hen our granddaughter Olivia was about a year old, she said her first sentence. It was short, but it was powerful: *"See me!"*

Her tiny arms raised in the air, she would clamor for attention, to be picked up, to be loved. We heard these words a lot at that stage in her life because it produced for her the desired results.

Don't we all, no matter our age or position in life, have that same need to be noticed, to be appreciated for who we are? Our unspoken plea is: *Don't pass me by! Don't ignore me! Don't forget me!* Each of us needs to feel important, even special, to at least one other person in order to be whole.

The good news is that there *is* Someone who regards you every moment of your life—and He thinks you are very special. He is always with you, will never abandon you, and is downright crazy about you, His very special child. What more could you ask of your Father than this?

✣ *God's thoughts are forever focused on you! Are yours on Him?*

— Susan E. Ramsden —

Forgiven More, Love More

"Who do you suppose loved him more after that?"
Simon answered, "I suppose the one for
whom he canceled the larger debt."

—LUKE 7:42–43

*I*t's hard enough to *forgive* them," I thought. "How can I possibly *love* them?"

I had sacrificed sleep, pulled strings, done all I could to help this man. Now his family was telling people that all of his problems were *my* fault. I was shocked, mystified, hurt, and angry.

In Matthew 18, Jesus describes a man who owes his king a huge sum of money that he cannot repay. He begs the king for mercy. Feeling compassion for him, the king cancels his debt.

As the forgiven man leaves the palace, he sees a fellow subject who owes him a much smaller sum. Ignoring his pleas for mercy, the man casts his fellow subject into debtor's prison. The king is outraged and reinstitutes his debt.

I cannot repay the debt I owe God. My *sin* killed His *Son*. When God embraces the cost of my sin, how can I angrily reject those who hurt me? Understanding God's decision to love me inspires me to forgive—and even love—my accusers.

✳ *False accusations against us should be reminders of God's love for us.*

— Steven Brown —

The Son Who Saved the Day

Gentle words are a tree of life.

—PROVERBS 15:4

I sighed as I looked at popcorn, soda cans, and dirty plates strewn around our TV room. The kitchen was a bigger disaster with trash coating the floor and the cabinet lined with bowls of cereal rotting in milk, stale ice-cream cones, and more.

I'd spent the day with my friend, a day of relaxation I sorely needed. But apparently my husband and kids had felt it was party day with Mom gone. Now, after I walked through one war-zone room after another, I became furious.

The volcano blew and I let my family have it. They darted wary glances at me as they reluctantly cleaned a few pieces of trash.

As I searched for the peanut butter lid, I felt horrible for losing my cool. Suddenly I felt strong arms wrapped around me. I turned to see the round face of my twelve-year-old son.

"I love you, Mom," he gently said.

Then with a hug, he was off to pick up the trash can.

The balloon of anger inside me deflated. The hardness inside melted and the tears finally came.

"Thank you, God," I whispered. "Thank you for a son who understands."

✻ *Gentle responses from a loving heart diffuse the most explosive situations.*

— Jeanette Gardner Littleton —

Harvesting Fields of Time

When you harvest the crops of your land, do not
harvest the grain along the edges of your fields,
and do not pick up what the harvesters drop.

—LEVITICUS 19:9

*W*hen the phone rang, I congratulated myself for checking caller ID.

Jennifer again. I let voice mail answer.

"Gaye, it's Jennifer. I . . . we haven't talked in a while and I just wanted to hear your voice."

And tell me the latest crisis in your life.

Jennifer seemed to call at the most inconvenient times. I grew adept at dodging her interruptions.

My husband, Jim, checked the phone and turned off my vacuum cleaner. "Sorry to interrupt, but why didn't you pick up?"

I blew strands of hair out of my face and let out a sigh. "Because it won't be a five-minute conversation, that's why—can't you see I'm swamped?"

Jim nodded. "As you are every day, sweetheart. Jennifer sounded like she needed a friend. Should she make an appointment? It's not like she was asking for a kidney."

I managed my time well, not one minute of the day wasted. Had I planned and scheduled myself right out of the lives of the very people God wanted me to serve?

✳ *Are you harvesting to the very edges of your field in terms of time?*

— Gaye Clark —

Truly Free

But the free gift of God is eternal life
through Christ Jesus our Lord.

—ROMANS 6:23

*H*ere's your free gift from St. Jude's!" the envelope proclaimed. Usually such mail goes straight into the circular file. But I could tell without opening the envelope that it included address return labels, and I could certainly use some of those. But on the other hand, I had no money to donate.

In a sense, I should be an ideal target for companies like this—I feel too guilty to use the labels or memo pads if I don't donate, even if they proclaim, "This is a free gift for you!" We all know they expect money in return.

But on the other hand, I'm not the ideal target because I'm so irritated by the fund-raiser manipulation that the mail generally goes in the trash unopened.

As I debated whether to use my "free gift" from St. Jude's or pitch it, I thought of Romans 6:23.

What a blessing it is that God has given us gifts—like salvation and His love—that are truly free. No strings attached. We can't earn it and God doesn't manipulate us into giving Him something in return.

✳ *God's gifts are free because His love is pure.*

— Jenni Davenport —

A Letting-Go Love

And I am certain that God, who began the good work
within you, will continue his work until it is finally
finished on the day when Christ Jesus returns.

—PHILIPPIANS 1:6

*P*erhaps the most painful part of being a mother is the letting go. I didn't realize this when I spent the first two decades of my life dreaming of happily-ever-after. And I didn't realize it during the next two decades when I carried diaper bags, volunteered in countless grade-school classrooms, and cheered from the bleachers. My mothering days appeared as endless as my love for my children.

Graduation brought a sober reality. As difficult as being a mom could be at times, nothing compared with the wrenching open of my hands as my boys became men. I wanted to cling to the past, and they wanted to embrace the future.

With compassion, God reminds me that I too was once a child. Every day since, He's led me, loved me, and taught me how to live. Yes, love can sometimes require a "letting go." But the same God who's been faithful to nurture me with His love will do the same for my children.

✻ *Confidence in God's perfect love for our loved ones frees us to release them into His capable hands.*

— Michele Cushatt —

A Forgiving Touch

Jesus reached out and touched him.

—MATTHEW 8:3

"Two hundred thousand dollars?" I gasped.

When my husband confronted his office manager—a long-time trusted employee—the sad truth came out. She'd been stealing money a bit at a time.

My husband and I felt angry, hurt, betrayed. We loved this employee.

For many days, I wondered how I'd ever forgive her.

God worked on my heart, and I sent a letter saying "I forgive you" and presented the Gospel.

Still, I felt led to extend forgiveness in person. How could I? My husband wouldn't want me to. She was fired, and the courts hadn't settled things yet.

One day I was in a store, and there she was down the aisle from me.

I don't remember my words, but when I reached out and touched her, I felt I was like Jesus touching the leper. Hadn't Jesus reached out to me when I was deep in sin?

I continue to pray for Joyce, especially when her monthly restitution check comes in the mail. My prayer is that she has found true riches—in Christ.

* *God wants us to extend the hand of mercy to others, just as He has extended it to us.*

— Andrea Jennings —

The One Who
Weeps With Us

Then Jesus wept.

—JOHN 11:35

*Y*ou'll need to memorize two Bible verses of your choice every week," our Bible professor informed us.

Most of the students trekked straight for John 11:35, which I quickly discovered was the shortest verse in the Bible.

Although that's the shortest verse in the Bible, it's also a powerful one for us to remember, and it has become one of my favorites over the years.

Lazarus, Jesus's friend, had died. By the time Jesus got to the visitation, Lazarus was already buried. He joined the mourners knowing He could raise His friend from the dead. Still, He wept. Perhaps He wept in sympathy and love. Perhaps He wept because life is cruel and death is inevitable for humans. But He cared enough to weep.

Jesus still cares enough to weep. I take such comfort in that. When we deal with difficult situations, or experience grief, or face whatever makes us want to cry, Jesus understands. He may not always stop the funeral, but He'll always weep with us.

✻ *Next time the tears roll, remember who cares enough to weep with us.*

— Ila Reed —

God Delights in Me

I will rejoice over Jerusalem
and delight in my people.

—ISAIAH 65:19

*D*ad is coming." One of us kids would sound the alarm, and we would scatter. Dad usually came home from work in a bad mood, so we tried to avoid his violent temper. He loved us by working hard to pay the bills, but he seemed incapable of demonstrating love with words or emotions.

My husband was not that kind of father. If I said, "Here comes Daddy," the kids would run to the front door, trying to be first to greet him. Delighted to see them, he would drop to his knees for a group hug.

He rejoiced over them, anxious to hear what they had to say. His smile and cheerful words communicated his love, acceptance, and approval.

I try to remember that my Father in heaven is like that with me. I never have to hide from Him in fear. He wants me to run to Him and enjoy His love, which He lavishes on me in a multitude of ways.

✳ *Since God delights in me, I can boldly run to Him.*

— Marcia K. Hornok —

Punkin Duke

Thank you for making me so wonderfully complex!
Your workmanship is marvelous—how well I know it.

—Psalm 139:14

I happened to find an old, handmade Father's Day card from my daughter under a box in our basement. She was a new college student at the time but wanted to convey the fact that she was still my little girl, at least in spirit. So she signed it, in her beautiful calligraphy, "Punkin Duke" Forever.

My eyes got misty as I recalled telling her when she was little that no one else had those exact big brown eyes or this private name of endearment. It belonged to her alone.

In Revelation 2:17, Jesus says that when we get to heaven, He will give us a white stone with a new name written on it that no one knows except the one who receives it. God loves each one of us in a unique and special way. And though we may not have a cute nickname for those close to us, we need to let them know that we treasure them as a one-of-a-kind.

We need to love each person as someone God has created to be unique.

— James Stuart Bell —

Being Instead of Doing

God replied to Moses, "I AM WHO I AM. Say this to the people of Israel: I AM has sent me to you."

—EXODUS 3:14

Carefully, I jotted down each task I needed to do. It was no surprise that my to-do list went on for pages. To-do lists not only help me organize, but they make me feel efficient and valuable as a person. I feel a renewed sense of self-worth as I mark finished items off my list.

We humans are so "do" conscious. We judge people's worth by what they do in life, their positions. As a result, sometimes I think we all try to do too much to prove that we are important.

In Exodus 3, God told Moses to demand that Pharoah set the Lord's people free. Moses knew the Egyptian leaders would want God's credentials before they'd release their labor force, so he asked what credentials to use. God's answer? Simply "I AM."

God could have elaborated on His many roles: Creator, Designer of the Universe, Omnipotent Lord, etc. Instead of focusing on the impressive things He *did,* He focused on who He *was.*

We can be pleased about what we do, but we also need to remember that although actions are important, the person behind the actions is more important!

⁂ *Remember that God loves you for who you are—not for what you do.*

— Jeanette Gardner Littleton —

Your Most Easterly Neighbor

For the whole law can be summed up in this one
command: "Love your neighbor as yourself."

—GALATIANS 5:14

I watched my new neighbor move in, and a week later I took her a gift. An elderly woman cautiously opened the door, thanked me, and closed it.

"What's she like?" Gary asked when I returned home.

"Have no idea. She wouldn't let me in—she doesn't appear friendly."

"Keep at it, you'll win her over." With Gary's encouragement, I kept going back, and one day Ethel let me inside. When I learned she had COPD and used oxygen, I left my phone number.

At Christmas I took her fruit and a Bible. She apologized for being rude the first day, and we exchanged email addresses. I worried about her being alone, but her daily emails assured me things were okay.

One day she signed her note, "Your Most Easterly Neighbor." I replied with a picture of bucking horses signed, "From Kat in the West."

When Ethel died, I realized how her independence, her humor, and her friendship enriched my life. I always thought I helped her—it turned out it was the other way around.

✲ *Neighbors are a gift to unwrap if we have the courage to knock on the door.*

— Kat Crawford —

Windfalls

He has showered his kindness on us, along
with all wisdom and understanding.

—EPHESIANS 1:8

An apple tree stands in the corner of our backyard, producing many miniature orbs. The immature fruit falls, littering our hammock area. It appears to have scarce redeeming value. In spite of my husband's threats to chop it down, there's something endearing about the ugly little tree that prematurely drops its fruit. I admire its continual production in spite of challenges.

Windfalls do serve a purpose, imperfect as they are. My husband's love of applesauce inspires his daily delivery to me of bucketsful of immature apples. Lots of spot removal is involved, producing more waste than fruit. However, the end result is a delicious treat laced with cinnamon and brown sugar.

I can think of windfall people with obvious imperfections. Sometimes we are too blind to see their purpose. For instance, my friend's mentally handicapped son has some irritating habits and actions, but his joy in life teaches me to have gratitude. He has great value in God's eyes.

✣ *Christ gave us infinite value on the cross.*

— Dianna Brumfield —

The Power of Words

Kind words are like honey—
sweet to the soul and healthy for the body.
—PROVERBS 16:24

I learned about God when I was a child. I met Him personally when I was a single mother of two toddlers.

My frustration level was high and my patience low. I became a screaming, swearing mom. When God blessed me with an emergency appendectomy, I was put on the sidelines. *Then* I could hear God; *then* I accepted Jesus into my heart; *then* I surrendered my miserable life to Him.

God lovingly showed me how blessed I was to have these beautiful children in my life. He showed me how disgusting it was when I screamed and swore at them. He made those words taste terrible in my mouth. He made my heart hurt whenever I hurt their little hearts. He taught me compassion and unconditional love.

Striving to reclaim their self-esteem and display the love of Christ, I began to show my children respect, to say please and thank you, and to be patient with them. I have determined that my words will build up and not tear down.

❖ *Words have an everlasting effect, bringing life or death. Resolve now that your words will bring life!*

— Kelly J. Stigliano —

Love Written on Stone

We love each other because he loved us first.

—1 JOHN 4:19

Father, it's such a beautiful morning. You know how much I love the shells and other gifts you send me in this tide pool. Can you please send a special treasure today?"

I spoke these words to my heavenly Daddy while strolling across the rugged lava shoreline on Hawaii's Big Island. I come here often and relish the intimate moments of communion we share together.

As soon as the words left my lips, I rounded a bend and instantly found His response.

The words "I love you" were carefully written out in large easy-to-read letters with the white coral that washes up on this beach. The stone-like letters contrasted sharply with the ebony volcanic backdrop, as if adding an exclamation point to His pronouncement. Because I am an artist, the beauty of the design made the message even more meaningful. God, my Creator, knew how to show me His love in the most intimate way. My heart trembled with gratitude.

"I love you too, Abba."

Though some ways are more obvious than others, God is always expressing His love for us through His creation.

— Karen Ellison —

The Investment

Love prospers when a fault is forgiven,
but dwelling on it separates close friends.

—PROVERBS 17:9

I felt sucker-punched as I realized Anna had not been honest with me.

"You lied!" burst out of my lips.

"Well, not really," Anna said with a frown, but she wouldn't meet my eyes. And I wasn't surprised when she avoided me at work and in social situations.

It hurt. Deeply. I'd considered Anna one of my closest friends. With her avoidance, I missed her camaraderie.

But she lied! She really hurt me! my heart cried out.

I knew I faced a choice. My inclination was to back off from Anna—not be rude to her, but to let the distance between us increase so she couldn't hurt me again.

But we'd been friends so long. In a sense, I realized, a friendship is an investment. And Anna and I had invested a lot in each other's lives for a decade.

The Lord nudged my heart. *Are you really going to let that time go to waste? You've had too many good years to let it be destroyed by this. It's really minor in the big picture of your friendship.*

I sighed. I asked God for courage and picked up the phone to call Anna.

✳ *A friendship is an investment that can yield great dividends over the long run.*

— Julie Durham —

Seeing Is Believing

For your brother was dead and has come back to life! He was lost but now he is found!

—Luke 15:32

My younger sister Cate always looked up to me—except when she looked down at me in terror when we were little and I convinced her to climb up a neighbor's outdoor antenna ladder. She would do anything for me, including jumping on the backs of bullies. I largely ignored her, and when I went away to college, I got involved in the worst of the early '70s youth culture, while she remained on the straight and narrow.

I then came home fired up with the message of Jesus, and my parents were greatly relieved that I had cleaned up my act. I thought intellectual arguments would help them embrace the truth. But they weren't immediately convinced that my gospel Christianity was real.

But my sister did receive the message. When I started loving my sister in multiple ways and we became close friends and went to fellowship meetings together, my father was blown away. He then saw that I was transformed by a power greater than myself, the power of the love of Jesus.

⁜ *They'll know we are transformed when our behavior truly changes.*

— James Stuart Bell —

A Gentle Pat

And he touched the man's ear and healed him.

—LUKE 22:51

*C*hurch was the last place I wanted to be that Sunday morning. I was suffering a bout of deep depression. Though I don't recall the circumstances surrounding my dark mood, I do recall how drained and blue I felt as I walked up the steps to the foyer outside our church's sanctuary.

I was stopped by someone and stood listening to him when Harold, an elder from our church, stopped to join the conversation. He greeted us with his shy smile and gentle words. He only stayed a couple of moments, standing next to me. Then as he turned to leave he gently patted me on the back.

I can't explain exactly what happened in that short moment, except his light touch on my back brought a great sense of affirmation. That simple pat encouraged and energized me, and the depression I had been experiencing faded. I still think of the results of that simple gesture of kindness and recognize the great power that comes from an affirming touch.

✢ *A gentle, sincere touch has as much healing power as mighty spoken words.*

— Steven Thompson —

The Still, Small Voice

Since God chose you to be the holy people he loves,
you must clothe yourselves with tenderhearted mercy,
kindness, humility, gentleness, and patience.

—COLOSSIANS 3:12

*R*esentment. That's what I felt. All the rookie high school teachers had lunchroom supervision. I *resented* it. Yet there I was pacing back and forth, patrolling my end of the cafeteria, attempting to ignore the nauseating odors of lukewarm lunchmeat. So when fifteen-year-old Dan refused to throw his garbage away, I fired back with a resentment-fueled directive to complete his task. His response—a refusal and an expletive—sent the two of us down to the dean's office. There was the usual consequence (detention and a call home) and we went our separate ways.

I was unprepared for a hallway encounter with Dan the next week. Should I (a) exercise my authority (*Do you have a pass?*), (b) make a sarcastic remark (*Did you throw your garbage away today?*), or (c) just ignore him?

Fortunately, in that split second, another option arrived in a still, small voice: *Just say hi.*

Eye contact, nod: "Hey, Dan." He was stunned. He expected resentment—and honestly, so did I. But we *both* experienced kindness that day.

✳ *When we express kindness, we can't help but experience kindness.*

— Elissa M. Schauer —

In Times of Trouble

Don't let your hearts be troubled.
Trust in God, and trust also in me.

—JOHN 14:1

I hate you! Get out of my room."

I stumbled out as if I'd been punched in the gut. My husband and I had poured ourselves into this girl's life. All we received in return? Violent threats and strings of obscenities.

Five years earlier we'd met Heather through our state's special needs program. Social workers warned that abused children had many problems, and we quickly found Heather was no exception. Separated from her birth mother at age four due to neglect and abuse, she'd lived in foster homes for nearly nine years.

God gave us a love for her, and we welcomed her in our home as a foster child. Nine months later, she became our daughter through adoption. At times we bonded and loved each other. But often her anger and hatred spewed out in hurtful ways.

During my quiet times, I cried out to God and learned to rely on His strength and wisdom. He revealed that the explosive outbursts and behaviors had nothing to do with us and everything to do with Heather's past.

God often reminded me that I am His child and because I am loved, I could love Heather.

�֍ *Because He pours His love into us, we can love others.*

— Margie Christenson —

Being "Named"

The Lord who created you says:
"Do not be afraid, for I have ransomed you.
I have called you by name; you are mine."

—Isaiah 43:1

*P*aul's the theological expert on our team," my new boss, Bonnie, explained. As she introduced me to my co-workers, she named each one's expertise, and I noticed more than one beam with pride at Bonnie's naming.

A couple of months later, I knew what my co-workers had felt, for Bonnie had also named me. When she introduced me to others or when we were in staff meetings, she often mentioned what she perceived as my special skill. Bonnie's naming gave me confidence in my abilities, but it also helped me find my place at work and in the world.

Thanks to Bonnie's example, I began to try to notice the unique gifts that my friends and family possessed. And I started naming those strengths and complimenting others on what was good and special about their lives.

Recently my friend Rhonda told me, "You know why I like being with you? You make me feel good about myself."

I grinned, delighted that I was succeeding in blessing others as Bonnie had blessed me.

✳ *Helping others see why they are special is a great way to remind them of how the heavenly Father loves them and has made them unique.*

— Jeanette Gardner Littleton —

The Ministry He Gives

Therefore, since God in his mercy has given
us this new way, we never give up.

—2 CORINTHIANS 4:1

*M*y friend Sally is my ideal of a Christian who serves. She has taken care of her elderly neighbors; she's walked through the valley of death with cancerous friends; she takes meals to people who need them; she volunteers at a thrift store that benefits the indigent. And those are only the things I *know* about.

I want to be like Sally. I want to love the world and make a difference like she does.

One day Sally came by my house to borrow a kettle—she was taking several pots of chili to the local mission.

I said, "Sally, teach me how to do good works. I want to serve like you."

She gave me a warm smile and said, "Kiddo, you have your hands full with your own ministry right now—those kids of yours and your job."

She was right. My ministry isn't dramatic like Sally's. It's not the stuff that looks good on a résumé or gets a person humanitarian honors. But God has given me my own ministry to focus on right now, just as He's given Sally hers.

✳ *Never underestimate the value of the ministry you have in the place where God has called you—even if it's "only" among your family and friends.*

— Jenni Davenport —

Carried by Him

He will feed his flock like a shepherd.
He will carry the lambs in his arms,
holding them close to his heart.
He will gently lead the mother sheep with their young.

—ISAIAH 40:11

I remember the last time my father carried me. It was fifty-one years ago. I was six.

I stayed behind with chicken pox while my parents and sister and brother went to a nearby town. Our school band was marching in a parade. I wanted to go, but because of the pox, I stayed with a neighbor.

When he arrived home, Dad came to get me. I wore pajamas, a housecoat, and socks. We started to walk across the yard, but after a few steps, Daddy asked, "Would you like for me to carry you?"

I let him pick me up.

He was tall—well over six feet—and strong. I recall how it felt to be in his arms, and the lurching ride of his long steps. I saw the world from his view, higher and farther from the ground.

Dad is gone now, but I remember the last time he carried me. I'm in our heavenly Father's arms now and feel His strength, His steps, and His care for me.

✻ *Our heavenly Father's arms are gentle, but strong enough to carry us and all of our burdens.*

— Brad Dixon —

Go Directly to Jail

If you are kind only to your friends, how are you
different from anyone else? Even pagans do that.

—MATTHEW 5:47

I snuggled the afghan over the shoulders of the distressed
boy. Both of us peered intently through my family room
window. In the darkness, police lights rhythmically slashed their
way across my neighbor's garage.

"Was your mom fighting with your stepdad again, honey?"

"Y-yeah. She's been out all night drinking."

Over the muffled sounds of cursing and the thud of her feet
against the cruiser's windowpane, I explained to the officer who I
was and that I would keep the woman's son for the night.

"When you're ready to release her, just give me a call."

I'd never seen the inside of the local lockup. But at 3 a.m. I
went to jail to pick up the volatile girl from next door and bring
her home with me. It was risky. It was inconvenient. And it was
scary to get involved. But if I show love to only those who love me,
what reward is there for that? That night my heart led me directly
to jail—and I followed.

✳ *Love in a way that those who don't know God will see your kindness and know Him because of you.*

— Jill Thompson —

I Love You More

Respect everyone, and love your Christian brothers and sisters.

—1 PETER 2:17

I was in a hurry to end a cell phone conversation with my girlfriend. "Good-bye, Lorraine," I said. "I love you!"

Oops! The "I love you" part slipped out by mistake. It wasn't meant for Lorraine at all, but for my husband, who was temporarily working out of town. Every night I told him I loved him before I hung up the phone. But this wasn't my husband. Lorraine was on the other end of the line!

To my surprise, Lorraine giggled. "I love you more!" she sang. It sounded as if she was grinning from ear to ear.

I flipped my phone closed. The next time we talked, should I confess that I'd said "I love you" out of habit? No. It might hurt her feelings. The truth is, I really did love Lorraine. Why was it so easy to tell my husband I loved him, but not my friend?

Now at the end of every phone call, Lorraine says, "I love you!"

I stifle a laugh and reply, "I love you more!"

❋ *We all need to hear the words "I love you."*

— Mary Laufer —

It's All Right to Be Human

Each time he said, "My grace is all you need.
My power works best in weakness."

—2 CORINTHIANS 12:9

*Y*ou human," two-year-old Aleson said. At first, I didn't hear what she was trying to say, but as she twirled her mermaid doll, Ariel, around in her hands and repeated, "You human," I finally understood. I am a human as opposed to Ariel, who is a mermaid.

Sometimes this truth frustrates me, but my humanity never takes God by surprise. He understands who I am and why I do the things I do. He loves me deeply regardless. He reminded me of His great love the very next morning in my quiet time when I opened my daily devotional. The first sentence was in bold letters: *It's all right to be human!* Yes, it is all right for my mind to wander when I'm praying. He even forgives me when I worry needlessly and comforts me when I grieve.

My weakness and wounds are the openings through which the light of the knowledge of God's glory shines. His strength, power, and love show themselves most effective in my weakness.

✳ *God uses precious children to speak His love into our lives when we need it most.*

— Susan Browning Schulz —

Muck and Frozen Snow

Instead, let the Spirit renew your thoughts and attitudes.
—EPHESIANS 4:23

I sat shivering in the small travel trailer with my arms wrapped around my shoulders. How on earth was I going to survive ten days of no electricity, breaking ice from the creek to carry water, and preparing meals for a group of hunters? Love for my husband had me agreeing to fill in as camp cook, but not even twenty-four hours had passed and I was ready to quit!

Then I heard two of my husband's clients talking outside by the fire pit. "I saved up all year for this trip," said one.

"Yeah," the other agreed. "It's gonna be great."

I laughed. The same hunting trip that had me cowering in a corner was a delight and treasure to the men outside. "Lord," I prayed, "please change my attitude."

That was over a decade ago, and the Lord was so faithful in His answer to that prayer that I haven't missed a hunting trip since. You couldn't pay me to stay away.

✳ *A lot of circumstances are more livable through a change of attitude.*

— Sandy Cathcart —

70 x 7 People

Then Peter came to him and asked, "Lord, how often should
I forgive someone who sins against me? Seven times?"
"No, not seven times," Jesus replied, "but seventy times seven!"
—MATTHEW 18:21–22

*W*hat is with her? Why does she keep doing this stuff?" I cried out to the Lord.

I was talking to Him about my stepdaughter, who had hurt me time and time again. In fact, at that stage in her life, she was pretty pleased with herself if she could visibly cause me grief.

I sensed the Lord telling me, "Forgive her."

"Again?" I responded. "How many times am I going to have to forgive her, God?"

Boy, I really set myself up for that one! Instantly, words from Matthew 18 flashed through my mind, including the "70 x 7."

I realized that morning that Nicole was my "70 x 7" person. The way our personalities clashed, I was sure she'd hurt me—intentionally or not—490 or more times. Or, as some theologians tell us Jesus meant here: endlessly.

All of us have people in our lives like Nicole—people who may be hard to love or cause distress in our lives but won't be leaving our lives anytime soon.

✳ *Keep showing love and forgiveness to those 70 x 7 people in your life, and let the Lord take it from there.*

— Janet Graham —

Friends Don't Let Friends Jump

Never abandon a friend—
either yours or your father's.
When disaster strikes, you won't have to
ask your brother for assistance.
It's better to go to a neighbor than to
a brother who lives far away.

—PROVERBS 27:10

*H*ey girl, what's happening?" Janie asked me as she answered her phone.

I didn't need a second invitation. And I didn't need to ease into the situation with small talk. Instead, I immediately poured out my soul. The job issues. The family challenges. The marital woes. They had all come crashing down on me at once until I felt I was going to drown in the undertow.

Of course, as always, Janie listened intently. And she knew exactly what to say, precisely what to ask, and the words I needed to hear to be able to get my bearings and breathe again. For the past thirty years, Janie's been there and been a dear friend through all the experiences that have shaped my life—deaths, marriage, childbirth, jobs. She knows the good and bad about me and accepts me anyway. Janie has been my example of true friendship—not just when I'm hanging off the ledges, but all the time.

That's probably one of the reasons why God gives us friends—to help us celebrate the good times, and to show us His—and their— love and concern in the bad times.

�֍ *Friendship includes talking others off their ledges, and letting them talk you off yours.*

— Jenni Davenport —

Teach Them Their Father Loves Them

But watch out! Be careful never to forget what you
yourself have seen. . . . And be sure to pass them
on to your children and grandchildren.

—Deuteronomy 4:9

*W*hen I was a girl, my mama must have told me a million
times, "Remember: Jesus loves you and so do I."

She called it to me as I climbed on the school bus. She whispered
it to me when she tucked me in bed. When I was a teenager, she'd
leave those words taped to my bathroom mirror, usually when I
needed them most. No matter how many dumb mistakes I made,
no matter how many times I disappointed my parents, I knew one
thing. I was loved by them. And I was loved by God.

Last week, my twelve-year-old son got his own email address.
"Send me an email, Mom. Here's my address."

Not sure what to write to the gangly, half-grown kid doing his
homework in the next room, I remembered Mama's words and
composed this note, "Hey, Hewson! It's Mom. Remember: God
loves you and so do I."

�֍ *If our children and others don't learn the love of the Lord from us,*
where will they learn it?

— Mimi Greenwood Knight —

Expecting Nothing in Return

Was I wrong when I humbled myself and honored
you by preaching God's Good News to you
without expecting anything in return?

—2 CORINTHIANS 11:7

*T*he young man wore only a thin coat. It was snowing out. I
happened to be in the church working when the secretary
told me he'd come in looking for a handout. When I met him, I
asked if he was hungry. He said, "Kind of."

So we walked to my house and I gave him some spaghetti. We
talked more and I found out he needed $40 to get home. "I'm
looking for a new start."

That seemed a perfect in-road to sharing the Gospel, so I did.
Finally, he said, "I know you believe those things, but I'm really
not ready to believe in God or Jesus."

After we talked a bit longer, I gave him the $40 he needed as he
left. Later, I thought about what I'd done. Was it a waste of my
money? Had he used it instead for drugs or alcohol?

I have learned that while people may use our gifts in ways we
wouldn't approve, God knows our hearts. He values the love of a
giving heart, and He will ultimately reward us for that love and
kindness we show others.

❖ *There is only one reward for sharing love, money, and help with
others: God's pleasure.*

— Mark Littleton —

Fair Dealings

Good comes to those who lend money generously
and conduct their business fairly.
—PSALM 112:5

*W*ant to buy cards?" he asked.
I couldn't believe it. A jacketless boy about seven years old stood outside my door late one snowy afternoon.

"You're selling greeting cards?" I asked incredulously. My thoughts raced. *Did his parents approve his peddling? Alone? On a day like this? Were they destitute?*

"Or, I can shovel," he offered.

"It'll snow all night. No point shoveling now."

"I'll come tomorrow!"

"Fine." What had I done? He was too young, too small.

He returned in the morning. But a high school boy saw him ring my bell and ran to the porch to vie for the job. I recognized the older boy as being from a nearby boarding school—one for delinquents referred by the courts.

"Work together?" I suggested. They agreed.

I watched from indoors and, when they finished, I gave them each $10. Then I asked the older one to stay. His expression clouded, as if he feared he'd done something wrong.

"Take this extra $10," I said. "The little boy was too young. You did the work and I want to be fair with you."

Appreciative, he smiled. "Thanks."

✣ *Be kind to the poor and treat others fairly, for both acts demonstrate love.*

— Helene C. Kuoni —

My Shattered Stained-Glass Soul

I will lead blind Israel down a new path,
guiding them along an unfamiliar way.
I will brighten the darkness before them.

—Isaiah 42:16

I was taking a stained-glass workshop at a time when my family fell in pieces around me. After tracing a pattern on colored glass, my wrists rolled outward to snap the pieces scored by a sharp, well-oiled cutter. Razor-sharp edges sliced my fingers. I cried. The pieces of my yet-unformed project represented my stained-glass story: the transparency of shattered dreams and the fragility of life.

Against all my hopes and spiritual beliefs, I was thrust into the role of solo mom with a nursing infant and an angry, hurting preschooler. Like molten flux flowing into the joints of a stained-glass frame, burning agony poured into every fiber of my being.

Depression descended upon my soul. Out of a heart of darkness, I opened the window of my shattered soul to *Jehovah Ori, The Lord is my Light.* I was blinded by torment, but the light of God's Word inched me forward, away from the tribulation of the past. Through faith in the true light, Jesus filled the deepest cracks in the broken window of my soul with His love.

Jehovah Rapha be praised—the restorer of my shattered soul. Jehovah provided light in the darkness and comfort in despair.

✣ *God loves to shine His light in our souls when we call out to Him.*

— Scoti Springfield Domeij —

Gold in the Ashes

Timely advice is lovely, like golden apples in a silver basket.
—PROVERBS 25:11

*T*he cedar fire roared through San Diego County in late October 2003, burning into early December. A few days into the fire, Ed and I learned nearly half the homes in a small community near our church were destroyed. We teamed up with Samaritan's Purse to help the residents.

Through the ash-covered back country, we drove up the mountain. I worked in the tent, sorting donations, helping residents find what they needed, praying, listening, and just helping them cope. Ed joined clean-up crews who cleared home sites of ash and rubble, allowing homeowners to save money and rebuild sooner.

One morning I worked with Sue, an older volunteer from a distant area, attaching wristbands to site clean-up volunteers—a looting-prevention practice. After one man walked away, Sue whispered to me, "Be careful, honey. Some of these guys are far from home and might not be completely . . . honorable. That last fella was making eyes at you."

"Thanks, Sue." I grinned. "That one was my husband."

From a caring heart, Sue offered wisdom, and also blessed two tired workers.

❖ *Strew nuggets of affirmation and caring along your path today; you never know whose day you'll brighten.*

— Mary Kay Moody —

Lessons From Big Bird

He humbled himself in obedience to God and
died a criminal's death on a cross.

—PHILIPPIANS 2:8

*M*y attorney father donned a large garbage bag covered in bright yellow crepe paper streamers. He strapped on a poster board beak and headpiece, and then slid into leggings and scuba flippers. With plastic jack-o-lantern in hand and grandchildren in tow, he set out to greet the neighbors with an energetic "Trick or treat!"

What would possess a grown man to dress like Big Bird and walk around in public? Not just anybody would, or could, parade around garbed in a bird costume. Daddy's love for his grandchildren outweighed the potential embarrassment. He humbled himself and entered their world; he became as a child.

While Jesus didn't dress like Big Bird, He did humble himself when He became one of us. He put on the trappings of humankind so He could fashion an eternal relationship with His children. With me. To some this sounds preposterous, but it is awesome. He entered my world.

✶ *Entering someone else's world is sometimes awkward, but the results can be eternal.*

— Sharron K. Cosby —

I Want It All

Give thanks to the Lord, for he is good!
His faithful love endures forever.

—PSALM 107:1

*E*very year in November, a toy store flyer we call "the book" arrives in our mailbox. When my son was three, my husband handed him the flyer, and Edson spent the next half hour lying on the floor gazing at each page.

After considerable deliberation, he stood, handed the one hundred pages of glossy toy ads to his father, and said, "I want it all."

We laughed, but I started thinking. I give my son gifts because I love him and it warms my heart when he expresses sincere thanks. How often do I tell God "I want it all" without being grateful for what He's already given me?

Now when I ask my heavenly Father for something, I picture my son with the toy store flyer, and I stop to say thank you first.

❖ *Before you ask for more, thank God for what you already have.*

— Katie Robles —

A Simple Act of Love

My dear brothers and sisters, how can you claim
to have faith in your glorious Lord Jesus Christ
if you favor some people over others?

—JAMES 2:1

*H*omeless Charlie smelled of dirty pavement and gasoline. His clothes hung like torn rags, and his hair was matted and greasy. But that didn't stop him from joining our writing class one night. For Charlie, it was an old habit from days gone by when our school housed the local mission. He had simply come in to get warm.

He plopped in a chair between Garret and Peggy, and I thought, *Now here is the real story.*

Peggy bravely remained in her chair so she wouldn't offend him, yet intermittently leaned far enough away to get a breath of air. Garret sported an enormous grin and laid a hand on Charlie's back. Nate quietly stood from his seat several positions away and filled a paper plate with food for Charlie.

I doubt if many of us remember much about the writing lesson that night, but all of us learned a firsthand lesson of what it means to love the unlovely and how much a simple act of kindness can accomplish.

✦ *Overcoming our own comfort is sometimes exactly what will comfort someone else.*

— Sandy Cathcart —

My Favorite Day

This is the day the Lord has made.
We will rejoice and be glad in it.

—PSALM 118:24

*M*y friend Joe, who's known me since high school, thinks I'm a bit wacky because today, November 3, has special meaning for me. Not because anything wonderful happened on this day. But as a bored young teenager, I sat in a barber shop on this day in 1967 and wanted to make it memorable. I bet myself that I could remember the day for the rest of my life. And the easiest way was to call it my favorite day of the year.

There were a few times in the early years that day slipped my mind. So to make it consistently memorable, I later decided to do something for others—namely, my wife. She's my built-in reminder. We go out to dinner on November 3 and review life since the previous one. Some years I'm riding high; on this day last year I was mourning the death of my father.

We've discovered that it's also a way to measure God's unfailing love and faithfulness, whatever the circumstances. Choose a random day to bless someone, and together celebrate God's extraordinary blessings in ordinary days.

✻ *No day is ordinary—God's loving presence and care pervades them all.*

— James Stuart Bell —

Love in a Dumpster

Do not withhold good from those who deserve it
when it's in your power to help them.

—Proverbs 3:27

One snowy day my friend and I noticed an elderly woman slumped beneath a tree at our college. We tried to approach her, but the woman waved us off with a flourish of her cane and a stream of shouts in what sounded like Russian.

We figured that, like many homeless in the neighborhood, this woman—whom we nicknamed Annie—had been released from the psychiatric hospital on the hill above our campus.

Thereafter we saw Annie sleeping on bus stop benches, wrapped only in a worn trench coat. Swollen ankles burst out of her torn sneakers. We wanted to help her but could not get close enough to try.

Then, after seeing Annie rummaging in a Dumpster by a pizzeria, my friend and I had an idea. We began "planting" food and gifts for Annie in that Dumpster—sandwiches wrapped in plastic, a warm scarf, a used winter coat, thick socks, serviceable shoes. We saw Annie wearing our Dumpster gifts, and I believe that these and our prayers helped her survive that winter.

⁂ *Lord, show me ways to help when I feel helpless.*

— Kathleen M. Muldoon —

Let It Snow!

"Come now, let's settle this,"
says the Lord.
"Though your sins are like scarlet,
I will make them as white as snow.
Though they are red like crimson,
I will make them as white as wool."

—ISAIAH 1:18

*S*now often doesn't fall in Kansas City, where I live, until about this time of year. When we get snow, we live on such a busy street that our snow is quickly dirty from all the traffic. However, when I was a kid, we lived on a seldom-traveled road, and with a huge park abutting our backyard.

Our house was on a slight incline, so my brother and I would place our sleds next to the house and then zoom through our backyard and into the park, trying to go farther each time. Then I'd find crisp patches of untouched snow to stomp in before heading back to the house to do it again.

Perhaps nothing is as crisply, cleanly beautiful as new fallen snow. That's the contrast painted in Isaiah. The ugly dirtiness of sin . . . and God is willing to turn it into clean, pure beauty, like snow.

I don't know how it works, but God, in His love, is able to take our messes and make them clean.

✳ *Take a quick peek into your life. If you're not happy with what you see, let God work a little snow magic.*

— Jeanette Gardner Littleton —

Why We Live

Knowing this, I am convinced that I will remain
alive so I can continue to help all of you grow
and experience the joy of your faith.

—PHILIPPIANS 1:25

One night as we lay in bed reading, my wife said to me, "Why
do you think I live, honey?"

A little too obvious an answer for me. I hemmed and hawed.
"Because I love you so much I want you around forever."

"To serve you and do your bidding?"

I knew I was entering a minefield. "No," I said. "I mean, I
appreciate all the things you do for me, for all of us. But I think
there's much more to it. There's companionship. Friendship. Like
us talking like this. I like that kind of stuff a lot."

"So you see me as a talking partner?"

Why did she always have to simplify it? "Okay, what are you
getting at?"

"I read this verse Paul wrote. He was about to be executed. But
he thought God wanted him to live on for the sake of the people
he ministered to. So is that why God lets people live longer? So
they can minister?"

I rolled over and gave her a big kiss. "And so I can have a kiss
anytime I want."

❖ *Why do we live but to serve, give, share, love, and comfort others?*

— Clay Taylor —

Can You Hear Him Now?

The Lord is close to all who call on him,
yes, to all who call on him in truth.

—PSALM 145:18

*M*arilyn asked me to take care of her daughters so she could get away for the weekend. The first night, after a story, prayers, and hugs, I tiptoed out.

"Auntie Susan, can you please come here?" Shannon called to me. "We want to know if God answers us when we pray."

"Well, God doesn't usually speak in a voice that we can hear with our ears, but I assure you that He listens when you pray, because you are very special to Him. If you are very quiet, you may hear Him whisper in your heart," I said.

Later, I heard the girls giggling and Shelly asking over and over, "Can you hear Him now?"

I grumbled, "What's going on in here?" My irritation dissolved in laughter when I found Shannon with her head planted on top of Shelly's little chest, listening with all her might.

Children take things so literally, I thought. *But at least they're trying to hear our Lord. I'm going to try listening more in prayer time myself,* I vowed.

✳ *When we love the Lord and seek Him in the stillness of our hearts,*
He hears us and answers.

— Susan E. Ramsden —

Enduring Love

The Lord will work out his plans for my life—
for your faithful love, O Lord, endures forever.

—PSALM 138:8

*A*s I stared at my biopsy report, only one word was readable to my watering eyes: cancer. My life as I had known it suddenly made a big turn I wasn't ready to take. Despair, shock, and fear flooded in to overtake my heart and mind.

Quickly turning to God's Word, I found this Scripture in Psalm 138. My name was written all over it. God was talking to me, but was I going to listen? Nothing had changed from the day before. God was still functioning in my life.

The lump in my breast and the spot on my spine weren't enough to stop the Lord's love from working out His plans. Indeed His love proves greater than cancer or anything else.

It's a love that picks us up when we need it the most. That carries us when we can only crawl. A love that doesn't stop at the first obstacle life puts in its way. It's a love that will endure forever.

�❖ *Thanks to His love, we too can endure forever no matter what may come our way.*

— Karen Gillett —

Make a Difference

Always be humble and gentle. Be patient with each other, making allowance for each other's faults because of your love.

—Ephesians 4:2

"I will never come back to this church again," said a grandma who had eight grandchildren attending our church. This was our first pastorate, so when I heard about her displeasure, I didn't know what to do. I prayed and remembered the verse about bearing with one another in love.

I went to her house with fear and trembling. I was a twenty-seven-year-old preacher's wife. She was a seventy-year-old grandma. I listened, I prayed, I told her we loved her, appreciated her, and wanted her to come back. Then I asked her what the problem was.

She told me. I showed her love. She came back to the church. One of the granddaughters is now the pastor's wife of that church. The eight grandchildren were able to attend and find Christ, and now their children are involved in the church. I can't help but wonder how it would have been different if I hadn't gone in love and listened.

⁂ *Can you make allowances for someone's faults because of your love?*

— Francine Duckworth —

Spiritual Wisdom

I pray for you constantly, asking God, the glorious Father
of our Lord Jesus Christ, to give you spiritual wisdom.

—EPHESIANS 1:16–17

I needed wisdom. My mother was now in assisted living to the
tune of $65,000 a year. I was far away in the Midwest where
my wife and I were having our own financial issues. I thought if my
mom's estate could pay, our family could move to Maryland and
take care of Mom in a house that would meet her needs and ours.

I was about to tell my brother and sister of this great plan, but
decided I should discuss it with my wife first. She said, "They won't
like you telling them this will solve our money problems, and they
will feel pushed into it. Also, it will take a lot more to care for your
mom than you've ever dealt with."

I prayed some more and realized my wife had given me wisdom
I didn't have. When you need wisdom from God, sometimes He
will speak himself. At other times He will speak through others
who love you like He does.

✣ *Always seek the wisdom of those who love you. They may have
just the right word for your situation.*

— Jerry Hamilton —

Thanks to a Vet

But encourage one another, especially now that
the day of his return is drawing near.

—HEBREWS 10:25

*A*s a teacher at a Bible college, I always find it a delight to encourage and support students during their graduation ceremonies, and it is one of the few things my husband, the mountain man, will don a suit coat to attend.

During one graduation banquet, a student was talking with me when I saw a young man approach my husband. "Are you Cat Cathcart?" he asked.

Cat nodded.

"Someone told me you are a Vietnam vet."

Arms folded tight across his chest, Cat nodded again. The young man leaned in close to my husband, and the two men talked quietly for several minutes. Soon, I saw rare tears form in my husband's eyes. Then the two men exchanged a strong man's embrace. Later, I learned that the young man was one of the last babies to be airlifted out of Saigon. He was the first person to thank Cat for his service to his country. Ever since that experience, I've sent thanks to every vet I know on Veterans Day.

✻ *Give thanks to people who are serving or have served you in some way.*

— Sandy Cathcart —

Love and Prayers

But you, dear friends, must build each other up in your
most holy faith, pray in the power of the Holy Spirit.

—JUDE 1:20

*J*eanette, has your father come to Christ yet?" David asked as
he did each time he saw me.

I looked into David's dark brown eyes. This man who lived in a
group home visited our ministry several times a week. He was shy
and had slight mental issues, but he loved people and God, and
he loved to pray. He constantly asked our staff for prayer requests,
and then he went to a corner of our building and prayed. David's
memory for these prayer needs was amazing.

"No, David. Dad hasn't come to Christ," I answered.

"I began praying for him September 28, 1980," David murmured,
mentioning the date from years earlier. "I'll keep praying." And I
knew he would.

I'd lost touch with David for a couple of decades when Dad
finally came to Christ—weeks before he died. Not long after that,
by chance I saw David's obituary in the newspaper too.

"He came to Christ, David," I whispered. "But I guess you've
probably already met him. Thank you for praying."

✣ *Love prays for others—as long as the prayers are needed.*

— Jeanette Gardner Littleton —

He Isn't Heavy

Then Jesus said, "Come to me, all of you who are weary
and carry heavy burdens, and I will give you rest."

—MATTHEW 11:28

*J*oey looked like a pro football player, only from the streets. In fact, he was overcoming a life of alcohol and homelessness. His slow and gentle mannerism soon put us at ease. When he felt safe, Joey told us why he had come to our grief recovery group. He had left home at an early age to escape an abusive father, yet he always felt guilty for leaving his mom and brothers to fend off his dad's rages.

To survive, he joined the military. When he was overseas, he found out his younger brother killed himself. Joey wondered if he could have prevented it. Two years later on the same date, his other brother killed himself. That's when Joey turned to alcohol to deaden his pain. It got even worse when his mother died. Joey came to the grief group after learning his dad died before he was able to forgive him.

My first reaction was, "Oh no! This is too heavy for me to help him with."

I felt God whisper to my heart, "It's not too heavy for me!" I couldn't handle his burden by myself, but I could help him carry it to the Lord.

✻ *Burdens become lighter when carried together to God.*

— Eva Juliuson —

God's Blanket of Protection

Answer me when I call to you,
O God who declares me innocent.
Free me from my troubles.
Have mercy on me and hear my prayer.

—PSALM 4:1

I left my home at 5 p.m., forgetting my winter coat. I thought, *I'll be home in a couple of hours, I'll survive.*

At 8:30 p.m. I stepped into six inches of icy white powder in toeless, backless shoes. I was coatless, and wet snow pouring from the sky soaked my hair as I scraped ice and snow off all four sides of my car.

My car started and inched forward on slippery roads. The gas gauge registered dangerously close to empty. Praise and worship music blasted from my radio. All around me, semi-trucks, cars, SUVs, and police cars with lights flashing sat sideways and backwards in ditches. The heavy snowfall blew across the road, blinding my vision.

"God, please help me get home," I prayed.

I broke free of the maze of stalled and stuck cars, continuing my glacial, ten-mile-per-hour crawl across slick, snow-packed roads. Two hours later, I pulled into my driveway and thanked God for His protection and safe passage home. Then I waded in ankle-deep snow to the warmth of my house.

✳ *When our cars—and our emotions—slip and slide, we can trust God to lead us home.*

— Scoti Springfield Domeij —

A Kind of Patient Love

Better to be patient than powerful;
better to have self-control than to conquer a city.
—PROVERBS 16:32

*M*y wife's school has a tight-knit faculty, but one special education teacher is an outcast. She has ADHD, which at age fifty-five is unattractive if not irritating—especially when she forgets her medication. She often interrupts, is flighty, scatterbrained, and just gets on everyone's nerves.

One day my wife, Linda, said, "All she needs is someone to love her like Jesus loves her."

Linda determined to be kind, giving, and patient with this woman. Over time, they became friends, and a few of the teachers who shunned her began to understand why she behaved as she did. Some even changed their attitudes toward her and began working more closely with her.

We cannot measure the value of patience and kindness and how that demonstrates tangibly that God loves someone. But if we will take the time to show patience, we can often change a bad situation to a good one.

✳ *Sometimes love means counting to ten more than once.*

— Jim Zabloski —

Carry a Friend to Jesus

Four men arrived carrying a paralyzed man on a mat. They couldn't bring him to Jesus because of the crowd, so they dug a hole through the roof above his head. Then they lowered the man on his mat, right down in front of Jesus.

—Mark 2:3–4

Sometimes Sally carries me. At other times, Rhonda is my transport. Sandy has been known to lift me up. And I could name a few others who have borne my weight over the years.

We all get paralyzed at times. Although we may not be physically paralyzed like the man in this Scripture, we may be emotionally or even spiritually unable to move like we should. Fears, worries, weariness, discouragement . . . all these things can impede our mobility.

But that doesn't have to mean we're finished.

That's one of the reasons God gives us friends. Through their words, prayers, and encouragement, they keep us going when we feel we can't move. They can even take us to Jesus when we feel spiritually paralyzed.

And in return, we can do the same for others. Do you know someone who needs a little help walking? Or maybe who can't see Jesus because of the crowds of people or concerns in his or her life? Maybe it's time to carry a friend to Jesus.

⁂ *None of us have to be paralyzed when we have friends.*

— Julie Durham —

My Mentor, Peggy

These older women must train the younger women
to love their husbands and their children.

—Titus 2:4

*W*hen you hear the term *mother-in-law*, what comes to mind? For many, those words are scary. Not for me. God put my mother-in-law, Peggy, in my life to teach me more about love.

Early in my marriage, I was seriously ill. I wondered if I would even survive. My in-laws took us in so Peggy could take care of me. She never complained about the extra work. That's love.

When my health improved, Peggy became more of a friend than an in-law. We frequently went shopping together. Little did I know, she was subtly teaching me how to shop. We spent time chatting in her kitchen; I learned to cook there. In our frequent conversations, I learned about life and loving others. She supplemented the lessons my own mom had taught me, without ever trying to take her place.

Without even knowing it, Peggy was also teaching me how to be a mother-in-law, and I intend to love my daughter-in-law the way Peggy loves me.

✻ *We serve a God who can make even in-law relationships wonderful!*

— Cindy Sipula —

On My Best Behavior

I will be careful to live a blameless life—
when will you come to help me?
I will lead a life of integrity
in my own home.

—PSALM 101:2

*W*hat do you *mean* you left the girls to sled at the park while you ran down the street and got a taco? They're not old enough to be left at the park alone! Someone could have grabbed them or they could have gotten hurt."

"Well, I was hungry," my husband said. "I guess it wasn't the smartest thing to do. I just didn't think about that."

The crazy thing is that he's brilliant. I call him my encyclopedia because he has an amazing array of knowledge. But my first impression of him was that he was an absent-minded professor type of guy, and I truly hit the nail on the head at the beginning.

I have lots of common sense, so sometimes it's *really* exasperating when my husband doesn't think. That's when my mouth goes into action with words I shouldn't say.

Why is it so easy for us, sometimes, to be unkind and cutting to those we love the most? I'm working at biting my tongue when my husband doesn't think or when my kids squabble. I'm trying to learn to be on my best behavior with those I love the most.

✳ *Kindness, gentle words, and loving forgiveness need to start at home.*

— Janet Graham —

Real Life and Love

It is through faith that a righteous person has life.
—Galatians 3:11

I tried to love people when I was an unbeliever. But it was difficult. It seemed I only saw their faults and the things that irritated me.

Then I became a Christian and God changed me. And God sent me one of the people I found hardest to love—a guy named Bob who worked at the ski lodge where I was an instructor and short-order cook.

Bob was arrogant. He used people, including me. He put others down constantly. And he accused me of being condescending when I told him about my faith in Christ.

I wanted to avoid him, but I had to work with him. I prayed about him constantly.

Then one day he rushed into the kitchen, terrified that some guy wanted to kill him because he'd stolen the guy's girlfriend. We worked together that afternoon, and I told him why I didn't fear people like I used to. He listened, accepted Christ, and became a good friend after that.

Some people are hard cases. You think you'll never have any influence. And then one day, everything changes. Love breaks through. And you and they are never the same again.

✷ *Show love; you'll be surprised what God can do through you.*

— Mark Littleton —

Do the Good Things

For we are God's masterpiece. He has created us anew in Christ
Jesus, so we can do the good things he planned for us long ago.

—EPHESIANS 2:10

*M*y daughter ran to me, terrified, to tell me about her big
sister's accident.

"Nicole fell off her bike and her knee is broken," she cried.

I rushed out and found Nicole in a heap, clutching her leg.

"Let me see it, honey," I said. There was a gouge in her kneecap,
and I could see the whiteness of bone beyond.

I rushed her to the ER, where a doctor probed the wound with a
long needle. Nicole screamed the whole time and I held her hand,
consoling, "It'll be over soon, honey. Just hang in there. It'll be
okay."

I'd never heard screams as loud as hers. But soon the doctors
had her in good shape. Afterward, I said, "I'm sorry I held your
hand so tightly, honey, but you screamed loud."

She said, "If you hadn't held my hand like that, Daddy, I would
have screamed worse."

It's funny in a way. But the situation wasn't. God came through
as always. I'm always startled to see God work like that. I shouldn't
be, for that is His nature. He wants to do good in our lives because
He loves us.

✳ *God's love is there even when someone is screaming.*

— Richard Holland —

The One in Charge

You intended to harm me, but God intended it all for good.

—GENESIS 50:20

*G*inger, we want you to train Brian to take over part of your job," my boss, Jim, said as he announced he was moving me from being full-time to part-time.

Brian had no experience in my field. He worked in a separate area of the company—one that was overstaffed. Financial cuts were necessary, and rather than just let Brian go from the overstaffed department, the company was putting me on part-time and keeping Brian full-time. I'd been hired later than Brian, I made more money . . . and Brian was related to the boss.

After several months of training Brian, I was laid off entirely. And Brian was moved fully into the position I'd been released from.

As I scrambled to find more work, I dealt with all the expected frustrations, hurts, and sense of unfairness of the situation.

But the Lord reminded me of Joseph in Genesis 37–50. Joseph didn't let the unfairness of his situations get him down. Instead, he trusted his loving Lord to take care of him no matter what people did. And sure enough, his faith was rewarded. Eventually, mine was too.

✻ *When people let you down, remember that your loving Father is still in charge.*

— Ginger Livingston —

You Fed Me

For I was hungry, and you fed me. I was thirsty, and you gave me a drink. I was a stranger, and you invited me into your home.

—MATTHEW 25:35

*W*hile my husband recovered from a near-death experience, God called us to manage housing for low-income and homeless people. This was far beyond our natural experience, but all God requires is love and obedience.

Often our residents struggled with making good life decisions including money management. Sometimes their cupboards were empty. With Thanksgiving approaching, God put it on our hearts to provide a Thanksgiving meal for them with all the trimmings. Dinner for forty-five people—we needed a miracle like the five loaves and two fish.

God supplied the food and I cooked a turkey dinner just like Grandma's. One-by-one they came, shocked that someone cared enough to prepare this feast. With smiles and words of thanks, they settled in to eat their meal. Through tear-filled eyes, I saw what an offering of love can do to mend a broken life. Love flooded the building that day as God touched their hearts and they hungered no more.

✣ *When God opens our hearts to love others, we can satisfy their hunger.*

— Barbara Hollace —

A Tarp and Two Boots

"You must love the Lord your God with all your
heart, all your soul, all your strength, and all your
mind." And, "Love your neighbor as yourself."

—LUKE 10:27

I rummaged through the box of donations and placed a wool
coat on the table in front of me. A disheveled man meandered
up to me. I said, "Good morning. Happy Thanksgiving."

He wiped his dirty sleeve across his mouth. "Hey, how's it going?"

I stared into his desolate eyes and couldn't believe he was our
friend's twenty-seven-year-old prodigal son whom I had been praying for. To see him face-to-face hit me like a brick. It pained me to
imagine her son sleeping on the forest floor each night.

My husband, Randy, sauntered over to us.

"Hi. Good to see you. What do you need to get you through
the winter?" he asked.

"Man, I could use a tarp to keep me dry, and some rain boots
too," he slurred.

"Meet me here next week, and I'll have them for you. Enjoy your
turkey dinner," Randy chimed.

The following week, we met him at our local church with the items.

He smiled. "Thanks, Randy. Did my mom tell you that I got
a job?"

"Yes, and I am excited for you."

On the ride home, I thanked God for restoring this man, and
for allowing us to be an instrument of His love.

✳ *Loving other people means meeting their needs, whatever those
needs may be.*

— Rebecca Krusee —

Let's Talk Turkey

The seeds of good deeds become a tree of life;
a wise person wins friends.

—PROVERBS 11:30

*T*hat special dinner I planned isn't going to work!" I told my prayer partner of many years.

"Why?"

"My entire family's coming. That's four adults and three kids. Our single neighbor and my husband's brother are coming, as well as Adri and her mom. I also invited our friend—now she's bringing five more people! I invited you, and you want to bring four more! That's twenty-four people! I don't have room enough for everyone. The last time I had a big meal like this, I was so busy that I missed enjoying the whole dinner!"

"Would it help if I don't come and don't bring my family?"

"But you're baking the turkey. I don't have oven space to pull all of this off."

"I can still bake the turkey and bring it over."

"You'd do that for me?"

"Yes, because I love you."

Not only did she bring over the turkey, but she also came over afterward and helped clean up!

✳ *A true friend not only hears and understands, but shows love in concrete ways.*

— Linda Jett —

Will I Sing Praise?

You turned my mourning into joyful dancing.
You have taken away my clothes
of mourning and clothed me with joy,
that I might sing praises to you and not be silent.
O Lord my God, I will give you thanks forever!

—PSALM 30:11–12

*A*fter my divorce, a silent shadow tiptoed up every fall, cloaking me in darkness. For several years, I failed to recognize its stealthy intrusion. As the Thanksgiving season raced toward me, looking at my china saddened me. I grieved over happier family times. Seeing the empty chair at our table was excruciating.

When hard-pressed, I dutifully and grudgingly expressed "what I'm thankful for," while my mind spit out a litany of what I wasn't thankful for. Too angry to embrace gratitude, I felt like the condemned Thanksgiving turkey celebrating against its will.

But in time, anguish no longer consumed all joy and thankfulness. Apart from some anxious gobbling, I began to appreciate the good things in my life again. I realized that being thankful was not what I *said* about God's blessings, but how I *used* them. I volunteered to serve Thanksgiving plates of grace to those less fortunate. I offered a listening ear and compassion to others newer on grief's path.

Now I observe Thanksgiving every day through "thanks-living" by praising the Lord for His blessing of everlasting loving-kindness.

✻ *Thanksgiving can be a way of life for us when we focus on the Lord.*

— Scoti Springfield Domeij —

His Understanding Is Unlimited

How great is our Lord! His power is absolute!
His understanding is beyond comprehension!

—PSALM 147:5

*M*om was dying, although I didn't realize it. Every day after
work, I drove forty minutes to spend the evening at the
hospital.

Besides work, the hospital visits, and caring for Dad, I also was
a volunteer youth worker and sang in the church choir. Leaders
at my church expected members to be there Sunday morning and
night, Wednesday night, and for teacher meetings, choir practice,
and other events.

After several weeks, I just couldn't keep up with it all. I couldn't
skip work, and I couldn't abandon Mom and Dad. So I began to
skip some church activities. This was not received kindly by some
people at my church. I felt guilty, tired, and like an emotional wreck.

One day I spent my lunch hour sobbing in my car at the worry
and weariness of it all. "Lord, I don't mean to be unspiritual," I
prayed. "But I just can't do it all."

"Don't worry; I understand. I love you," He answered. With
those words, He released me from others' expectations. Nothing
else seemed to matter as long as I realized He knew what I was
going through and knew I was doing my best.

✳ *The One who loves us most always understands the challenges we*
face. His understanding is unlimited.

— Jossy Grey —

Reconciliation Begins at Home

So if you are presenting a sacrifice at the altar in the Temple and
you suddenly remember that someone has something against
you, leave your sacrifice there at the altar. Go and be reconciled
to that person. Then come and offer your sacrifice to God.

—MATTHEW 5:23–24

I asked our youth pastor to invite Jon to church this week,"
Dan told me. Dan and his teen, Jon, had experienced a falling out, and Jon had gone to live with his mother. Months later,
Dan still fumed about disrespectful words his son had said, and he
hadn't talked to Jon since then. But now Dan's church was having
a special teen night and Dan wanted Jon there.

"Dan, it's not the youth pastor's responsibility," I gently pointed
out. "It's yours. Why don't you call Jon and invite him."

"But he was so rude to me!" Dan said. "And he's never said
he's sorry."

"Yeah, but he's a kid," I reminded Dan. "He doesn't know how
to apologize. He needs you to show him how to mend the broken
relationships in life."

Dan ended up calling Jon. Jon came to the event, and their
relationship was eventually transformed.

✳ *The first step to reconciliation is the willingness to breach the gap.*

— Ila Reed —

God's Heartwarming Hug

I will answer them before they even call to me.
While they are still talking about their needs,
I will go ahead and answer their prayers!

—ISAIAH 65:24

*I*t was a very cold, windy, winter day. The funeral service for our good friend was in the morning. His wife had died six months earlier and he had been sick a long time. After the service, we reached out in love to his daughter with cookies and hugs.

Several hours later, we were at the cemetery for another longtime friend. The bitter cold wind swept the words away, but knowing he loved the Lord made it easier. Having hugged the family, we went home.

I felt drained and exhausted. Before I had time to pray, the doorbell rang. In came our pastor friend, who gave me a great big bear hug. It lifted my spirits. About fifteen minutes later, our associate pastor friend also came in, bringing another bear hug. It was a double affirmation from God of His love and care. He filled my cup to overflowing, enabling me to reach out again.

�֍ *God's love is always there, and He sends His messengers to strengthen you.*

— Kay E. Combs —

Endless Treasures

Though I am the least deserving of all God's people, he
graciously gave me the privilege of telling the Gentiles
about the endless treasures available to them in Christ.

—EPHESIANS 3:8

*T*he speaker held my attention like a vice. He was exciting,
eloquent, and most of all, passionate about evangelism. "If
you don't have a Gospel tract in your pocket when you go out in
the world, you aren't dressed right," he said.

And, "If you're not ready at all times to share the Gospel, you
aren't ready to eat or drink either."

At the end of the meeting, he simmered down a little and told
us how the Gospel was the greatest treasure we had. "Not money.
Not food. Not a great house or career. Not even a great spouse is
as much a treasure as the Gospel. For it is available to everyone."

I thought a lot about that and even began carrying tracts with
me to pass out everywhere I went. Have you ever thought that the
greatest love you can show anyone is to share the Gospel with him
or her? It is, and we should all be ready at any opportunity. Always
be ready. It's a sign of the real love in your heart to speak the truth,
even in situations where it's not wanted or expected.

✻ *Telling others the Gospel message is one of the best ways to love
them.*

— Jerry Hamilton —

Epicurean As a Second Language

Don't be concerned for your own good
but for the good of others.

—1 CORINTHIANS 10:24

*W*ell, *they say a girl marries a man like her dad,* I thought.
Though I wouldn't say my dad and husband are just alike,
they do have similarities, I realized as I watched my husband relish
his meal. Mark sure does love his food.

Dad was the same way. After Mom died, he missed her desperately—especially her cooking. Mom made country comfort food
to perfection.

Unfortunately, I didn't get that melt-in-your-mouth-creations
gene, nor did Mom teach me her secrets.

And frankly, I don't have a distinguished palate. My husband
can detect a hint of rosemary adorning a dish. I'll eat anything
that's set before me, and I don't need to have any idea what's in
it. I regularly cook, but my meals tend to be simple. Food is just
another chore to get out of the way.

We were a ways into marriage before I realized just how important food is to my husband. In fact, it's one of his love languages.
When I make an effort to cook something well, my husband feels
loved.

I'm still rather ESL—epicurean as a second language—but I'm
learning to speak a language that he'll understand.

❖ *Part of loving successfully is learning what says "I love you" to
those in our lives.*

— Jenni Davenport —

Repent, Christmas Is at Hand!

*Can't you see that [God's] kindness is
intended to turn you from your sin?*

—ROMANS 2:4

*I*t was a typical kick-off sermon on the first Sunday in Advent. My distinguished-looking pastor with his green accented robes admonished us to make room for the Christ child in our hearts, etc. But then he inserted the word *repentance*, and I was startled.

Being a liturgical Christian, I thought of Lent as the time of repentance, moving toward Good Friday and Easter. But he explained that the early church saw "making room" in their hearts during Advent as a cleansing operation. When the Christ child "arrived" around four weeks later on Christmas, the room in their hearts would be swept clean of habitual sins. Then they would be more fit to celebrate His arrival.

I've adopted that idea. It doesn't mean that I'm now somber in Advent, in a state of mourning. But I hope to make room for God and others by denying myself more often and putting them first. And then, on December 25, I'll have even more room to celebrate!

�֎ *Making room for God and others means first putting off the old self.*

— James Stuart Bell —

University of Adversity

And if you give even a cup of cold water to one of the least of my followers, you will surely be rewarded.

—Matthew 10:42

One December day, a blizzard was brewing. I would miss a day of fifth grade because school had been cancelled.

"Brrrrr." The blast from the frigid temperatures made my mother's teeth chatter. "It's freezing out there."

When I spoke, my warm breath fogged over the cold pane of glass. "Glad I'm inside where it's warm."

As Mom admired the white landscape, a dark shadow loomed in the distance. "Who on earth would be traipsing around in this weather?"

I squinted, trying to catch a glimpse of the mysterious person. "It's Keith—the homeless man!"

Mom bolted out the door and frantically waved her arms. "Keith! Woo hoo! Have you had breakfast?"

A thin, shabbily dressed man who resembled some character from a Dickens novel entered our home and eyed the bacon sizzling in the pan. "Sure smells good."

"We're glad you could join us for breakfast today." Mom poured a steaming cup of coffee for our guest of honor.

"Me too."

Even though school was cancelled that day, I learned a valuable life lesson about caring for those who've seen a tough life.

God always makes room for those special souls who have graduated from the University of Adversity. Shouldn't we?

— Dixie Phillips —

God's Rules Rule!

What is more pleasing to the Lord:
your burnt offerings and sacrifices
or your obedience to his voice?
Listen! Obedience is better than sacrifice,
and submission is better than offering the fat of rams.

—1 SAMUEL 15:22

*M*y daughter loves to ride her bike but hates to wear her helmet. My husband, however, strictly enforces the helmet rule. My daughter was unhappy about this until the day she ran into the house and announced, "I fell off my bike and hit my head, but because I had my helmet on, it didn't even hurt. Dad's rules rule!" I had to laugh. That "terrible" rule became great because it helped her.

It reminded me about God and His rules. God doesn't want us to hate His rules, but to love them. They keep us from getting hurt, just like that bicycle helmet.

One important rule is to love God, and to love others as much as we love ourselves. My husband loves our daughter so much he can't bear the thought that she might get hurt. And that's exactly why God gives us His rules too.

I'm glad I have a Father who loves me so much . . . just like my daughter has a father who loves her.

✳ *Spend some time thanking God for loving us enough to give us His rules.*

— Kelly Combs —

Love In, Fear Out

I prayed to the Lord, and he answered me.
He freed me from all my fears.

—PSALM 34:4

*I*t was not love that took me down the long, cold corridors
of the jail, but fear.

I had retired and was suddenly part of a jail ministry team that
our pastor thought I should try. Even though I'd completed the
training, I knew this ministry was not for me. I was a Sunday school
teacher and enjoyed working in women's ministry. I never thought
about people behind bars. I told God what He already knew—I
did not care about these women. I told Him that He would have
to change me if He wanted me to minister well.

Then, the women dressed in orange walked into our meeting
room. I felt fear leave; God's love entered. I looked at these women
and reached out and hugged them. I did not see alcoholics, thieves,
murderers, and drug addicts. I saw mothers, daughters, and wives
who had made bad choices. I could not wait to share the abundant
love of the Father with them. God had shown His love to me. It
changed me.

❖ *God's love changes our hearts and opens our eyes.*

— Bev Schwind —

The Escape Hatch

The temptations in your life are no different from what others experience. And God is faithful. He will not allow the temptation to be more than you can stand. When you are tempted, he will show you a way out so that you can endure.

—I CORINTHIANS 10:13

*M*ommy, what's happening?" my daughter asked, looking from me to the angry man on our front lawn. The man's dog was defecating on our lawn when our chow pushed out the front door, barking furiously. Instantly my son grabbed our dog and dragged him away. But the rattled man let me have it, ignoring my repeated apologies. My adrenaline surged.

Don't say it! Just walk away! The Holy Spirit shouted at me.

I paused, but then gave in to the temptation by answering my daughter. "This guy's just a jerk, honey."

That did it. The man punched the number for animal control into his phone and reported us for having an unrestrained dog.

So then, of course, I had to deal with the hassle of animal control and an unpleasant neighbor—stress factors I could have avoided if I'd just obeyed the Holy Spirit's directions.

We all face temptations. But God loves us enough that He helps us overcome them. We never *have* to give in to a temptation because God always provides an escape hatch we can choose to exit through.

✣ *When temptation heats up, look for the way of escape our loving God has provided.*

— Jossy Grey —

Love Your Neighbor

Do not seek revenge or bear a grudge against a fellow
Israelite, but love your neighbor as yourself.

—LEVITICUS 19:18

*K*aren was the classic tough girl at the ski lodge where we
worked and roomed. She was living with my friend at the
lodge who wasn't a Christian, but who asked me many questions
about Christ. One day I told him that he should stop living with his
girlfriend because God considered this a sin. Apparently, he went
back to his room and told Karen. The next thing I knew, Karen
stood at my door with a knife in her hand.

"You keep tellin' Joe about this God stuff," she said, "and I'll
come in here one night and cut you open like a Christmas turkey."

Later that night, I told Joe what happened and he said, "Don't
worry about it."

We kept talking about God.

One day, Karen ran into the room where some of us were holding a Bible study.

"He's come back," she said, ranting about her boyfriend before
Joe, who'd now returned to the lodge. "And he'll beat me up."

It was then that I really talked to her about Christ. She decided
to believe in Him and became a stalwart member of our group.

It's the law of love: keep on loving, even the unlovely, and one
day you'll break through. It might not be soon. It might be a long
time. But love has real power. God's love can clear away all the junk
and speak the truth so they believe it.

✣ *Love others even when they're not nice; they might be the next ones
God draws to himself.*

— Mark Littleton —

Blanket of Love

And I will pray the Father, and he shall give you another
Comforter, that he may abide with you for ever.

—JOHN 14:16 KJV

*E*xperiencing the loss of a soul mate had me emotionally beaten.
One rainy night, I was driving home on curvy mountain roads.
The lights of the cars behind me were painfully blinding me as I
drove around the curves. I kept trying to adjust the mirror until it
broke off in my hand. That was the last straw. I broke down.

Arriving home, I could not calm myself. In the midst of all this
grief, I prayed, *"Father, Your word says that you are the Comforter.
If you are, I need you now."*

I curled up in bed and immediately felt as if someone was pulling
a warm comforter over me. I settled down into the first peaceful
night's sleep I'd enjoyed in more than a year.

The next morning the sun was shining through my window,
warming my face. I reached down to move away the comforter
that I had felt the night before. There was none.

I still giggle twenty-five years later. That night when I prayed
to God, I did not ask to be comforted. I asked for a Comforter.

✻ *God has a Comforter available to be our Advocate whenever we
need someone to warm us and be on our side.*

— Sheila Embry —

The Love Habit

Let us continue to love one another, for love comes from
God. Anyone who loves is a child of God and knows God.

—1 JOHN 4:7

I love you," I murmured and patted my son's hair.

"I love you too, Mama," he replied, a secure smile on
his face.

The interchange only took a couple of seconds while I walked
through the room and while he sat playing his Nintendo DS. But
it added a little brick to the bridge of love connecting us.

I was raised by wonderful parents, but they weren't touchers
and didn't verbally express love, so I grew up not quite sure that
my parents even liked me.

When I became an adult and had kids, I realized the depth of my
parents' love and understood that they came from a non-expressive
background. But I decided I never wanted my kids to doubt my
love. So I purposely worked to construct a love bridge between us.

The bridge of love between each of my kids and me isn't built
of big blocks of sacrifices. Instead, it's like a Lego bridge—made
of little pieces. With each touch, each kiss, each expression of love
or admiration, I add a brick to the bridge and make it stronger. I'm
getting into the habit of building the bridge continually.

❊ *Whether with our kids or others, expressing affection and building
a bridge of love is a habit we develop.*

— Jenni Davenport —

Everyday Living for Jesus

Loving God means keeping his commandments,
and his commandments are not burdensome.

—1 JOHN 5:3

I don't have any great lion's den experience like Daniel. I've never been asked to go through a fiery furnace like Shadrach, Meshach, and Abednego. My life is so ordinary that sometimes I wonder if people really see Jesus's love through me. My husband is a youth pastor, and by the nature of being his wife, I am involved in the lives of many teens, but I wonder, *Do I really make a difference?*

Then I think about young adults who were previously in our youth group. Many aren't where I would like to see them spiritually, and I'm still praying that will come. However, others have grown so much and are even leaders in their own churches now.

Sometimes it isn't the exotic experiences but the everyday lives we lead that help those around us see Jesus in the real world. Most of us will never slay a giant with a sling, but we serve the same God as those great men of faith. When we live out our faith in our ordinary lives where He puts us, we can help others see Him.

✳ *Obeying God's commands means living where He puts us.*

— Leta Deering —

God Cares

Your Father knows exactly what you
need even before you ask him!
—MATTHEW 6:8

*I*t was winter not only outside, but inside as well. Our lives felt cold and wanting. Christmas would soon be upon us and we were broke. My husband had been in the hospital and we were in a hard place. We'd had four children within six years.

Our second child, a daughter, was about eight. All she wanted for Christmas was a pink sweater. I looked everywhere. None of the stores I frequented were carrying pink that year. My daughter was praying for a pink sweater, and I was too. I know it's not a big thing, but I wanted my daughter to know that God cares about the smallest detail of our lives.

Several weeks went by, then one day someone came to the door with a bag of secondhand clothes. I carefully went through the bag and got near the bottom with a sinking heart. When I pulled out the last item, it was a soft pink sweater in just the right size.

✻ *God cares about every detail of our lives.*

— Kay E. Combs —

Being a Refuge

But let all who take refuge in you rejoice;
let them sing joyful praises forever.
Spread your protection over them,
that all who love your name may be filled with joy.

—PSALM 5:11

*M*aria definitely didn't approve of everything her daughter did. Seventeen-year-old Lucy was living with an abusive boyfriend.

"I'd like to beat him up myself, but that wouldn't help any," Maria commented crisply.

Maria encouraged Lucy to come to the house frequently. And when Lucy did, Maria made sure she didn't scold Lucy about her lifestyle.

"The rest of the world beats her up emotionally," Maria said. "I want home to be the place of refuge, where she can always feel love and acceptance."

As a result, Lucy spent a lot of time at home. And one day when the boyfriend abused her, she thought, *I'm treated way better than this at home* and returned to live with her parents.

While not everyone is enmeshed in an abusive situation, far too many people we encounter are dealing with tough stuff—sometimes it's because of bad choices, and sometimes it's just life.

Our human inclination is often to scold, blame, preach, and put in our two cents' worth. But sometimes all others need is a kind word, a shoulder to cry on, a place of acceptance—a refuge where they can find peace, love, and God's grace in the middle of a crazy world.

✣ *We can be a refuge for others, just as God is for us.*

— Jossy Grey —

Exposing Evil

Carefully determine what pleases the Lord. Take no part in the worthless deeds of evil and darkness; instead, expose them.

—Ephesians 5:10–11

My friend, whom I'd led to the Lord months before, suffered a relapse. He sat in a bar drinking his life away once again. His wife called me and told me what was going on. I drove down to the bar and stepped in.

"Hey!" Seth cried as I walked in.

I sat next to him at the bar. "What are you doing, Seth?" I asked fiercely.

He said, "Sit up, I'll buy you a drink."

"I don't want a drink," I retorted. "I want you out of here and back to what you have become."

"Aw, come on. It's just a little drink."

"For you, no. You can't have 'just a little drink,' because it strings itself into many drinks, until it's your whole life, Seth."

His eyes fell. "I'm sorry. I'm sorry."

I led him out of there and he got his act back together.

Stepping in to stop evil is the most loving thing many of us can do—wherever we find it, wherever we see it, even if it will arouse anger.

✣ *Expose evil when you have to, even fiercely, for it is speaking the truth in love.*

— Jerry Hamilton —

Going My Way?

Look! The virgin will conceive a child!
She will give birth to a son, and they will call him
Immanuel, which means "God is with us."

—MATTHEW 1:23

Hey, Elsi! Do you mind giving Sharona a ride home from church today?"

Actually, I thought, *I do mind. I'm not going in that direction, I've got a lot to do, and I'm in a hurry.*

But what I say is, "Sure, I'd be glad to!"

Sharona, who usually takes the bus, has a box of groceries to take home. We slide the box into the car, and she climbs into the backseat. She has to sit there because Karyn is in the front. Karyn lives fifteen minutes away, in a different direction. She is thrilled that she can attend church, which only happens because I'm willing to give her a ride.

There are times when going out of my way is a problem. But, I remind myself, Jesus went out of His way to come to me. So how can I do less?

⁂ *It's worth going out of our way to show love.*

— Elsi Dodge —

Quiet Servant

Watch out! Don't do your good deeds publicly, to be admired by others, for you will lose the reward from your Father in heaven.

—MATTHEW 6:1

*P*arents love it when daughters tell them how much their spouses care for them. My oldest daughter, Rosheen, was describing her husband, Mike, and one thing she said struck me as significant. "He does a lot of good things that nobody knows about."

I wanted to ask what those deeds were, but that would somehow defeat his very purpose.

There are dozens of needs surrounding us, yet we often address those that will bring us recognition. If we love, we want to be seen as a loving person. Jesus speaks in hyperbole when He says that when we give to others, we shouldn't even let our left hand know what our right hand is doing. That's a strict standard, but if we aren't concerned about the rewards here, we will certainly receive them in heaven.

My daughter recently had a skiing accident that will provide Mike with many more opportunities for service. But let's keep that hush-hush.

✢ *Acts of love done in secret will keep us humble.*

— James Stuart Bell —

The Game of Encouragement

So encourage each other and build each other
up, just as you are already doing.
—1 Thessalonians 5:11

Mommy, I got 60,000 points!" my son cried. I was talking with his father, so it took me a minute to focus. But then I realized he'd been playing our vintage pinball game that he's finally tall enough to operate.

"Whoa! I don't know if I've ever gotten that high!" I said. "Here, let's play together and see who gets the highest score."

He was, of course, game for the competition. I pulled the release and started flipping the flappers on the machine. *Ding! Ding!* My score was climbing perilously close to his record.

He started shouting—I assumed he was shouting in grief that I was catching up to him. But no, I listened to the words, "Way to go, Mommy! Keep it up!"

My competition-loving son was more interested in seeing me do my best than in being able to brag that he beat Mommy.

Wow! What a lesson for all of us! Sometimes we all treat life like a competition and others like our competitors. How much better when we don't worry so much about our lives but focus on helping others reach their potential.

✻ *When we cheer each other on, we're all winners!*

— Jenni Davenport —

The Christmas Carol

Love does no wrong to others, so love fulfills
the requirements of God's law.

—ROMANS 13:10

*C*aroling to the neighbors would be so much fun!" I exclaimed
as my friend and I shared coffee.

Suzanne asked, "What if we sang O *Tannenbaum* in German
to Mary?"

A gruff-sounding older lady, Mary had escaped Nazi Germany,
settling in our area years ago. Some on our block were put off by
her ways, but Suzanne and I had tried to reach out to her.

A week later, the singers gathered at my house for hot chocolate
before beginning our trip around the block. The group ran through
our special song. I was sure we had butchered the language.

A knock at Mary's door yielded nothing. We began to sing. The
door soon opened a crack. We sang another carol. The door opened
a bit wider. We then began to sing our German lyrics. The door
flung open, and Mary came out on the front porch, singing with us.

Her face almost broke with the wide smile, tears streaming down
her cheeks. She told us later it was the best gift she had ever received.

✳ *Love means thinking of what might please someone else.*

— Betty Ost-Everley —

Loving Fruit for Christmas

I am the vine; you are the branches. Those who remain
in me, and I in them, will produce much fruit.

—JOHN 15:5

*C*hristmas shopping, what a challenge! But I approached the
mall with a smile on my face, keeping in mind that Jesus is
the reason for the season.

I found exactly what I was looking for in the first store and
proceeded to the checkout. I got behind a lady whose cart was
overflowing with items that needed to be wrapped by hand, as
they included glassware and porcelain.

Finally the clerk rang up her total of $69.50. I couldn't help but
comment, "Wow! What a bargain. You got all of that for a great
price!" The lady looked around at me, stunned by my pleasant
tone in the face of an endless wait. "You have been so patient.
Thank you so much," she said. As the clerk helped the lady take
her loaded cart out of the store and left me waiting in line, the
customer thanked me and kissed me for being an example of the
Christmas spirit. "Have a Merry Christmas!" she exclaimed.

✳ *Without the Babe in the manger, I am a broken branch; as I abide in
the love of Christ, I am enabled to bring forth the fruit of the Spirit.*

— Patricia A. Moyer —

Showing His Love

Give as freely as you have received!
—MATTHEW 10:8

*W*hen my brother, Steve, and I were ages eight and nine, our parents often treated us to a Saturday afternoon at the movies.

I remember one Christmas time when we were done with the movies and waiting for our parents to pick us up. It was cold, but we didn't mind because we were waiting in front of a store that had a wind-up train on display in the window.

The shop owner saw us mesmerized by the train and kept winding it up for us. After a bit, he came with a box and packed it all up. We were heartbroken when he took it away, out of the window.

The next thing we knew he came out the front door and gave the box to us, saying, "Merry Christmas!"

That was more than fifty-five years ago, but I still remember to this day the joy that filled me when he handed us that box.

✤ *The joy that comes from giving, even if it is something small, can last a lifetime.*

— Bruce Dalman —

Giving Christmas Coffee

You should remember the words of the Lord Jesus:
"It is more blessed to give than to receive."

—ACTS 20:35

*W*hy isn't the coffee ready?" asked Diane.
"I'm sorry," I said, tempering my voice. "I just got to work."

"Well, that's no excuse. It's your job!" Diane snapped.

Diane was the charge nurse and she definitely lived up to her reputation! No matter what I did, it was never enough.

The week before Christmas, I drew Diane's name for the office gift exchange. My heart sank when her name glared back at me. What could I possibly give her?

On the day of the Christmas party, I received an email that Diane's only daughter was in critical condition from a car accident. I grabbed my Thermos of coffee and headed for the hospital.

When I arrived, Diane was sitting alone in the waiting room, wiping tears from her face. I inched next to her, pulled the Thermos from my purse, and offered her a cup of coffee. With a weak smile, she grabbed the cup from my hands and took a sip.

"Thank you. It's just what I needed," Diane whispered.

Ten years later I'm still celebrating the miracle of Christmas over a cup of coffee with Diane and her daughter!

✻ *Giving is so much better than receiving when it's generated by an act of love—especially at Christmas!*

— Connie Pombo —

No More Holiday Grumbling

Do everything without complaining and arguing.

—PHILIPPIANS 2:14

*P*recious time slipped away as I inched along the snowy streets. I'd never get to the supermarket with all this holiday traffic. I felt like canceling my Christmas party. Company coming, and me not ready!

Grumbling, I snagged the last cart and frowned when I saw the mobs at the deli. And it was no better at the seafood counter. A quick grab for the last item and I raced for the checkout.

Thank heaven for the express line! There was only one person in front of me, a woman in a wheelchair. Her blue eyes danced merrily as she chatted with the cashier about her party—which was also starting in a couple of hours.

"Merry Christmas!" she called with a bright smile as she rolled away.

She was the perfect example of a cheerful hostess! Challenging circumstances and last-minute errands wouldn't interfere with this woman's gracious hospitality. What a timely reminder! My mind was set . . . no more grumbling for me. I left the store looking forward to a great time with my guests that night.

✢ *Hospitality doesn't have to be perfect, just heartfelt.*

— Susan A. Karas —

The Gifts of Christmas

The Lord is with you!

—LUKE 1:28

*P*ain pillaged the first Christmases my sons and I spent without their father. I felt as helpless as that babe in a manger thrust into a cold, inhospitable world. Haunted by the spirit of happy Christmases past, I mourned the loss of our family's meaningful rituals.

What single parent has not experienced Mary's feelings? Astonished, perplexed, afraid, anxious, and incredulous.

On *the* first Christmas, Mary and Joseph confronted a difficult moral situation—a pregnant bride-to-be. Wagging tongues surely gossiped. Their social prestige was near zero. The innkeeper rejected Mary and Joseph, forcing them to find shelter wherever they could. Their precious baby was born into poverty.

The financial hardship and emptiness of my lonely Christmas engulfed me in depression. And then the God of disguise and surprise came to reside right where I lived, just as He did that first Christmas. The words of the real God, the warm God, engaged my cold heart right where I was—needy, helpless, despondent, weak, and angry. Emmanuel—God with us—wrapped me in His amazing gifts—new life and the true spirit of Christmas.

✳ *Just as God was with the people of the first Christmas in their scary situations, He is with us.*

— Scoti Springfield Domeij —

Knock, Knock, Who's There?

It is a sin to belittle one's neighbor; blessed
are those who help the poor.

—PROVERBS 14:21

Danny lives under the bridge next to my home. No, he's not a troll. He's my neighbor and he is homeless. He knocked on my door a few weeks after I moved in and introduced himself: "I'm Danny and I live under the bridge."

I was caught off guard and unsure how to respond. I sensed that I had offended him by my demeanor.

Months passed, and Danny was on my mind a lot, especially when it was cold. I decided to go apologize to him and take him a Christmas present. He invited me into his humble abode under the 293 Highway bridge, and we laughed and became friends.

A few days later, he knocked on my door again. He shared that he had gone to the local church and met the Lord. He had come to invite me to his baptism, which I attended. Danny still lives under the bridge, he is still my friend, but he is no longer homeless. He has been adopted into God's kingdom.

Even at our front doors God will use us to draw others to Him.

— Vince Byrd —

The Big Event

Jesus was born in the town of Bethlehem in
Judea, during the reign of King Herod.

—MATTHEW 2:1

*J*esus probably wasn't born on December 25."

I listened intently to my Bible professor. I'd never heard this before. He explained that some theologians think Jesus's birth was in the spring because shepherds would have been out with their sheep at night during lambing season. Others speculate it wasn't during the winter months because travel for the census would have been too difficult.

The celebration of Jesus's birth had landed on December 25 because it was tied with a secular celebration, he explained.

I'd had no idea. I'd just assumed that Christmas was Christmas. I didn't know what to think about it.

That was years ago, and I still celebrate Christmas on December 25. Somewhere along the way, I've just filed away my curiosity about the actual date with other questions I don't know the answers to. I've discovered what's important is not having all the answers, but having faith in the One who does!

✳ *It doesn't matter when Jesus was born—only that He lives within us.*

— Jeanette Gardner Littleton —

Finishing My Christmas List

Give, and you will receive. Your gift will return to you
in full—pressed down, shaken together to make room
for more, running over, and poured into your lap.

—LUKE 6:38

I awoke Christmas Eve, pleased my shopping was done. Still, I hadn't asked Jesus what He wanted for His birthday. I felt I could offer Him little as I issued a quick prayer asking what was on His birthday list.

Instantly I was struck by a surprising request. "Go visit Bernice." Bernice had been a friend of my deceased parents, and years before I had attended church with her. Recently I had heard she'd been placed in a nearby nursing home.

I gathered some small gifts, and as evening approached, I anxiously headed toward the care facility. I hadn't seen Bernice in years and wondered if age had stolen her mental faculties.

I found Bernice sitting on the side of her bed. She instantly recognized me. After I presented the gifts, she asked if I would stay. Our visit lasted a couple of hours as we laughed and recalled memories.

I headed home that dark, crisp Christmas Eve, recognizing that Jesus's birthday list had blessed Bernice and me as much as it had blessed Him.

✵ *God's gift lists often contain blessings for us.*

— Steven Thompson —

Still Seeking Him

> They entered the house and saw the child with his
> mother, Mary, and they bowed down and worshiped
> him. Then they opened their treasure chests and gave
> him gifts of gold, frankincense, and myrrh.
>
> —MATTHEW 2:11

I looked at the tree that had been surrounded by presents an
hour or so earlier. I knew I needed to work on the traditional
meal, but I was too exhausted to get up.

Christmas is my favorite time of the year, but it can be so tiring.
Seeing Christmas lights, decorating, attending programs, watching
traditional movies, making cookies, finding gifts. Amid the hustle,
it can be hard to *really* find Jesus.

Maybe that's why I connect with the wise men so well.

We don't know much about the wise men. We don't really know
where they were from or exactly who they were. We do know it
wasn't convenient for them to hunt down Jesus. They had to follow
a star and ask for directions. It cost them time and money. And
they had to go out of their comfort zones to find Christ.

Sometimes worshiping Christ is not convenient for us. With
rising gas prices, it costs money to attend church activities. Worshiping Christ may cost us someone's approval. Sometimes our
circumstances are not convenient, and worshiping God may mean
leaving our comfort zones.

But whenever we get up and get out to worship Christ, we will
find Him and be rewarded.

✳ *Searching for God is not always easy, but when we seek Him, we'll
find Him—at Christmas and any other day of the year.*

— Jenni Davenport —

Surprised by Service

For even the Son of Man came not to be served but to serve others and to give his life as a ransom for many.

—MATTHEW 20:28

*J*osh is doing dishes!"

Quickly the message spread through the hundred-member staff in our youth ministry. Why was it so amazing that Josh was helping wash dishes after the luncheon? Because Josh had just *spoken* at the luncheon. He was a bestselling author and an enormously popular speaker, leading a week of evening meetings and a couple of lunch banquets.

On other days, Josh was out in the freezing weather, helping with construction for the youth ranch our ministry was building. No one would have thought twice if Josh had rested during the day while preparing to share God's Word at night to the packed-out crowds. Instead, he encouraged us by entering our world, by becoming one of us, by actually being a servant to us.

What an odd thing for Josh McDowell to come to my mind during the Christmas season. But then again, maybe not. For isn't that what this time of year—and this Christian lifestyle—is all about? God stepping down to be one of us, and teaching us to enter others' worlds with love too.

✳ *Who can you surprise with your service this week?*

— Janet Graham —

He's Watching

The eyes of the Lord watch over those who do right;
his ears are open to their cries for help.

—Psalm 34:15

*W*hat?" my son asked when he looked up and saw me watching him. I smiled and shook my head. "Nothing."

He went back to his task and I kept watching. Soon he looked up again. "What?" he asked. "What did I do wrong?"

"Nothing. I just like watching you," I said. "You're cute. And I love you so much."

Different verses in the Bible tell us that God's eyes are on us. I used to feel uncomfortable to think of God watching me. Waiting for me to slip up and fail, I assumed.

Then I heard entertainer Mark Lowry talk about God's eyes being on us—but not because He is like the traffic cop waiting to catch us doing something wrong. Instead, He loves us so much that He can't keep His eyes off of us. God is proud of us, fascinated with us, and probably even thinks we're cute.

So now, when I think of His eyes on me, I think of the way I love to watch my kids. And I just smile.

✣ *God gets a kick out of you, so relax!*

— Julie Durham —

Follow His Leading

Since we are living by the Spirit, let us follow the
Spirit's leading in every part of our lives.

—GALATIANS 5:25

*M*y wife and I wanted to work toward buying a house. But a huge debt to the hospital from having our first daughter dragged us down. We hadn't had any health insurance, and the bills mounted into the thousands. It looked like years before we could ever begin to amass the money for a down payment. I kept praying about it, and it seemed God said, "Just follow my leading."

I did, and one day my dad came to me and said, "Joe, if you want to start looking for a house, your mom and I are in position to help you get one."

Amazed, I gave him a list of all the problems we had. He said, "Don't worry about money, just worry about finding something nice but not too expensive."

We did, and six months later we moved into a nice duplex my wife called the "Taj Mahal."

God led us every step of the way. I'm amazed that when a path or goal looks impossible, God can step in and make it happen. I've seen it happen many times in my life. God is never daunted. His plan will come to pass.

✣ *God loves you so much that He will not let His plan fail you.*

— Joseph Compaine —

God's Always Right

For everyone who asks, receives. Everyone who seeks, finds.
—MATTHEW 7:8

*G*od didn't answer the prayer." I was bothered by that statement. The person seemed to be totally ignoring the fact that God sometimes says no. God always hears and answers prayers. Sometimes He may not directly say no, but I believe He brings unexpected alternatives. He knows what's needed more than we do.

Years ago this was proven to me when I was invited to pray for a friend's dying husband. My ministry focused on memory healing. Memory healing is a procedure where, through prayer and probing questions and the Holy Spirit's direction, we help people go back to painful moments in their lives and seek the Lord's healing of those traumas.

As my prayer partner and I ministered beside the hospital bed, God quickly brought meaningful healing to the man behind the oxygen mask, and I expected his health to improve, as it often does after a healing.

The next day, when his wife called to report he had died in peace, I was puzzled. But his wife knew that memory healing prayer was what her beloved needed to die peacefully. God brought him what was best.

✣ *If God tells us to come to Him with our requests, we can trust Him to bring the needed answer.*

— Sally Edwards Danley —

A Friendly Kiss

Greet all the brothers and sisters with Christian love.
—1 Thessalonians 5:26

*I*n my first years after graduation from college, I dreaded New Year's Eve. My friends always threw a big party with lots of drinking. But the hard part for me was having no wife or girlfriend on such occasions.

One year, when I was about twenty-three, two of my close friends, Jeff and Judy Winter, had converted to faith in Christ. They attended the annual party, and it was good to get together and talk about our mutual faith. Again that year, all my friends were there, some quite drunk, and everyone with a girlfriend or wife in tow. Except me. As everyone talked excitedly, the final moment came. I shrank back into the shadows and just hoped to endure it without feeling too depressed.

Dick Clark rang off the numbers and everyone connected. But then, before she even kissed her husband, Judy walked over and planted a big one on my lips. "That's for telling us about Jesus," she said, and then melted into the crowd.

I will always remember it as a moment of compassion directed at a lonely guy on a dark evening. Sometimes you just have to look out for those on the edge, people who aren't fitting in at the moment, and show them God's love. They'll treasure it.

✶ *Give a little love to someone who may be feeling lonely during this season.*

— Mark Littleton —

Pressing Ahead

No, dear brothers and sisters, I have not achieved it,
but I focus on this one thing: Forgetting the past and
looking forward to what lies ahead, I press on to reach
the end of the race and receive the heavenly prize for
which God, through Christ Jesus, is calling us.

—PHILIPPIANS 3:13–14

The end of the year stresses me somewhat. I can't help but think of all the things I planned to do that year—and didn't get done. I not only think of goals I haven't met and tasks I haven't done, but also people I didn't get to spend time with as I'd wanted to, birthday cards I didn't send, and other ways I didn't meet my goals of showing I cared.

As I face the new year, I have to consciously put the old year behind me—its surprises, its disappointments, its failures, and even its successes. If I don't consciously do this, I enter the new year so focused on the failures of the year before that I am hindered mentally and emotionally.

Today I'm praying Paul's words in Philippians 3:13–14. I'm asking God to help me forget the past, and to press ahead toward all that He has for me this year and beyond! I'm asking Him to help me remember and make time to do the things I need to accomplish, especially when it comes to showing love to the others in my life.

✣ *As you enter this new year, forget what's behind you—and press ahead with faith and love.*

— Jeanette Gardner Littleton —

About the Contributors

Beverly Abear is a retired English teacher, painter, and writer in Minnesota.

Jane M. Abeln is celebrating fifty years as a Missionary Sister.

Charlotte Adelsperger is an author and speaker from Overland Park, Kansas.

Gloria Ashby writes from Colleyville, Texas.

Sandi Banks works with Summit Ministries: www.anchorsofhope.com.

Linda Beach enjoys writing children's curriculum and being a mom and grandmother.

James Stuart Bell is the owner of Whitestone Communications, a literary development agency.

Sarah Bergman writes from her home in Paola, Kansas.

Brenda Black is an author and speaker: www.thewordsout -brendablack.com.

Faith Bogdan is a writer and speaker living in Gillette, Pennsylvania.

Doug Bolton wrote *Signs of Hope: Ways to Survive in an Unfriendly World.*

Loretta Boyett is author of *Face From the Past,* a romantic suspense novel.

Laura L. Bradford writes about the ways God's love has changed her life.

Kathleen Brown divides her time between Texas and the Colorado Rocky Mountains.

Steven Brown is a physician and author of *Navigating the Medical Maze.*

Dianna Brumfield works for a recovery home and lives in Spokane, Washington.

Diane Buller is a former college writing instructor from central Illinois.

Debbie Burgett is a missionary with New Tribes Mission: www.ntm. org/rand_burgett.

Vince Byrd is the senior minister of Omega Missions, Inc.

Sue Cameron is a speaker and Bible teacher: http://my-own-little-corner.blogspot.com.

Susan Campbell founded More Than You Imagine ministries for women.

Renee Shuping Cassidy is a real estate agent and an equestrian.

Sandy Cathcart is a writer, artist, and photographer in southern Oregon.

Kitty Chappell is a speaker and award-winning author: www.kittychappell.com.

Laura Chevalier coordinates programs for international students and short-term missions.

Margie Christenson and her husband, Steve, live in Colorado Springs.

Jan Christiansen is founder of Inspired Ink Writer's Group: www.janiceeileen.com.

Gaye Clark is a cardiac nurse and has been married to Jim for twenty years.

Virginia Colclasure is a retired librarian and book reviewer, and does genealogy research.

Liz Collard is author of the BUILDING A GODLY MARRIAGE series.

Kay E. Combs is a wife, mother, grandmother, and deaconess from Massachusetts.

Kelly Combs is a wife, mother, writer, and speaker. Visit her at www.kellycombs.com.

Joseph Compaine lives in Missouri and loves the guitar.

Jerry Constance is still working, but looks forward to retirement.

Sharron K. Cosby is passionate about writing and speaking about families and addiction.

Linda Cox retired from her job with the Illinois Department of Natural Resources.

Kat Crawford is a cancer survivor and former pastor's wife from Nebraska.

Karl Cumberland is married with four kids and one grandchild.

Michele Cushatt writes stories, articles, and devotionals based on everyday experiences.

Tracey Dale-Akamine is a missionary and church planter with her husband, Brian.

Bruce Dalman lives in Gladstone, Missouri.

Betty J. Dalrymple travels, plays golf, and enjoys being a retiree.

Sally Edwards Danley is a leader with Celebrate Recovery.

Jenni Davenport is self-employed in the publications field.

Zach Davidson enjoys antiquing with his wife in their spare time.

Zeta Davidson works in Christian education and English as a Second Language classes.

Jean Davis is married to her high school sweetheart and lives in Delaware.

Angela Deal writes from her home in Alberta, Canada.

Leta Deering is a nurse and youth pastor's wife in New Mexico.

Brad Dixon is regional vice president for the Missouri Baptist Foundation.

Elsi Dodge travels the continent in a thirty-foot RV: http://RVTourist.com/blog.

Jane Doelan serves God by volunteering in her kids' public schools.

Scoti Springfield Domeij helps single parents embrace new life and lead their families.

Sam Donato not only writes books but also enjoys collecting signed books.

Pamela Dowd is the author of *All Jingled Out*.

Francine Duckworth is a pastor's wife in Colorado.

Julie Durham is editorial assistant for a teen magazine.

Agnes Lawless Elkins has authored or coauthored seven books and numerous articles.

Lynnda Ell writes about nonfiction book writing and healthy living: http://LynndaEll.com.

Karen Ellison has art and a greeting card line you can enjoy at www.karmelcreations.com.

Julia D. Emblen is a former public health nurse.

Sheila Embry is from Arlington, Virginia.

Harry Erb has retired from being a manager in a machinery company.

Georgeanne Falstrom is a writer from Irving, Texas.

Gene Farmer works in a factory.

Michael K. Farrar, a doctor of optometry, practices in Northern California.

Jim D. Ferguson is an exercise enthusiast who enjoys being with his family.

Jeannie Fields-Dotson is a middle school teacher, wife, and mother of two children.

Louise D. Flanders is a member of the Christian Authors Guild in Woodstock, Georgia.

Dianne Fraser works for Cornerstone Christian College in Busselton, Western Australia.

Peggy Frezon is a pet specialist: www.peggyfrezon.com.

Katherine A. Fuller lives in Maryland with her husband, stepson, and mother.

Sarajane Giere is a former reading teacher from East Quogue, New York.

Linda Gilden directs the CLASS Christian Writers Conference and teaches for CLASSeminars.

Karen Gillett writes from her home in Powell Butte, Oregon.

Tina Givens writes articles and advertising copy for Christian nonprofit organizations.

Verda J. Glick is a missionary in El Salvador.

Martha Pope Gorris is an author and speaker who lives in San Diego, California.

Marge Gower writes from her home in Auburn, New York.

Janet Graham writes personal experience articles for a variety of magazines.

Jossy Grey enjoys being a homemaker and pastor's wife.

Sunny Marie Hackman is a Rocky Mountain storyteller: www.sunnymariehackman.com.

Jerry Hamilton has four kids, two dogs, and two cats.

Pat Harris enjoys teaching the Bible to children in her neighborhood.

Mary Fran Heitzman is coauthor of *Starting from Scratch When You're Single Again.*

Tammy L. Hensel is a devoted wife, mother, and church leader in Bryan, Texas.

Sandy Heuckroth is a former teacher, secretary, stay-at-home mom, and journalist.

Jennifer C. Hoggatt is a writer, speaker, and vocalist: www.myjavawithjennifer.com.

Barbara Hollace writes from her home in Spokane Valley, Washington.

Richard Holland is a former pastor who still loves to teach the Bible.

Helen L. Hoover and her husband volunteer with Sowers, an RV ministry for Christian retirees.

James Hopkins passionately loves his wife and kids.

Marcia K. Hornok writes from her home in Salt Lake City, Utah.

Joyce McDonald Hoskins is a writer from Stuart, Florida.

Donna J. Howard writes from her home in Orfordville, Wisconsin.

Robbie Iobst lives with her family in Colorado. Visit her at www.robbieiobst.com.

Andrea Jennings is a freelance writer living in the southeastern United States.

Linda Jett practices therapeutic massage and participates in her church's drama ministry.

Pat Stockett Johnston is a former missionary from the Middle East.

Eva Juliuson writes from her home in Oklahoma City, Oklahoma.

Sheila Sattler Kale is owner of The Closer Walk Christian Bookstore in Fredericksburg, Texas.

Susan A. Karas lives in Yaphank, New York.

Sudha Khristmukti writes from her home in Gujarat, India.

Sara King is a writer from Dallas, Texas.

Kirsten B. Kline is the owner of Révérence Studios in Mechanicsburg, Pennsylvania.

Mimi Greenwood Knight is a mama of four living in South Louisiana.

Kathleen Kohler is a writer and speaker from the Pacific Northwest.

Rebecca Krusee has a B.S. in Industrial Technology.

Helene C. Kuoni is editorial assistant for *The Secret Place* devotional magazine.

Mary Laufer is a substitute teacher living in Forest Grove, Oregon.

Julie Lavender is the author of five books and several magazine articles.

Jeanette Levellie authors a bi-weekly humor/inspirational column in her local newspaper.

Bobby Lewis serves as pastor of The Sanctuary Church in Dublin, Ireland.

Dawn Lilly is a wife, mother, and grandmother in Washington.

Jeanette Gardner Littleton is celebrating her thirtieth year as an editor.

Mark Littleton is a full-time writer of one hundred books.

Ginger Livingston is an avid fan of vintage arcade games and jukeboxes.

Susan Lyttek writes early mornings in the shadow of our nation's capitol.

Margaret M. Marty launched a memoir-writing business, Portraits in Prose.

Sandra McGarrity authored three novels and contributes to books, magazines, and e-zines.

Edie Melson is from Simpson, South Carolina: www.thewrite conversation.blogspot.com.

Jonathan D. Miller is a teenage author who lives in a small Iowa town.

Pat Miller is a published author and ordained Assemblies of God minister.

Katherine Mitchell coauthored *Don't Settle for a Fairy Tale: A True Love Story.*

Patrick Mitchell enjoys sharing the Gospel with others.

Mary Kay Moody enjoys walking through waves in the Pacific Ocean: www.MaryKayMoody.com.

Peggy Halter Morris writes from her home in Largo, Florida.

Peggy Morris is a pastor's wife who loves to encourage others through her words.

Patricia A. Moyer is an inspirational speaker and writer who loves digging into the treasures of God's Word.

Kathleen M. Muldoon authored *Sowing Seeds: Writing for the Christian Children's Market.*

Dena Netherton invites you to visit her inspirational blog: http://denanetherton.blogspot.com.

Ramona Nicks is an engineering assistant and math tutor when she's not writing.

Juanita Nobles is a retired reading teacher in De Soto, Missouri.

Lloyd O'Donnell is interested in genealogy.

Mary Beth Oostenbrug is executive director for a Christian organization serving disabled adults.

Emily Osburne is author of *Everyday Experts on Marriage:* www. emilyosburne.com.

Betty Ost-Everley lives in Kansas City: http://betty-ost-everley.blogspot. com.

Kristianne Ovenshine is an empty-nester from western Pennsylvania.

Jane Owen lives with her husband of forty-three years in the mountains of West Virginia.

Cynthia Owens has a passion for encouraging others to embrace their walk with God.

Kristi Paxton is a substitute teacher, freelance writer, and Mad House-wife spokesmodel.

Nora Peacock enjoys her husband of forty-two years, children, and grandchildren.

Wayne A. Pearson is a retired worship pastor and public school music teacher.

Elizabeth W. Peterson is a retired English teacher in Summerville, South Carolina.

Diane Petree writes from her home in Mechanicsville, Virginia.

Dixie Phillips specializes in writing for children and adults alike.

Sherry Poff teaches high school English in Chattanooga, Tennessee.

Connie Pombo is a "retired" author and speaker from Cuenca, Ecuador.

Tricia Propson directs Rekenekt, a ministry that connects parents and youth: www.cornerstonecomm.org.

Marty Prudhomme has taught Bible studies and leads a friendship evangelism team.

Susan E. Ramsden enjoys spiritual poetry, devotionals, and speaking engagements.

Ila Reed engages in sewing and making cakes for special occasions.

Kelli Regan loves prison ministry, mission trips to Haiti, and backpacking.

Susan J. Reinhardt enjoys reading, writing, antiquing, gardening, and family time.

Nancy Reinke blogs at www. joyfulaltitude.com and http:// mtnmanna.blogspot.com.

Don Richards lives in central Missouri and loves eating out.

Katie Robles is a former Spanish teacher who loves gardening and reading.

Linda W. Rooks is the author of *Broken Heart on Hold: Surviving Separation.*

Bobbie Roper shows God's love in Sydney, Florida.

Mona Rottinghaus is an instructor with the National Alliance on Mental Illness.

Carol Russell writes from her home in Fort Scott, Kansas.

Kenneth Santoro is from Cherry Hill, New Jersey.

Alyssa Santos ministers through an organization in Ethiopia.

Elissa M. Schauer is a wife, mother, and writer living near Chicago, Illinois.

Doris Schuchard is a writer in the areas of family and education.

Susan Browning Schulz blogs at www. thelisteningheart.blogspot.com.

Bev Schwind is a teacher at a rehab mission.

Cheryl Secomb enjoys writing fiction for children.

Kim Sheard lives in Virginia with her husband, Henry, and their dog, Freckles.

Pauline Sheehan, RN and Certified Diabetes Educator, wrote *Hugs for Caregivers.*

Patti Shene is executive editor for *Starsongs* magazine.

Carrie Shepherd is a seasoned international speaker.

Cindy Sipula enjoys scrapbooking, her granddaughter, and her son's foster kids.

Susan Kelly Skitt loves to write and speak about life with Jesus Christ.

Debra R. Stacey writes from her home in Independence, Iowa.

Patricia L. Stebelton lives in Fort Myers, Florida.

Kelly J. Stigliano enjoys speaking and writing: www.kellystigliano.com.

Rebecca Stuhlmiller is a speaker and church leader who encourages people.

Jessica Talbot is retired and lives on a hobby farm in British Columbia.

Clay Taylor likes to study the origins of words.

Jill Thompson is author of *Soul Battle: It's Not Against Flesh and Blood.*

Steven Thompson writes from his home in Osage, Iowa.

Mac Thurston is a graduate of Dallas Theological Seminary.

Donna Collins Tinsley, wife, mother, and grandmother, lives in Port Orange, Florida.

Christine Trollinger is a writer from Kansas City.

Brian Varney is a former pastor from Maryland.

Ann Varnum is a television talk show hostess at WTVY-TV in Dothan, Alabama.

Deb Vellines enjoys traveling with her husband, her grandchildren, and writing.

Benjamin Venable enjoys cooking, board games, reading, and juggling.

Caitlin M. Vukorpa writes from her home in Saint Joseph, Michigan.

Dorcas Annette Walker is a columnist, speaker, and photographer from Jamestown, Tennessee.

John C. Westervelt has been an engineering supervisor on the Apollo project.

Lori Wickline is a bookkeeper and teaches Bible studies.

Jean Ann Williams writes articles and short stories for children's magazines.

Deb Wuethrich is an editor at *The Tecumseh Herald* in Tecumseh, Michigan.

Brenda J. Young writes from Defiance, Ohio.

Jim Zabloski is a freelance writer and adjunct education professor.

Pam Zollman is the award-winning author of forty children's books.

Since 1979, **Gary Chapman** has written more than twenty books. His book *The Five Love Languages* has sold five million copies in English alone and has been translated into thirty-six languages, including Arabic and Hindi. He has his own daily radio program called *A Love Language Minute*, which can be heard on more than a hundred radio stations across the United States.

In addition to his busy writing and seminar schedule, Gary Chapman is a senior associate pastor at Calvary Baptist Church in Winston-Salem, North Carolina, where he has served for thirty-eight years. Gary and his wife, Karolyn, have been married for forty-seven years and have two adult children and two grandchildren.

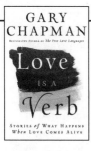